self-esteem
comes in all sizes

self·esteem comes in all sizes

[
how to be happy and healthy at your natural weight
]

REVISED EDITION

CAROL A. JOHNSON, MA

gürze books

Self-Esteem Comes in All Sizes
How to Be Happy and Healthy at Your Natural Weight
Revised Edition

©2001 by Carol A. Johnson

Gürze Books
PO Box 2238
Carlsbad, CA 92018
(800) 756-7533
www.gurze.com

Front cover design by Dunn+Associates, Hayward, WI
Author's photo by Anthony Loew

The first edition of this book was published in hardcover and trade paperback in 1995 by Doubleday, a division of Bantam, Doubleday, Dell Publishing Group, Inc. Material from the Spiegel *For You* catalgogue and *Tufts University Diet and Nutrition Letter* are reprinted with permission. The case studies in this book have been thoroughly disguised to preserve confidentiality.

Library of Congress Cataloging-in-Publication Data
Johnson, Carol A.
Self-esteem comes in all sizes / Carol A. Johnson. — revised ed.
p. cm.
ISBN 0-936077-37-9
1.Self-acceptance.   2. Body image.   3. Psychology   4. Weight loss—
Psychological aspects.   5. Self-esteem.   I. Title.
BF575.S37J64   2001
158'.—dc20   2001 131681

The authors and publishers of this book intend for this publication to provide accurate information. It is sold with the understanding that it is meant to complement, not substitute for, professional medical and/or psychological services.

1 3 5 7 9 0 8 6 4 2

*With Love to Ron and Mom
and in loving memory of my father,
R. Donald Johnson*

contents

acknowledgments 9

preface: looking back... xi

foreword by Gary Foster, Ph.D. xv

introduction: the journey begins xvii

1 born big 23

2 separating fact from fiction 31

3 bound by culture 54

4 acceptable discrimination 72

5 creating your own ideals 102

6 what are you waiting for? 119

7 self-esteem comes in all sizes 137

8 creating personal style—in a big way 179

9 I'm only telling you this for your own good 209

0 lose weight and call me in the morning 238

1 movers and shakers 255

2 so you still want to lose weight? 272

3 the size acceptance movement 313

4 fitting in 325

epilogue 331

notes 335

recommended reading 353

plus-size resources 357

acknowledgments

The concept of health, happiness, and self-esteem at any size did not originate with me. Many others helped to pave the way, including the National Association to Advance Fat Acceptance (NAAFA), the Council on Size and Weight Discrimination (CSWD), Largesse, and many other local and regional size acceptance organizations.

Heartfelt thanks to:

• Gary Foster, PhD, of the University of Pennsylvania, who reviewed the research chapter of the book and contributed the Foreward.

• David Allison, PhD, of Columbia University, who also helped to review research material.

• Thomas Wadden, PhD, and Albert Stunkard, MD, of the University of Pennsylvania, who have lent their support and have asked me to provide "the voice of a larger person" in many of their projects.

• Supermodel Emme who has been one of our supporters and cheerleaders for a number of years.

• Bill Fabrey of the Council on Size and Weight Discrimination for his insights and contributions to the discrimination chapter.

• Alice Ansfield, editor of *Radiance Online Marketplace,* for promoting Largely Positive in her publications.

• My colleagues at the Planning Council for Health and Human Services, my "day" job, who have provided lots of support and encouragement.

• My friend and colleague Debbie Seyler, who had been saying to me for years, "You need to write a book!"

• My friend and colleague Ann Schmitter, who always comes to my rescue when I need computer skills that exceed my own.

• Milwaukee physicians Drew Palin and Anthony Machi for their belief in this concept and for helping to bring it to the attention of other health professionals.

• Milwaukee psychotherapist Sandra Blaies and Milwaukee registered dietitian Anne Sprenger for their ideas, encouragement, and contributions to several chapters.

• Francie Berg, editor of the *Healthy Weight Journal,* for her support and promotion of Largely Positive through the years.

• Magazine writer and editor Sandy Szwarc for sharing the Largely Positive philosophy with her readers.

• Carol Story of *CBS This Morning* for her belief that this message needed to be heard by a national TV audience—more than once.

• Many size acceptance colleagues including Dr. Cheri Erdman, Ellyn Satter, Lynn McAfee, Miriam Berg, Pat Lyons, Joe McVoy, Karen and Richard Stimson, Susan Weber, Debbie Powell, Rochelle Rice, and Linda Omichinski for their friendship and collaboration over the years.

And special thanks and hugs to my editor and publisher, Lindsey Hall, and her husband Leigh Cohn, for believing that this book had a "second life" and for "breathing life back into it!"

I am grateful to all the members of Largely Positive who have had the courage and conviction to embrace this concept and stand up for it, even in the face of society's attacks. I would like to single out our original group of facilitators, Kari Young, Opal Collier, Lorraine Oulton, Mary Gardner, Linda Poth, Lori Olson, Jean Woodmansee, and the late Wendy Shockley.

My mother, Bernice Johnson, and my father, Donald, now passed away, always believed I could be anything I wanted to be, had faith in me—even when I didn't—and loved me unconditionally. My wonderful husband, Ron Bundy, has loved, respected, and encouraged me every day for 25 years. He is truly the "wind beneath my wings." My mother-in-law, Thelma Bundy, always has compliments and encouraging words for me. Other special people who have provided support and encouragement include Valorie and Jerry Kohn, Faye and Ken Miller, and my adopted "brother" Jim Carroll and his wife, Kathy.

Finally, I want to say a special word of thanks to the many people I have encountered who, though not large themselves, have become allies in the battle to end size discrimination. You are all extra special!

PREFACE

looking back...

When the first edition of this book was published, I sat and waited for the world to change. Six years later, I am still waiting. Am I discouraged? I would be lying if I said there have not been moments when I questioned my sanity at having taken on this challenge. I have been waiting six years for Oprah to call. I dreamed of opening the newspaper and seeing my book on the *New York Times* bestseller list. It never happened. Talk shows I was on were sometimes cut short or canceled for breaking or more important news. I sat in bookstores, waiting for people to line up around the block for me to sign their books. I was often lucky if several people came.

But there have been many other moments of exhilaration and joy. The book has introduced me to many fine people who are also committed to this cause. It has opened doors for me that probably would not have opened had I not had a book with which to knock. It helped connect me to the research community and a whole new audience of professionals. And it has brought me the most wonderful testimonials from readers who are determined to stop letting their weight interfere with their lives. My husband often says to me, "If you have helped one person toward better self-esteem and a happier life, you have succeeded." And I know he is right.

Here is the preface I wrote for the first edition of this book—it still holds true:

The promise held out to me was that if I got thin, I could like myself. So until I was 40 years old, I tried to get thin, but despite my best efforts, I never made it. Then I began to wonder if I could like myself just as I was. No one really wants you to, and if you say you do, no one believes you.

But I knew I had to try because I didn't want to spend another 40 years looking for the pot of gold at the end of the diet.

My first step was to become familiar with the scientific research on that awful word "obesity." I was amazed, because what the research really says and what most people believe are two entirely different things. I didn't think I should keep this news to myself, so I set out to share it with other large people in the form of an organization called Largely Positive. Its mission, I decided, would be to educate and to promote health and self-esteem among large people.

For best results from this book, you must wipe your mind clear of everything you have ever heard about the condition known as "being overweight." As I said, a lot of what we've been taught about issues of size and weight is simply inaccurate, and a lot of it is driven by prejudice.

My second step was accepting myself and my body "as is" and living in the present, not the future. Is that "giving up?" Absolutely not! Giving up means not trying any more, abandoning hope. If I were really talking about giving up, I'd say don't bother with healthy habits. Don't bother fixing yourself up. Don't bother going anywhere. Just stay inside the house, wallowing in self-pity, with a box of bonbons by your side. This is *not* my message.

I like to think of it as taking charge. We're becoming educated about issues of size and weight. We're trying to educate others. We're getting a life—making the most of who we are right now, not who we think we might be five years from now. We're developing a healthy lifestyle. Some of us are losing weight, some aren't. But we're liking ourselves a whole lot better, and society will be amazed at the contributions we can make with a new positive attitude!

Large women are sick and tired of hearing what's wrong with them. They're ready to hear what's right. Weight is only one tiny piece of who we are. It's come to symbolize way too much of the human condition, and it needs to be cut back to size.

Only human

Lest you think I am "terminally positive," let me assure you that I am human. I have my moments of "not-so-largely positive." Rude remarks still hurt—but not for as long. Sometimes I am frustrated when clothes I want don't come in my size. There are times I'd like to whittle off 25 pounds—especially when I'm squeezing my hips into a small theater or airline seat. I feel confident most of the time, but not always. If I could take a pill and wake up 25 pounds thinner, would I do it? Probably—provided there were no unpleasant side effects. I'd also take a pill to give me thicker hair and longer eyelashes. In the end, it all falls under the heading of "might be nice, but I can live—fully and happily—without it." I have become a *person* with a weight, not a *weight* dragging around a person.

Even though I may wish for some changes in size or symmetry, I can accept my body in its present format. I can live in it. I can, and want to, treat it with respect. My weight and my self-esteem are no longer glued together. I don't let my weight prevent me from living my life to the fullest. No matter what I want to do, there's usually a way to do it. I am no longer playing the "waiting game" with my weight.

A word about terminology

There is some difference of opinion among size acceptance activists over what word to use to describe large people. The term "overweight" generally is shunned because the methods used to label a person "overweight" have been called into question. I may not be "overweight" for my own physiology, but someone else at the same weight might be. The word "obese" is uniformly rejected in the size acceptance community. Researchers will tell you they need to use the terms "overweight" and "obese" because they are quantifiable.

Another difference of opinion arises over use of the word "fat." Many size-acceptance advocates feel strongly that we should call ourselves fat because, plain and simple, it's what we are. To them, the word "fat" is just another descriptive adjective, like short, tall, blond, or freckle-faced. Any other word is simply a euphemism and a cop-out. I don't disagree with them in principle, but I have found in my work with large women that, no matter what argument we use, very few are ready to use the word "fat" to describe themselves. The word has so many negative connotations and is so often linked to other negative words—fat and lazy, fat and ugly, fat and stupid. There was actually an article in the March 2000 issue of *Men's Health* magazine titled "How Not To Be Fat, Lazy, or Stupid."

I have chosen to settle, for the most part, on the more neutral term "large." But whatever words we use to describe our bodies, I believe we are all working toward the same basic goal—preventing weight discrimination and enhancing the health and self-esteem of larger people.

There's something in this book for just about everyone in America! If you're a large person yourself, if you live with a large person, if you're a health professional who treats large people, if you're a journalist who writes about issues of health, even if you are a person of normal weight who has no weight issues, this book will help you to see large people in a whole new light—a light that's not obscured by prejudice, ignorance and insensitivity.

foreword

Self-esteem comes in all sizes: it seems like a simple enough proposition. What does not seem logical is that among all of one's physical, emotional, intellectual and interpersonal qualities, body weight would serve as a central measure of worth. Yet, women in industrialized societies, especially young women, have been led to believe that they cannot and should not feel good about themselves if their bodies do not resemble that of a fashion model. In this context, it is a shame that this book had to be written, but I am grateful that Carol Johnson had the insight and courage to do so.

I read the first edition in 1995 when preparing to conduct a study at the University of Pennsylvania on alternative approaches to weight management. I anticipated that it would be similar to other books I had read, which suggested that persons of size stop trying to manage their weight because it was hopeless. What I found instead was a call for these individuals to take themselves and their situations seriously. Although this did mean learning to accept the varying sizes of their bodies, it also meant taking whatever steps possible to live full and healthy lives.

This message was so fundamentally sound and so articulately presented by Carol that I began to recommend her book to my patients; it struck a cord with many and helped them see themselves differently—no easy task for large women in this culture. This same message is the cornerstone of her revised second edition. Once again she has done a superb job of helping large persons rethink how they view and treat themselves. This edition also contains timely updates on research and many relevant issues. Given the mounting misinformation about body weight regulation, such updates are imminently useful. Carol is right that education is the key to acceptance.

For readers of size, this book won't change your life; you'll have to do that. But it will give you a candid, humorous and thoughtful perspective on living and thinking in a new way. Research indicates that modest weight loss has significant physical and psychosocial benefits. It is also just as clear that not everyone who eats the same and exercises the same weighs the same. So, putting life on hold until you lose weight makes your life dependent on factors over which you may not have total control. Play in the mother-daughter softball game, wear colors you like, do those things you have been delaying until "after I lose weight." In short, eat healthy, be active, and live life—NOW.

For healthcare professionals, given the increasing prevalence of overweight and obesity in our society and the significant discrimination against larger persons, I recommend that you read this book to challenge your own views about weight and worth. Moreover, recommend it to your large patients who face the real dilemmas that Carol outlines. Any effort you make to help them understand that their weight describes them but does not define them may be among the most significant things you can offer.

Gary D. Foster, Ph.D.
Clinical Director of the Weight and Eating Disorders Program
University of Pennsylvania School of Medicine

INTRODUCTION

the journey begins

Buckle up!

You are about to take a journey unlike any you've ever been on before—at least in this society, because by the time we reach our destination, a place called "Largely Positive," you will no longer allow your size and weight to measure your self-worth. Heck, you may decide to throw your scale in the trash! We'll be making a number of stops along the way, to talk about things like:

- Why people come in all sizes (and it may have very little to do with how much you eat).
- How to know if you're really a binge eater (and why).
- Why it doesn't necessarily follow that "If I lost weight, anyone can."
- Why self-esteem does not stop at size 12.
- How to get compliments and command respect in an ample body.
- How to get your priorities in order and start living your life now.
- And, O.K., how to better manage your weight *once and for all*.

The "un" syndrome . . .

Do you have a case of the "un's"? Chances are you do if you're one of those people society calls "overweight." You feel that you're "un" everything—unattractive, undisciplined, undesirable, unmotivated, undeserving, uninvited! I was an "un" myself until I learned that weight has very little to do with willpower and a lot to do with physiology, and that human beings are in some ways like flowers. Flowers come in all colors, shapes and sizes—and they're *all* beautiful. Somehow when it comes to human flowers, and particularly the female flower, we've forgotten the beauty that is inherent in variety and diversity.

This book is about removing the "un's." It's a book to help you polish up your self-esteem, start living now, discard weight as a measure of self-worth, and replace self-blame with self-understanding.

Starting with an empty slate

I'm going to have to ask you to do something right now, before you read any further: Wipe your mind clean of everything you thought you knew about issues of size and weight. I'm going to be challenging a lot of the things you've probably believed for years about your body and why it's the size it is. And who am I to do this? I'm someone who has spent the last 12 years studying the research on obesity and wondering why more people don't know about it. If they did, they'd stop torturing their bodies with diets that seduce and then backfire.

I'm also someone who has been big her whole life and who understands what it's like to turn on the TV or open a magazine and see nothing but thin people. I know that society really would prefer not to have to deal with fat people at all—at least not while they're still fat. But the fact of the matter is that one-third of the people who comprise this thing called "U.S. society" are people who fall into the category of "overweight," so ignoring them is becoming increasingly difficult.

Finally, I'm a trained sociologist, and that makes me curious about society and the people who live in it. Part of my job is to try to understand how we acquire our values, how "norms" come into being and what makes us tick.

Like individual human beings, societies are not perfect. They have their strengths and their weaknesses. Although our society is great in many respects, one of its chief flaws is the emphasis it puts on physical appearance and a definition of beauty that excludes the majority of its citizens. A size 12 woman is now the "before" picture in a diet ad. This is crazy, and has to stop.

I know you . . .

We haven't met, but I'm well acquainted with you. I know, for instance, that the numbers on the scale dictate how you feel about yourself and determine whether you:

- Say, "Yes, I'd love to come to the party," or "No, I can't make it. It's my night to remove lint from my navel."
- Buy a drab, "hope-they-don't-notice-me" muumuu or a "here-she-comes" fuschia jumpsuit, boldly accessorized with dangly earrings.
- Set sail on a Caribbean cruise or stay home and watch reruns of *Love Boat.*
- Go back to school and earn your degree or remain hidden away in a cubicle where no one will notice you.

You've been on every diet that's appeared in print—and some that haven't. You've contributed your fair share to the $50 billion diet industry by investing in exercise gadgets, books, potions, pills, creams. You've even sent away for some of that stuff advertised in the back pages of magazines, knowing that it's probably a rip-off but secretly hoping for a miracle (I have, too!).

Somewhere along the way you convinced yourself that you're a compulsive eater with no willpower or self-control. Otherwise, why would you still be struggling with your weight?

Every decision you make—or don't make—is influenced by your weight. But, you console yourself, as soon as the pounds evaporate, all that will change. You'll feel good about yourself and life will be the proverbial bowl of cherries (not chocolate covered, of course!). You continue to soothe your wounded self-esteem with the salve: This time next year I'll be thin and my problems will have vanished along with the weight.

Guess what? You don't have to wait until next year. You can have it all now! You can feel good now, look good now, be the best you can be—right now! Why? Because your problems, for the most part, are not caused by your weight; they're caused by how you feel about yourself and how society feels about larger people. You can do a lot about the former, and we'll work together on the latter.

Giving up or taking charge?

I know you're skeptical. You think that if you decide to accept yourself "as is" you'll be giving up. But it's not giving up. It's taking charge—perhaps for the first time—of your life, your body, your self-image, of this unique being that is you and only you. You're going to stop soaking up negative messages about your weight, stop accepting misinformation and start focusing on being the best you can be in the body you have right now!

Sometimes people who come to our workshops ask: "Can I still come if I'm dieting?" The answer is, "Of course you can!" And you can keep reading this book if you're dieting. Ultimately, your decisions about your body and your weight are personal, and I respect your right to make the choices you feel are right for you. My purpose is not to convince you to stop trying to lose weight, but to stop basing your self-worth on the results of that process. And this, I believe, is something that would be of great benefit to every woman in America—and many other societies like ours, where weight-watching has achieved the status of near-religion.

I would like it if I could at least convince you to get off of the diet merry-go-round. The word "diet" can have a lot of meanings, but I'm talking about the old-fashioned kind characterized by deprivation, rigidity, frustration, and failure. If traditional dieting has been a flop for you—as it has for 95 percent of the people who've tried it—why not stop? Doesn't it make sense to give up something whose success rate is as dismal as that?

There are lots of other reasons to give up repeated dieting. Evidence is mounting that dieting, far from improving your health, may pose risks of its own. Dieting also takes an emotional toll. If "losing weight" is your only goal, weight loss becomes your only measure of success. If the weight loss isn't all you hoped for, or if it's short-lived, you feel you've failed, and your self-esteem takes another beating. Redefine your goal as "developing a healthy lifestyle" and you've got dozens of chances for success. Maybe you switched to skim milk, went out for a walk, or banished a negative thought from your head. These are all successes and you need to keep a running total.

What you do about your weight is your business. What I want to reduce are those negative thoughts that weigh heavily on your mind and prevent you from living your life to the fullest.

Health as the brass ring

When I suggest to people that they give up dieting, they usually ask, "But what will I do instead?" It scares them to think about giving up something that has always held out the promise of changing their lives and making their dreams come true. I know it was like that for me. I always believed that my "real" life would start when I lost weight and became thin. I often had daydreams of what my "thin" life would be like—I'd be successful, admired, sought after, and confident. Ironically, I am now all of these things—I'm just not thin.

As I said before, my purpose is not to discourage weight loss. There are legitimate reasons for some people to try to do that. But the process will work much better if self-esteem leads the way rather than being "on layaway" until the end of the diet. And it will work better if you understand what's going on with your weight biologically and physiologically. Most of what we do to lose weight directly contradicts what science says we should do.

So, once again, is there a better alternative? Yes. Instead of focusing specifically on weight loss, why not make health your goal? Get to know yourself and what health means for you. Chances are you've been so preoccupied with issues of body size, you've never really gotten to know yourself apart from your weight. If you are at a point where your weight defines who you are, you look at yourself and you see a person who weighs too much. Period. Weight has obscured any deeper self-perception and has erected a barrier between you and life. Together, we will gently remove that barrier so you can accomplish the things that are really important.

Before we do that, let me share with you what it was like for me growing up in a thin-obsessed society.

1

born big

As a child, I prayed every night for God to make me thin. I couldn't figure out why my prayer was never answered. It's clear to me now. I didn't know it then, but I had a mission to fulfill.

—CAROL

I was a big gal upon arrival. At six months, I had already been proclaimed "too heavy" by the medical profession. Since a six-month old infant probably isn't hiding food in the closet or eating to numb the feelings of a relationship gone sour, it seems to me my genes were already programmed for a Rubenesque edition. Pictures of me as a toddler reveal a pudgy, apple-cheeked, cheerful tot. Little did I know what lay in store for me, all because of a few extra pounds.

The genetic determinants of weight are evident in my family. Both of my grandmothers were large women, and doctors always told my father that he was overweight. Assorted aunts, uncles, and cousins are also of the larger persuasion. Of my immediate family, only my mother escaped the "battle of the bulge."

My earliest memories of feeling "different" from the other girls date back to grade school when it became hard to find clothes that fit, and my grandma had to make my dresses. They were pretty, always with a bow that tied in back, but by sixth grade they seemed childish. I wanted to wear what the other girls were wearing. It was important to "fit in." The problem was "fitting into" the skirt I so desperately wanted—a "slim" skirt—all the rage at the time.

My mother took me to Lane Bryant, the only place chubby girls could shop in those days. We found a slim skirt. It was powder blue with a black belt. I'm not sure how flattering it was, but my mother tactfully kept her mouth shut and bought it for me. I was elated, but the joy soon turned to tears when the kids made fun of me. I became known as "Carol the barrel."

Forget the tooth fairy! I wanted the "thin" fairy to appear, wave her wand and make 30 pounds vanish. Each night when I concluded my prayers, I added, "And please God, make me thin."

The dieting Olympics

I knew then that the only way I would ever be as good as the other girls was to lose weight. Let the dieting begin! The doctor recommended a 1,200-calorie diet. Feeling that he was the expert and wanting to do what was best for me, my mom went along. I began toting brown-bag lunches to school, often containing a sandwich, celery and carrot sticks, and a piece of fruit. Well-balanced, yes, but by the end of the school day I was hungry. So when my friends wanted to stop at the soda fountain for ice cream cones and candy, I knew I shouldn't, but it was hard to resist, and I came away feeling I had done something "bad."

Despite the low-calorie diets, I was not losing weight. Although I did occasionally indulge in unauthorized "goodies," I was not eating excessively—no more than what my friends appeared to be eating. I just wasn't eating little enough to lose weight. But something new had arrived: over-the-counter diet pills. The ones I decided to buy were called *Regimen Tablets*. They were all different colors, and you had to take a fistful several times a day. I knew my mother wouldn't approve, so I got an older friend to buy them for me. I waited for the weight to melt away, but pretty soon it became evident that I was not going to "thaw." I tossed them.

Liquid diets are nothing new. We had Metrecal. Eating one meal a day seemed like a surefire way to lose weight, and it was so easy! A can for breakfast, another for lunch, and then a "balanced dinner." Okay, I thought. I can do that. And I did. But, once again, I was so hungry by the end of the school day that the ice cream parlor became my oasis on the way home to my "balanced dinner."

Through all this, my self-esteem continued to erode. One of my dreams always was to be a cheerleader. When tryouts were announced in the seventh grade, I signed up immediately and practiced night and day. After tryouts, I knew I had given a flawless performance. It was not to be, however. The physical education teacher, who was judging the competition, took me aside and gently told me that although I was one of the best candidates, she simply could not choose me. The reason? I was too chubby. My body was unacceptable for public display.

Shortly thereafter, I became intrigued by the baton and decided to take twirling lessons. You would have thought the cheerleader episode had deterred me forever, but somehow it didn't. I felt awkward at first, but soon the baton seemed like an extension of my arm and I graduated to more complicated routines, such as practicing high tosses and twirling two batons at once.

I dreamed of leading the marching band down the football field and, adept as I was, I thought there was a pretty good chance this dream would become reality. Reality did set in, but not the one I had dreamed about. Once again I was trying to do something that chubby girls weren't supposed to do—put themselves on display. This time I didn't even try out. I was told not to bother because the uniforms wouldn't fit me. And the message pierced deeper: You're not acceptable.

Hormones started to stir, especially at get-togethers and dances. We had "basement parties," and while they were fun, I began to dread sitting in the corner all evening. I got asked to dance so infrequently that when I did, I was afraid of being clumsy and awkward and stepping on my partner's feet. Most young boys, I learned time and again, are not looking for a plump girlfriend.

You may be wondering, How heavy was she? Maybe she really looked grotesque. The truth of the matter is that my weight in high school exceeded the weight charts by no more than 30 pounds. Now, when I look at my high school pictures, I don't think I look at all heavy. Yet, at the time those 30 pounds felt like the weight of the world.

Losing weight had become the most important thing in my life. I truly believed, deep in my heart, that I was not as good as the thinner girls. Only by losing weight could I become their equal. Every summer vacation I vowed I would lose weight by the time I returned to school in the fall.

The summer before my junior year in high school, my dream came true, thanks to blue-and-white speckled pills called amphetamines (known in street vernacular as "speed," I later learned). My doctor suggested I try them. It was a miracle! I had no appetite. Eating became a chore, and as an added benefit, I had more energy than I knew what to do with. Within 24 hours, I could clean the house from top to bottom, write a 20-page term paper, catalogue my entire record collection, and have energy to spare. I became engulfed in a whirlwind of tasks—some necessary, some bizarre. Sleeping was an annoyance. But I was losing weight—rapidly.

I bought new clothes in a smaller size and couldn't wait to get back to school. I stopped taking the pills since they'd done their job and I didn't think I'd need them anymore. By the following summer, the weight had returned, but I now knew what to do. I asked the doctor for more blue-and-white speckled pills. No problem! He wrote a prescription, and so it went for the next few years.

I went through several bouts with amphetamine diet pills before I realized that their power to produce weight loss was offset by their power to wreak havoc with my body and mind. It became clear to me that these little babies could easily become addictive and they had to go. I was still preoccupied with losing weight. I just had to find a pill-free way to do it.

My mother, always loving and supportive, was quick to point out that I excelled in other areas: I was in the top-ten of my class scholastically and graduated as class salutatorian. I could play the piano by ear and frequently entertained at school assemblies. I captured the lead in the sophomore, junior, and senior class plays because, unlike the cheerleading and major-ette advisors, the drama coach did not believe that being thin was a pre-requisite for appearing on the stage. Talent, she said, was the primary cri-teria, and I will always be grateful to Betty Jean O'Dell for seeing past my weight and recognizing my inner abilities. I wish I could have realized that my weight was a very small part of my sum total, but at 17, few kids have that kind of wisdom.

I was lucky in one respect. My parents didn't belittle me because of my weight. I have heard of others who were downright cruel—one woman's mother called her a "fat little pig" and told her she'd never get a boyfriend, and another's father said he found it difficult to love her when she was fat. Even as a big girl, I was truly "Daddy's little girl." I know my father adored me. He constantly assured me I could be anything I wanted to be. But even though my parents were proud of me, they couldn't insulate me from the outside world. And when you're young, your parent's opinion isn't as important as the appraisal of your peers—especially those of the opposite sex.

I remember liking a boy in junior high and sending my cousin to find out if he liked me. Returning from her mission, she said: "He says he'd like you if you weren't so chubby." There were other similar episodes, and the message became more deeply entrenched: You're flawed. You're inferior, you're just not desirable. As we all know, appearance is especially important when you're young, and teenage boys want girls who look as if they're headed for the *Sports Illustrated* swimsuit issue. I finally did meet one who thought I was "the greatest" in the body nature gave me, but he was about the only one—until I met my husband.

I kept trying to diet, but those fat cells just didn't want to budge. And my mind played the same tapes over and over: If only I had more willpower. There must be something wrong with me!

Enter the "diet doctors" and their books. One recommended mostly protein and water. I persuaded my mother to broil me steaks every night and cook turkey breasts for lunch. I washed it all down with eight glasses of water a day. I lost about 40 pounds before I started having nightmares about meat! If there had been an Olympics for dieting, I would have surely earned a gold medal.

Between diets I managed to finish college and earn both bachelor's and master's degrees. I got my first job as a hospital social worker and had to have a physical. I looked away when they weighed me. My weight had truly become an albatross and I didn't want to know how much that albatross weighed!

In the late 70s, liquid diets became popular again—something called "liquid protein." At least you didn't have to think about what to eat or what not to eat. It seemed ideal. I got a two-week supply. It tasted vile, and I was hungry. I was told the hunger would go away. It didn't. After a week of being hungry constantly and drinking that horrible concoction, I decided I'd had enough of quick-weight-loss schemes and threw the rest away.

In the years that followed, I went to group weight-loss programs periodically, but since I was never able to reach my "goal" weight, I always eventually gave up. Each time I'd think that I'd failed once again, instead of realizing that my body had probably reached the weight it considered appropriate—even if that wasn't the weight called for by the program's charts.

Changes toward the positive

Without my realizing it at the time, my self-esteem had started to climb. My career was going well, and I was being judged not by appearance, but by the work I was producing. Supervisors and clients praised my achievements and my weight didn't seem to be an issue at all.

Some things, however, did remain the same. I knew that there must be men who found larger women attractive, but I wasn't meeting any of them. Just as I was about ready to give up completely, one of my best girlfriends called to say she had found the man of my dreams and wanted to arrange a "blind date." The guy sounded great, but previous experience had taught me that verbal descriptions were not accurate predictors of outcome. Still, she persisted, and since I was batting zero in the dating game, I finally agreed to meet this "young executive who drives a Cadillac."

The evening arrived. I was nervous as always about how I looked. I tried on everything I owned, searching for the outfit that made me look least fat. We went for dinner. He was nice, funny, easygoing, attentive. I had a great time. He said he'd call me. Experience had taught me that they never do, but he did call back, and three years later we were married. In the past I had found love to be conditional—conditional on losing weight. Not this man. He said: "I love you because of who you are, and I think you're beautiful, both inside and out."

I didn't become "largely positive" overnight, but I was starting to re-evaluate my beliefs about my weight, my image and my value to the world. Let's start with image.

One evening, some friends urged me to go with them to a local department store to have our "colors" done. It sounded like a fun thing to do and I learned that I was a "summer." I had to admit the colors did look good on me. That sent me on a shopping spree to buy new makeup and clothes. I also decided to transition from tiny, barely perceptible earrings to big, bold ones. All my accessories became dramatic. As the final step in my makeover, I had my hair highlighted blonde. Before I knew it, I had developed a personal style that felt right to me. Somewhat to my surprise, it was a pretty flamboyant style that couldn't help calling attention my way. There was a time when my fashion goal would have been to attract as little attention as possible.

Then a funny thing started happening—people began to compliment me—on my clothes, my hair, my jewelry, on how I looked in general. And it was having a very positive impact on my self-esteem!

I continued to do well in the world of work. I changed jobs, feeling that I was better suited to the world of social research and community planning. It was a good move and I flourished in the human services arena. My size was never mentioned. My colleagues respected me and my reports won praise. All in all, I was feeling pretty good about myself.

This doesn't mean I had lost interest in losing weight, and one day while browsing in a bookstore, I came upon a book called *The Dieter's Dilemma* by William Bennett, M.D., and Joel Gurin. The title intrigued me. Dieting had certainly been a dilemma for me. Maybe I'd find out why. I did get answers, but not the ones I expected. I didn't find out how to lose weight; I found out instead *why* I was a large person and *why it's dieting, not the dieters, that have failed.* The book was a revelation for me because for the first time someone was saying it wasn't my fault. There was no need to blame myself. "Fatness, in most cases," claimed the authors, "is not the result of deep-seated psychological conflicts or maladaptive eating behaviors; usually it is just a biological fact." I felt liberated, vindicated—finally someone who understood I was not behaving like a glutton.

About this time a friend asked me to accompany her to a diet group neither of us had tried before. I said yes. It still seemed like something I ought to do for my health, even if my self-esteem no longer required it. So we went. My progress was slow, and some weeks I didn't lose at all. I understood from my newly-acquired education about issues of size and weight that slow was actually best. But the group leader didn't appear to know it. She didn't seem to be familiar with any of the research. When I lost very little or nothing at all, she'd ask: "Do you know what you've been doing wrong?" I knew I hadn't done anything wrong. I knew that very slow weight loss, punctuated by plateaus, was the best way to go about it. People who lost ten pounds in a week were applauded and congratulated. I wanted to scream: "This is not good! You'll gain it all back." But I didn't.

The final straw came one evening near the Fourth of July when our group leader decided that, in keeping with the impending holiday, we would make a list of all the "freedoms" we lose when we're overweight. This struck me as a pretty negative thing to be doing and I said so. "I may want to lose some weight," I told the group, "but I don't feel I've lost any freedoms." The leader scowled. After all, I was throwing a monkey wrench into her planned activity. She needn't have worried. The group made the list. Years of negative messages about their bodies made it easy for them.

After I got home that evening, I said to my husband: "I don't need to spend money to go someplace where I'm encouraged to feel bad about myself. Why doesn't someone start something that's positive?" That evening, Largely Positive, the organization I created to promote health and self-esteem among larger people, was born.

♥ ♥ ♥ From The Heart ♥ ♥ ♥

A Big Little Girl's Prayer

When I was a little girl and said my evening prayers, they always ended the same way – "And, God, could you please help me to get thin?" Then I waited to slim down. But it didn't happen, even though I tried as hard as any little girl could. I just needed God's help, I kept telling myself, and needed to pray harder. But it still didn't happen.

"Why?" I would ask. What was I doing wrong that God was punishing me by not answering my prayer? I was a nice, kind little girl. I always tried to do my best. I obeyed my parents. I helped other people. I didn't think it would be that difficult to zap a few pounds off of me. But although I said this prayer for years, my body did not change. I even became angry with God. I did not think my request was unreasonable.

It took me a long time, but now I realize that my prayers *were* answered. God could not allow me to become thin because plans had already been made for me. I did not see it then. I see it now.

2

separating fact from fiction

I was born an O (circle person), not an I (straight up and down) person. The circle could get smaller, but it's still a circle.
—CELESTE

Most of what we are routinely told about how fat is gained or lost is either wrong, misleading or meaningless.
—WILLIAM BENNETT, M.D.,
THE DIETER'S DILEMMA

Recently I was asked to present a workshop to fitness instructors about creating an exercise program for large people. I began by asking them what they envisioned when they heard the word "fat." Here are some of the words from their list:

- Overeater
- Out of control
- Undermover
- Depressed
- Lazy
- Unmotivated

- Unhealthy
- Feel sorry for them
- Jolly

I wasn't offended; in fact, I expected it. It's what we've all been taught. It's what I believed about myself for a long time—until I started digging and found out that what the research really says and what most people believe are two entirely different things.

This research does *not* contain the promise many are seeking—of pounds shed painlessly and permanently. So why don't the real facts find their way to the general public and why don't people want to hear them? Because the truth may be regarded as too hopeless, depressing or unprofitable for most of them to hear.

For me, learning the truth was a relief. In fact, it was liberating. It gave me peace and the ability to finally get on with my life. Most importantly, it showed me that I was not at "fault." I did not need to "blame" myself for what I weighed. It was not an issue of blame, it was an issue of biology.

I want the same for you. I want you to stop blaming yourself for your weight. I want you to stop beating yourself over the head every time you eat something you think you shouldn't. I want you to stop feeling that your ample size means that you are a weak-willed person. I want you to stop making apologies or accepting substandard treatment because you feel it's what you deserve.

And after you've stopped doing these things, I want you to start doing some other things. I want you to start realizing that your weight is not a measure of self-worth. I want you to start accepting yourself just as you are. I want you to start living your life in the present. I want you to start strutting yourself down the street as the confident and attractive large woman that you are. I want you to start taking your rightful place in your family, in your community and in the world—but most of all within yourself.

When it comes to obesity, myths abound

One of the things that struck me most when I began my journey toward a better understanding of obesity is that I had never before heard any of the stuff that's in the research. Not from my doctors. Not from my teachers. Not from the popular press. Not from *anyone*. And I couldn't figure out why. It made me angry. Actually, it made me very angry because, had I known about the research, I would not have spent half my life mired in self-blame and self-reproach. I could have chosen to stabilize my weight and be healthy, instead of embarking on a futile roller coaster ride of weight loss and gain.

By the way, many of these findings are not new. Some of the information has been around since the early 1900s, which makes it very hard for me to understand why it has been ignored so systematically. A fitness instructor at one of my workshops admitted: "I know I've read some of this stuff before, but I guess I've just chosen to ignore it." Why? The idea that large people are just stuffing themselves is so entrenched that research contradicting it is quickly overpowered by widespread prejudice and disbelief. It's sort of like "don't confuse me with the facts. My mind's made up."

Advice we could do without

- "Excess weight is unsightly and unhealthy."
- "Packaging is of prime importance. A terrific product deserves to be well presented. The smart woman knows this."
- "Excess weight can be a financial burden, social handicap, and health hazard . . . The key is discipline."

These are comments made by a nationally syndicated advice columnist regarding larger women. By pronouncing excess weight "unsightly," she has just labeled one-third of American women unattractive. Her second remark implies that a large woman cannot be "well presented." Even more disturbing is the statement that "packaging is of prime importance" and that "smart women know this." The implication is that large women are not smart, because if they were, they'd all slim down so as to "present" themselves well.

Her contention that extra weight is a social and financial handicap may be partially true, as shown by a study done at the Harvard School of Public Health. Large women, investigators found, earned less money and were less likely to marry, but they did *not* conclude, as did the advice columnist, that "the key is discipline." They concluded that the real cause is discrimination and the key is to put an end to it!

Getting the facts out to people about issues of size and weight—and having them believe it—is one of the hardest things I have ever done. But as my friend Kari said to me: "The guy who had to sell the fact that the world is round probably had a hard time too!"

Most people probably think they know what causes obesity. If you're fat, you just eat too much. Pure and simple. Case closed. End of story. But the story is nowhere near finished. Reputable researchers will tell you that the underlying causes of obesity are still elusive, that they're finding out more all the time, and that there's still a lot they don't know. One of the things they do know, however, is that there's a lot more to it than what you eat.

"Obesity is not a moral failure—it's a disease with a clear-cut biological and genetic basis," said Richard Atkinson, a physician from the University of Wisconsin at Madison, speaking to the North American Association for the Study of Obesity (NAASO) in Milwaukee. "We have been using a behavioral type of treatment for a disease that we now all realize is much more complicated," he continued.

Rudolph Leibel, another conference speaker, said that scientists are making strides toward identifying genes, key substances, and regulators in the body that predispose certain people to be fat. But until all of those genetic and biological factors are identified, efforts to treat obesity by controlling diet, exercise, and other behavioral factors are like treating malaria with aspirin— providing temporary relief of symptoms, but not resolving the underlying condition.

Most people assume that if you're fat, you just eat too much and don't get enough exercise. But it's far more complicated than that. Let's try to understand what *is* currently known, keeping in mind that:

- There's still a lot that remains unknown. An exhibit of diet products at the Smithsonian Institute ended with these words: "There is no known cause for obesity. There is no known cure."

- Obesity researchers don't always agree among themselves. Debate continues over how obesity affects health, how it influences metabolism, and how much of it is due to environmental vs. genetic factors.

Types of obesity

The first thing to understand is that people are big for different reasons, meaning that there are different types of obesity.

Childhood vs. adult onset

Childhood obesity is usually more severe, is characterized by an increased number of fat cells, is more resistant to treatment, and may be more genetic in nature. A team of researchers at St. Luke's-Roosevelt Hospital Center, Columbia University, led by David Allison, Ph.D., estimates that genes account for 75 to 80 percent of the body fat in children.[1] Studies have even shown that certain body chemicals, such as dopamine, behave differently in people with childhood-onset obesity than in people with adult-onset obesity.[2]

Apple vs. pear

What kind of fruit do you resemble? Where's your extra weight located? If it's around your middle, researchers like to call you an "apple" (usually referred to as "android" obesity in the scientific literature). If it's primarily in your hips and thighs, you're a "pear" (scientific term: gynecoid obesity).[3,4] Studies have shown that high blood pressure, coronary heart disease, and diabetes are more common in people with android obesity than in those with gynecoid obesity.

Quick weight loss may put you at even greater risk. Here's why: Weight lost rapidly is almost always regained. And where is the regained weight deposited? Around the middle. This happens because regained weight contains more fat than muscle, and fat tends to accumulate around the abdomen, making you more like that not-so-good apple shape.

One provocative new theory is that high levels of stress may cause fat to build up in the abdomen. Stress causes a steady release of the hormone cortisol, and abnormal levels of cortisol can cause excess fat deposits in various areas of the body, including the abdomen. More research is needed, but learning stress management techniques might not be a bad idea.

Body weight regulation

Do you have a "predetermined" weight? You may have heard the term "setpoint," which supports this idea. However, because that term implies everyone has an exact, predestined weight, leaving no room for even small variations, experts now prefer the concept that each person has a weight *range* which his or her body can comfortably maintain.

A person's weight range, say experts, probably varies by about ten percent either way. People may be able to keep their weight at the lower end of their range by watching what they eat and exercising. But changing the range itself is quite difficult.[5] Interviewed for an article titled "Gaining on Fat" which appeared in the August 1996 issue of *Scientific American*, obesity expert Rudolph Leibel said:

> If . . . the treatment of obesity were like an appendectomy, where you go to the doctor, you get your appendix taken out, and that's it, then what we would hear is that people went to such-and-such a place, got their obesity treated, and it never came back again. That is definitely not the case. The actual ability to reduce body weight is not a particularly difficult problem . . . But what does characterize the vast majority of humans is that they are very resistant to the maintenance of body weight below whatever 'normal' for them is. Whatever goes on when we lose weight, it seems to set off a bunch of metabolic alarms. The body will not tolerate that willingly . . . and we just don't understand all of the components of this thing.

It seems clear that a variety of factors interact to regulate body weight and people do have biological weight boundaries. Let's look at some of the major ones.

It's in my genes

Scientists do not believe that there is a *single* gene that causes obesity except in very rare cases. Many genes have now been identified, each capable of causing obesity in mice, and each with a human counterpart.[6] There is considerable evidence that heredity plays a major role in determining your size, shape, and weight. Some of the evidence:

- In at least two major studies, identical twins who were raised apart were found to weigh almost the same.[7, 8] One of those studies even took into account environmental factors, or outside influences, thought to contribute to obesity and found that they "had little or no modifying effects on the genetic influence on body fatness or obesity."

• Adopted children have been found to resemble their biological rather than their adoptive parents in terms of shape and weight.[9]

What you may actually inherit is a combination of metabolic factors, behavioral predispositions, and the tendency to store calories in one type of tissue (e.g. fat) more than another (e.g. muscle). Research has demonstrated that children of heavy parents tend to have lower metabolic rates.[10] More recent studies have linked specific genes to resting metabolic rate.[11] Also, recent evidence supports a genetic effect on food intake.[12,13]

The leptin influence

Chances are you have heard of "leptin" in the news. Leptin is a hormone produced by a gene, previously called the "ob" gene, and now simply referred to as the leptin gene. Leptin is believed to play a major role in regulating appetite and body weight. The discovery in the mid-90s that mice with a defective "ob" gene did not make leptin— and became very fat—generated great excitement in the scientific community because of speculation that overweight people might have the same problem.

Then another fat mouse came along, and, unlike its rodent cousin with the defective "ob" gene, this mouse had a defective "db" gene (now called the leptin-receptor gene). Instead of having no leptin, the "db" mouse had more than enough leptin, but the mouse's body "ignored" it. This is similar to people with Type II diabetes, who have a condition known as "insulin resistance" in which their bodies make too much insulin, but their cells are resistant to it. Although most overweight people are not quite like the "db" mouse, they do tend to have excess leptin—in one study, four times more than people of normal weight.[14]

The initial hope was that maybe people could be given extra leptin and they would lose weight, but when daily leptin injections were given to humans, some of the people lost moderate amounts of weight at best, and there was little effect except at the highest dose. A few people actually gained weight.[15] Scientists are not sure whether leptin will ultimately play a role in weight management, but they feel this new "molecular approach" to understanding the regulation of body weight is one of the best examples of real progress in biomedical research.

Those pesky fat cells!

Once a fat cell, always a fat cell. True or false? This one is true. "No, we probably can't reduce the number of cells once formed," said Susan Fried, Ph.D., speaking to members of NAASO. "The number stays constant even with large weight loss."[16] What is termed "mild obesity" is essentially linked to an increase in fat cell size, but people who are very large (or that unfortunate medical term "grossly obese") also have many more fat cells—in some cases, at least twice as many as normal.[17] Excess numbers of fat cells have been observed in heavy children shortly after one year of age, and by age 11, these larger children had more fat cells than average weight adults.[18]

People on treatment programs tend to stop losing weight when their fat cells reduce to "normal" size, Fried said. Therefore, people with excess *numbers* of fat cells will still be fat, even though their cells are of normal size. Maintaining a fat cell below its normal size appears to cause biological stress, Fried added. She suggests that weight reduction might be more successful if patients with large numbers of fat cells reduced only until the cells were of normal size.

People inevitably ask: "Can't I liposuction my fat cells away?" The fact of the matter is that liposuction is *not* a weight loss procedure; it is a contouring procedure. The number of fat cells that such a procedure sucks out is quite trivial.

What color is your fat?

"Brown fat may be key to obesity," reads the headline in the December 12, 1993 edition of the *Milwaukee Journal*. The article, reprinted from *Newsday,* reveals: "An obscure substance in the body called brown fat seems to make much of the difference between being fat and being skinny." Brown fat is a poorly understood substance that seems to act differently from white fat, the ordinary stuff of bulging waistlines. Brown fat burns energy rather than conserving it, as white fat does, said endocrinologist Bradford Lowell at Beth Israel Hospital in Boston. In essence, it "wastes" calories. Animals seem to have more brown fat than humans.

Based on animal experiments, Lowell found that loss of brown fat led to gross obesity. It is theorized that large people may have a deficiency of brown fat activity, causing them to burn fewer calories. Lowell concluded that "brown adipose tissue dysfunction can cause obesity."[19]

High school biology revisited

We all learned in biology class about enzymes and proteins—but most of us have probably forgotten much of what we learned. You might want to rekindle an interest in the subject, because it turns out that some of these substances behave differently in fat people than they do in thin people. Among them:

- Lipoprotein lipase (LPL): LPL is an enzyme that acts like a sponge, mopping up fat traveling in the bloodstream and depositing it in fat cells. The higher the LPL, the more fat stored. It has been discovered that LPL levels drop early into a diet, but rise again after weight loss—as though the body was fighting to regain the weight. Researchers studying LPL found that "weight loss in very obese subjects leads to the increased activity and expression of lipoprotein lipase, thereby enhancing lipid [fat] storage and making further weight loss more difficult."[20]

- Galanin: Galanin is a brain protein that urges the body to consume fat-rich foods. Rats with high levels of galanin, when given a choice of foods, went straight for the lard! Those with normal galanin levels ate equal portions of all available foods. Scientists believe that the same reaction may occur in humans.[21, 22]

- Adipsin: Adipsin is a protein produced by fat cells. Animals that are fat for genetic or metabolic reasons make much less adipsin than those of normal weight or those that are fat because they were purposely fed too much. Scientists speculate that some forms of obesity, particularly where genetics is a factor, may be tied to a lack of adipsin.[23]

An obesity virus?

One new theory being proposed is that in some people, obesity may be caused by a virus. Researchers at the University of Wisconsin have been able to bring on obesity in animals by inoculating them with a human adenovirus. They concluded: "Data from these animal models suggest that the role of viral disease in the etiology of human obesity must be considered."[24]

Weight cycling

The debate over yo-yo dieting, or "weight cycling" as researchers call it, started in the 80s and continues on. When the topic first filtered down to the public, it was because of research indicating that dieting leads to a slowdown in metabolism and that repeated, or yo-yo, dieting further aggravates the problem. More recently, these findings have been called into question. So what gives? I'll try to sort it out.

Does yo-yo dieting alter your metabolism?

More recent research indicates that people's metabolic rates fell while they were dieting, but bounced back to pre-diet levels when they regained the weight they lost. This led to the conclusion that that weight cycling does not *permanently* slow down your metabolism.[25] But to *keep the weight off*, other scientists found that you will need to eat 15 percent fewer calories than a person who weighs the same as you, but has never been heavy.[26] And a comprehensive review of all major studies on weight cycling revealed that *formerly* overweight people had, on average, a three to five percent lower metabolic rate than people of the same weight who had never been overweight—which "is likely to contribute to the high rate of weight regain in formerly obese persons."[27]

It looks like:

1. Your metabolic rate falls while you are dieting, but bounces back if you regain the weight you lost. So it does not keep getting lower and lower with each successive diet.

2. If you want to maintain your weight loss, you will have to eat significantly less than someone who weighs what you now weigh, but has never been "overweight."

Does exercise prevent the fall in metabolism? It does, but not completely. In a 48-week study comparing dieters who exercised with those who didn't, metabolic rates fell during the first eight weeks whether people were exercising or not. By Week 24, people who were doing regular aerobic exercise had a smaller reduction in metabolism than people who were just doing strength training or not exercising at all. However, by Week 48 "there were no significant differences," probably, investigators speculated, because people were not exercising as regularly as they had in the beginning.[28]

Does yo-yo dieting change body composition? Some say yes, some say no:

- *Yes:* Repeated bouts of weight loss and regain may promote abdominal obesity and contribute to long-term health risks.[29]
- *No:* Body fat distribution was unchanged throughout the study.[30]

Does weight cycling cause psychological damage? "Definitive conclusions about the presence or absence of psychological consequences of weight cycling are premature, given the small number of studies," say the research team of Foster, Sarwer, and Wadden.[31] In their review of the few studies that have been done on this topic, they could not find widespread support for the idea that yo-yo dieting is associated with depression or other psychological malfunctioning. They did note that its effect on *self-esteem* has not been studied.[32] And in at least one study, the more diets a person had been on, the lower his/her self-esteem.[33]

Are there health consequences to yo-yo dieting? Some researchers believe that yo-yo dieting can lead to high blood pressure. For instance, Paul Ernsberger, Ph.D., of Case Western Reserve University, found that weight cycling elevates blood pressure in rats.[34] Other studies have found no such effect,[35] while there are those who feel that it is the combination of yo-yo dieting and the "apple" or abdominal type of obesity that strongly raises the risk of hypertension.[36] Weight cycling may be associated with decreases in glucose tolerance.[37]

One of the more interesting and disturbing findings is the link between weight fluctuation and excess mortality.[38] Scientists are not sure why, but they do acknowledge that there appears to be an association "between body weight variability and negative health outcomes, particularly mortality from coronary heart disease."[39] In one major study, both weight loss and weight gain were associated with significantly-increased mortality, and the lowest mortality rates were observed in men maintaining stable weight.[40]

Myths and unsolved mysteries

I hope you're getting the point. Larger people are biologically and physiologically different from thin people. It has nothing to do with willpower. It has nothing to do with your character. Now it's time to shatter some myths.

You just eat too much

This is, admittedly, an area of debate. Researchers David Garner, Ph.D., and Susan Wooley, Ph.D., looked at the eating habits of larger people in the early 90s and concluded: "Although occasional studies have found overeating by the obese, the majority have found no difference in food intakes of obese and lean infants, children, adolescents and adults." [41]

But now we have a more sophisticated technique, called the "doubly-labeled water" method, for measuring food intake. Explains David Allison, Ph.D., of Columbia University, who has studied and used the procedure:

> *Doubly-labeled water (DLW) is a biochemical technique developed in the early 1980s. It involves drinking water that is labeled with two isotopes. By looking at the differential rate of excretion of the two isotopes in urine a week or two later, scientists can determine how much oxygen a person is consuming and how much energy is being expended. Newton's first law of thermodynamics states that matter and energy can neither be created nor destroyed, but only converted. The DLW measurement tells us how much energy a person expends and takes in. Thus, DLW allows us to determine how much energy (calories) a person consumes without having to ask them.*

Through the use of this technique, it has been found that the *average* food intake of larger people, as a group, exceeds the *average* intake of thinner people, but the question is how much more? Studies have shown that the majority of larger people are not binge eaters (more on this in Chapter 12). It is also true that not all larger people eat more than average-weight people. And some thin people are probably eating more than you. Here's what a five-foot seven-inch, 113-pound model had to say when she was asked during a magazine interview if she watches what she eats: "Actually I eat like a man. If I have the day off, I'll have eggs Benedict, potatoes and coffee for breakfast, a turkey sub for lunch, and then I could always go for some Italian food for dinner." She also admitted that she does not regularly work out.

3,500 calories = one pound?

3,500 calories may *not* add exactly one pound to your hips. When identical twins who volunteered for a study were overfed intentionally, the siblings gained weight at about the same rate, but unrelated people gained anywhere from 9.5 to 29 pounds, even though all had eaten the same number of calories.[42] In a similar experiment, 12 pairs of identical twins were purposely overfed by 1,000 calories a day for three months. Although weight gains varied considerably between pairs, the gains within pairs were quite close.[43]

When a group of university students was asked to deliberately over-eat, each should have increased his or her weight by 20 percent, according to the mathematics of calories, but most found it difficult to post even a ten percent weight gain.[44] Finally, a group of lean prisoners volunteered to overeat for 200 days with the goal of gaining 20 to 30 pounds. Even though they virtually doubled their food intake, most struggled to gain weight. Only two did so easily. Not everyone reached the goal, and those who did could only maintain it by continuing to overeat. Once the experiment was over, weight loss came readily to all but the two who gained most easily (who were eventually found to have an unrevealed family history of obesity or diabetes).[45] Such experiments make it clear that simply the num-ber of calories consumed cannot explain weight loss or gain.

You have no willpower

If willpower is defined as having the strength to resist temptations such as candy, cookies and cake, large people have demonstrated vast quan-tities of it. Most have been on countless diets requiring them to avoid foods they enjoy for long periods of time. I often wonder how many thin people could deprive themselves of favorite foods and endure a continual undercurrent of hunger for weeks at a time.

Of course, this can't last. As obesity expert John Foreyt, Ph.D., explains in the book he co-authored with G. Ken Goodrick, Ph.D., *Living Without Dieting:*

> *We feel that losing weight by dieting is not unlike breath holding. The body will take over control after awhile, and it will cause breathing and eating even if the mind doesn't want to. After breath holding, a normal person will inhale a vast quantity of air to make up for the oxygen deficit. After a prolonged diet, the body will take in a large number of calories to make up for calorie deprivation.*

If the definition of willpower also encompasses strength of character, then large people have lots of it. First, it takes a lot of grit to live large in this society. Second, put food aside and think of all the situations in your life that required strength and perseverance:

- Have you survived the death of someone close to you? And have you found the strength to integrate cherished memories into your life and continue on?
- Have you met the challenge of an illness or disability? Perhaps it was you. Perhaps it was someone close to you who needed your help.
- Have you faced a fear and did you overcome it? Maybe it was a fear of flying, of speaking in public, of trying new things?
- Have you extricated yourself from a bad relationship or marriage and gone on to rebuild your life?
- Have you taken on a new job despite being scared to death? Have you gone back to school despite being absent from the classroom for years?
- As a large person, have you remained undaunted and resilient in the face of constant prejudice and discrimination?

Now who says you've got no strength of character or "willpower?"

You must have emotional problems

Noted obesity researcher Albert Stunkard finds it incredible that obese people are as mentally healthy as they are, "given all they have to put up with." He and his colleague Thomas Wadden have found that "overweight persons in the general population show no greater psychological disturbance than do non-obese persons."[46] They also found that there is no single personality type that characterizes the "severely obese."[47] Other researchers have found that factors once thought to be a *cause* of obesity, such as depression and anxiety, appear to be *consequences* of being a continual target of discrimination.[48]

Yes, some larger people have psychological problems, and so do some thin people. But it is often assumed that all larger people must have psychological problems, or else why would they be heavy? Generalizations such as these are dangerous. The general consensus about the psychological health of large people seems to be: Most large people are in good psychological health. Those who are not often visit mental health professionals. The same statement could be made about thin people. And some large people who seek counseling might have avoided it if ours was a more compassionate and tolerant society.

But it's unhealthy to be fat

Everyone *knows* how unhealthy it is to be fat, right? Some researchers aren't so sure about this and the issue has generated considerable debate in scientific and academic circles. Once again, the general public has been left pretty much in the dark. Why is this? People, even those who are supposed to objectively report the news, are reluctant to acknowledge that obesity could be anything but detrimental. Francie Berg, editor of the *Healthy Weight Journal*, recalls being at a prestigious meeting convened in 1992 by the National Institutes of Health, in which the benefits of weight loss were called into question. Several researchers had reached the surprising conclusion that instead of prolonging life, weight loss sometimes is associated with earlier death. The press, she said, was reluctant to report the findings of these studies. "We can't print that!" they said.

Researchers Susan Wooley, Ph.D., and David Garner, Ph.D., note that there are "conflicting opinions on the health risks associated with obesity, and the conclusion that obesity is dangerous represents a selective review of the data." This means that data supporting a link between obesity and health risks will be printed, while data contradicting this view is often suppressed. According to an article in the October 2000 issue of *Shape* magazine:

> *When the New England Journal of Medicine reported that the extra risk of dying associated with being fat was much more modest than expected, press coverage was minimal—it showed up on page 19 of The New York Times. After all, what a non-story: Being fat won't kill you!*

While plenty of studies can be found linking obesity to diabetes, hypertension, high cholesterol, sleep apnea, arthritis, coronary artery disease, stroke and certain types of cancer,[49] conflicting evidence exists. I will focus in this chapter on the conflicting evidence simply because it so rarely reaches the general public.

Deaths caused by obesity

It is often reported that more than 300,000 deaths per year can be attributed to obesity. But:

- A 1998 editorial in the *New England Journal of Medicine* said, ". . . that figure is by no means well-established. Not only is it derived from weak or incomplete data, but it is also called into question by methodological difficulties of determining which of many factors contribute to premature death."[50]

- A 1993 article in the *Journal of the American Medical Association* attributes the 300,000 deaths per year to diet/activity patterns, not to obesity.[51]

- A 1996 publication by researchers at the National Center for Health Statistics and Cornell University found that moderate obesity (no more than 50 pounds over ideal body weight) increased the risk of premature death only slightly in men and not at all in women during follow-up periods lasting up to 30 years. In fact, they found that thin men had a risk of premature death equal to that of men who were extremely overweight.

Of course, there are those who disagree, and another study, done in 1999, supports the 300,000 annual deaths figure.[52] What we don't seem to know is how many larger people are not among these statistics because they are taking steps to keep themselves fit and healthy.

Obesity and heart disease

Most of the studies that have looked at the relationship between body fat and atherosclerosis (clogged arteries), find that fat people are no more likely to have clogged arteries than thin people.[53] The International Atherosclerosis Project of the late 50s and early 60s concluded, after 23,000 autopsies, that there was no relationship between body weight or body fat and coronary vessel disease.[54]

In March, 1994, Steven Blair, an epidemiologist at the Cooper Institute for Aerobics Research in Dallas, told people at an American Heart Association meeting: "One of the fundamental tenets of the weight loss industry is if you get people to eat less, they'll lose weight. And if they lose weight, they'll be better off. And there is no evidence to support either one of those." Blair studied 12,025 Harvard University graduates. Those who said they were "always on a diet" had a heart disease rate of 23.1 percent, more than double the 10.6 rate of those who said they never dieted. Men who kept their weight steady, even if they were overweight, had less risk of disease than men whose weight fluctuated by as little as ten pounds.[55]

Obesity and Hypertension

I know many thin people with hypertension, so there has to be something more going on here than weight. It appears that this is true. The relationship between obesity and hypertension is *not* straightforward and "most likely represents an interaction of demographic, genetic, hormonal, renal, and hemodynamic factors."[56] Studies have found that the presence of abdominal fat or the "apple" type of obesity is more apt to be associated with hypertension in larger people.[57]

Obesity and Diabetes

There is plenty of evidence that obesity and Type II diabetes are strongly linked. But the newest research is focusing on a condition called "Syndrome X" which is characterized by the clustering of insulin resistance, diabetes, high blood pressure, high cholesterol, and abdominal obesity.[58] People bearing this profile do need to be vigilant about their health and make sure they are getting regular check-ups.

The Study of Health Outcomes of Weight Loss (SHOW) is a new study that will follow 6,000 people with Type 2 diabetes for four to seven years. The study will see how people who lose weight and maintain it fare in comparison to those who are treated for their diabetes and other health problems, but do not lose weight.

I'm a food addict

Some large people have convinced themselves that they're "food addicts" or "sugar addicts." Yet there is no real scientific evidence to support these claims. According to noted endocrinologist C. Wayne Callaway, M.D.,: "There is no such thing as a 'foodaholic,' at least not in the same way as people become addicted to alcohol or drugs."

John Foreyt, Ph.D., agrees. "There is no evidence," he says, "for addiction to any particular food such as sugar or white flour, even though some people swear they have such addictions." Again, people may mistake a natural reaction to food deprivation—eating—for a food addiction.

The popular belief that sugar is addictive stems from the fact that sugar produces a quick rise in blood sugar—a "sugar high" as some people like to call it. However, bananas or raisins, when eaten alone, actually raise blood sugar more than an equal amount of calories from table sugar.

True addiction has two characteristics: (1) tolerance, meaning that you have to increase the dose progressively to achieve the effect originally produced by a smaller amount, and (2) withdrawal, meaning that unpleasant symptoms will occur if the substance is discontinued abruptly. On neither account do experts find sugar addictive.

The U.S. Food and Drug Administration (FDA) has concluded that "high consumption of added sugars is not related to overweight." In FDA investigations, those who consumed more sugar consistently ate less fat, and did not weigh more than other groups, even when their total calorie intake was higher; in fact many weighed less.[59]

Also not true is the belief that sugar triggers diabetes. According to Richard Jackson, M.D., a researcher at Boston's Joslin Diabetes Center: "If you don't have the genes for diabetes, you can't bring it on simply by eating sugary foods." Diabetes is a hereditary disorder characterized by inadequate or ineffective insulin, the hormone responsible for regulating blood sugar levels.

Most nutritional experts agree that sugar poses no threat to health when eaten in moderation as part of a healthy lifestyle that includes exercise and balanced eating.

You have an ideal weight

If you were at your ideal weight, would you also be at your healthy weight? Not necessarily. So what's the difference? Ideal weight is what that old chart in your doctor's office says you should weigh based on your height and "build." (William Bennett, M.D., author of *The Dieter's Dilemma*, contends that the research upon which these tables are based "was so badly designed and inadequately presented that it cannot be taken as evidence of anything.")[60] For some women, ideal weight is the weight that finally allows them to zip up a pair of size 2 jeans.

"Healthy weight," a term coined more recently, takes into account the belief, discussed earlier, that each person has a natural weight range. But how do you know what constitutes a healthy weight? Who better to ask than Francie Berg, licensed nutritionist, adjunct professor at the University of North Dakota School of Medicine and editor of the *Healthy Weight*

Journal? Says Berg: "Healthy weight is the weight the body naturally adopts at this time in one's life when eating well and living actively."

Getting the experts to agree on the definition of "healthy weight" isn't always easy. Women's health consultant Pat Lyons and exercise scientist Wayne C. Miller, Ph.D., point to the "lack of scientific agreement on what constitutes a healthy weight for a given individual." The National Center for Health Statistics, World Health Organization and Shape Up America all use different cutoff points for defining who's overweight and who isn't.[61] It's not even enough any more to know what you weigh. You need to know your "body mass index" or "BMI," which is a ratio between your height and weight. If your BMI is 25 or more, the government considers you "overweight." If it's 30 or above, you're "obese."

The good news is that people who are considered overweight or obese may not need to lose as much weight as they thought to achieve a healthy weight. (The bad news is it probably won't be enough to fit into those size 2 jeans.) Although most dieters strive to achieve "ideal" body weight, there is now plenty of evidence that a modest weight loss can result in significant health benefits. Says George L. Blackburn, M.D., of the Nutrition/Metabolism Laboratory at New England Deaconess Hospital: "You cannot overestimate the value of the five to ten percent weight loss."

Healthy weight sounds good in theory, but the idea may lack popular appeal, especially among women. Why? Because the media and diet industry promote the idea that those at healthy weights are still "fat." Women in diet advertisement "before" pictures are often wearing anywhere from a size 10 to 14. Many were probably at healthy weights before they started dieting. In a University of Pennsylvania study, 60 women were asked to specify their goal weight and four other weights: "dream weight," "happy weight," "acceptable weight," and "disappointed weight." The women's goal weights were nearly three times the amount of their average weight loss. Almost half ended up at a weight they had defined as worse than "disappointing."[62]

My fat protects me from intimacy

The title "When Food Becomes a Substitute for Sex" jumped out at me from the pages of a women's magazine. In a study of patients undergoing psychoanalysis, 47.7 percent of those who were large said they used food to avoid sexual relationships. While I don't want to deny or minimize problems such as these, the majority of large women are not in psychoanalysis. Many are enjoying intimate relationships and robust sex lives. Once again, we make the mistake of generalizing the legitimate problems of a minority to the majority.

Researchers at Chicago's Michael Reese Hospital were actually startled to find that large women had a stronger sex drive than thin women. They had started out with the opposite hypothesis: that women become large and stay that way as a means of insulating themselves from the give and take of mature sexual relationships. When psychologist Colleen Rand scrutinized psychiatric evaluations of both patients awaiting weight loss surgery and others in psychoanalysis, she concluded, "There are no data which indicate that the obese individual has significantly greater or fewer sexual problems than nonobese individuals."[63] In a more recent study, Cornell University researchers found that body weight is not associated with most aspects of marital quality; indeed larger women were happier with their marriages.[64]

I hardly think that I made a conscious decision as a pudgy infant to acquire that layer of fat to shield myself from romance or other intrusions from the world around me. I have never shied away from romance or affection, and I have never regarded my ample flesh as a suit of armor to insulate me from the outside world. No one could accuse me of trying to "hide" or recede into the background.

Once again, you *must* think for yourself. Don't accept theories which may or may not apply to you. Always say to yourself, "Am I buying into this because I've heard it for so long or because it really applies to me?"

Larger women have a history of sexual abuse

Another popular assumption is that a history of sexual abuse is common among larger women. In one study, "significantly overweight" patients reported a greater prevalence of childhood sexual abuse than did a group of "always-slender" adults.[65] But in another study of women of all sizes, "nearly one woman in three reported unwanted sexual experiences before the age of 16."[66]

Some speculate that it is not weight *per se*, but eating disorders, that are linked to sexual abuse. Researchers who reviewed the available studies concluded that "around one-third of eating-disordered patients have been sexually abused in childhood," but then they add that this figure is *relatively comparable to rates found in normal populations.*[67]

Large women will have difficult pregnancies

While there are studies to support this claim, there are also those that dispute it. For example:

- In a study of 208 very heavy, pregnant women, there was "no significant increase in the incidence of urinary tract infection, diabetes, breech presentation, Caesarean section, forceps delivery, or maternal and infant morbidity.

- Another study of more than 4,200 women found that "overweight and obesity are only weak predictors of labor complications, given a normal pregnancy."

Dr. Paula Adams Hillard, an obstetrician and instructor at University of Cincinnati Medical Center, said in *Parents* magazine, "I do not feel it is appropriate or necessary to discourage pregnancy for women who are quite heavy. Although there is some potential for pregnancy-related problems, the risks are not markedly increased, especially if appropriate prenatal care begins early."

Dr. Jonathan Scher, an obstetrician, gynecologist and professor at Mt. Sinai School of Medicine in New York, agrees. "Extremely large patients can encounter minor difficulties," he says, "but most of the problems of larger women's pregnancies have solved themselves through technology." What about doctors who advise large women to lose weight before getting pregnant? Dr. Scher considers this a waste of time. "Large size pregnancy is a perceived problem," he says. "I think this whole section of the textbooks has to be rewritten. And doctors should get a bit kinder."

If I did it, so can you!

Occasionally someone will lose weight and decide to reveal their weight-loss "secrets" to the public. "If I did it, you can too!" is the rallying cry. What's wrong with this? First of all, as we have seen, people are different biologically and physiologically, and their bodies respond to dieting differently. Second, research has clearly shown that an individually tailored weight management program generally works better than someone else's.[72]

A *Consumer Reports* magazine survey of 95,000 readers found that dieters who decided to "go it alone" lost a modest amount of weight, about ten pounds on average. Those who went to a commercial program and followed it for about six months lost 10 to 20 percent of starting weight, but gained almost half that weight back within six months of finishing the program and more than two-thirds within two years.

I am not out to do battle with people who have lost weight and want to share their game plans. I know for them it represents the achievement of an important and difficult goal, and I'm sure some genuinely want to help others by presenting themselves as a role model. I can understand that. But they need to understand that the factors responsible for my weight may be different than the factors governing their weight, and that what helped them may not work for me. Their advice will be helpful to some, but others will be better off "flying solo."

How do you feel now?

How does this information make you feel? Liberated? Vindicated? Exhilarated? I hope it produces these reactions, but sometimes it doesn't. Sometimes people are disillusioned. "Are you saying it's hopeless, that I'll never lose weight?" they ask. "No," I reply. "I'm simply trying to help you gain a better understanding of the factors that are responsible for your size and weight so you can make more informed decisions about how to best manage your weight." It may mean switching your focus from an "ideal" weight dictated by a chart to a more realistic and healthy weight set by your body.

For some, this may require a period of "mourning" the passing of the "ideal weight" dream, especially if they've been putting their lives on hold waiting for that dream to materialize. For some who mourn too long or too intensely, I recommend therapy. But once the mourning is completed, you'll stand at the threshold of a whole new and exciting adventure— your life!

♥ ♥ ♥ From The Heart ♥ ♥ ♥

"No one ever told me . . . "

- No one ever told me about fat cells, that once you have them, they're yours for life, or that how many you have probably limits the amount of weight you could lose.

- No one ever told me about "weight ranges"—that we're all programmed to carry a certain amount of weight and that when we try to change it, our bodies defend that pre-programmed weight like crazy.

- No one ever told me about the genetic underpinnings of weight or asked me if there were heavy people in my family.

- No one ever told me that repeated dieting could have metabolic consequences.

- No one ever told me that dieting often fails to produce lasting weight loss.

- No one ever told me that attributing excess weight to overeating is simplistic and that biological and physiological processes play critical roles in determining a person's weight.

- No one ever told me that weight loss might carry its own health risks and that losing weight is no guarantee of a longer life.

- No one ever told me to stop blaming myself and instead blame the fact that obesity remains a poorly understood condition.

- No one ever told me that it might be possible to be healthy even if I did not reach my "ideal weight."

Why didn't someone tell me these things sooner? I could have spent a lot less time blaming myself and a whole lot more time appreciating the positive aspects of my life and myself.

3

bound by culture

The beauty of the human race is that everyone is unique and that uniqueness creates its own beauty. It is a shame that standards of appearance prevent people from knowing one another.

—Kari

Who defines beauty?

Two women are walking down the street. One is slender, one large. The slender woman is the recipient of whistles and other male noises of approval, while the large woman is subjected to oinks and jeers. One is considered beautiful, the other fat and ugly. Who made this decision and why? Who decided that the word "fat" could be linked only with negative adjectives?

Ideals of beauty are defined by cultures. "Black teeth, red lips or a stark white face appear attractive to someone conditioned to appreciate them," says body image expert April Fallon.[1] Aesthetic preferences for body shape and size have varied widely over time and across cultures. Anne

Scott Beller reports that out of 26 tribes from around the world who have gone on record as expressing a preference, only five preferred their women slender.[2] In trying to understand what men find attractive about the female body, Charles Darwin surveyed different cultures and concluded that, with respect to the human body, there is no single standard of beauty.[3]

The definitions of attractiveness are learned, explain writers Linda Tschirhart Sanford and Mary Ellen Donovan in their book, *Women and Self-Esteem.*

> *None of us came into this world believing we had to be attractive to be worthy. Nor did any of us come into the world with the idea that being attractive means being thin or having particular looks. We had to be taught to equate our worth with our attractiveness, and we had to be taught just what it is that's considered attractive in our culture at this particular point in history.[4]*

Women of the world

We know that in America and most Western cultures, many women feel they need to be extremely thin to be considered attractive. But this isn't true in other parts of the world. Our obsession with diets and thinness would seem strange to most of the world's inhabitants. It's not that women in other cultures aren't concerned with their appearance and their figures. Women everywhere want to look good. It's just that "looking good" means different things in different cultures. In fact, in many, a woman's plumpness is a sign of beauty, good health, prosperity and sexual appeal.

In Nigeria, gaining weight improves a girl's chances of getting a husband. The girls are put in special fattening rooms to pile on the pounds. Calling a Nigerian woman a "slim princess" would be an insult.[5] When Indian women were asked to describe the ideal shape for a woman, many ended up describing their own current shape.[6] (Sounds like they think they're fine just the way they are!)

And from an article in *Marie Claire* magazine titled "You're Not Fat, You're Living in the Wrong Country," we learn:

• In the Yucatan peninsula of Mexico, a heavy woman is not called fat but "substantial."

- In Mali, near the Sahara, a fat wife is envied.
- In Fiji, body weight is a measure of beauty and a symbol of how well your community takes care of you.
- Also in Fiji, a woman's calves are thought to be the sexiest part of her body. The worst insult you can offer a Fijian woman is to say she has thin legs.

Unfortunately, findings from a 1998 Harvard study presented at the American Psychiatric Association's annual meeting revealed that the widespread introduction of TV to Fiji in 1995 (with mostly American programs) has led to an increase among young Fijian girls in eating disorders, dieting, and body image disorders. Before then, only three percent of Fijian girls reported they vomited to control their weight. Three years later, 15 percent reported the behavior.

There are some signs that attitudes about the attractiveness of large people may be changing. In a national survey conducted annually by the NPD Group, a market research firm, one of the questions is whether "people who are not overweight look a lot more attractive." In 1985 a majority of respondents agreed with this statement. By the year 2000—once again, according to the NPD Group—only 24 percent agreed.

Fashion and beauty

It has always been my contention that there are no "bad" bodies, just bad press. That the fashion industry has had a substantial influence on our definition of beauty, especially in terms of size and shape, is undeniable. When I page through a fashion magazine or catch a designer runway show on TV and no one looks like me, I quickly learn that bodies like mine are not acceptable for public viewing. Although some top designers have now discovered that large women exist and have money to spend on quality apparel, others feel that plus-size designing is beneath them. One top designer was reported to have said that under no circumstances would he create clothes for plus-size women. If he had wanted to go into the upholstery business, he snorted, he would have!

For years the fashion industry paid little attention to us. Oh, we were grudgingly given some frocks called tents and caftans, along with the well-known double-knit polyester pants, but in general, the industry didn't care and thought *we* didn't care. Then a light bulb clicked and clothing manufacturers discovered that large women comprise a sizable percentage of the population. We hold jobs, go to parties, engage in leisure activities—and have money and credit cards in our wallets.

But it's still obvious, since we continue to be absent from the mainstream fashion venues, that no one wants to look at us, and thus the unspoken message remains: You're not pleasing to look at. We'll design for you, but we'll keep it under wraps as much as possible.

Occasionally, these industry ideals are challenged by some forward-thinking people, such as photographer Kurt Markus, whose work has been featured in *Mirabella* magazine. "I find," he says, "that the concept of beauty as defined by fashion is so limited that it has no application to real life." I wish a whole lot more people thought like you do, Kurt!

A moral imperative

The single characteristic of body size is thought to reveal a person's health status, degree of self-discipline, even state of mind. Indeed, weight has become a measure of a person's moral character. Says Hillel Schwartz: "This is a society in which feeling fit has become a spiritual category, where fitness means you are prepared to deal with everything in today's society and you are morally just. This is a society in which fat represents not only unfitness but spiritual backsliding, or an utter failure."[7]

Being fat isn't regarded just as a health problem; it's viewed as a "sin." *People* magazine recently published an article titled, "Diet Winners and Sinners," which lavished praise on the newly reduced and denounced the gainers. Talk shows regularly rake large people over the coals, sometimes while they sit beside their disgusted spouses, who issue weight loss ultimatums; sometimes while people who have triumphed over weight dispense their particular brand of advice; and sometimes in conjunction with health professionals who offer stern lectures. "We just have to hope you don't drop dead here on the stage," a doctor snapped at a friend of mine when the two appeared on a talk show dealing with weight issues. My friend is a healthy, attractive woman who has a Ph.D., is a college instructor and swims regularly. She also happens to be a large woman.

The large among us are assumed to be unhappy people who have little self-respect and no self-control. Yet similar assumptions are not made about people who have health-compromising habits, such as smoking, or high cholesterol. Why is this? Many feel it's the element of visibility. A rotund body is taken as visible proof that its owner has no control over what she puts in it, and that she indulges nonstop in goodies that slimmer people know how to decline—even though repeated studies have shown that many larger people are not eating excessively.

"Her body is an admirable reflection of her discipline," I once read about a celebrity who spends hours each day perfecting her physique. What's so admirable about this? Once we get past the point of exercising for health and well-being, it seems to me that it becomes not "admirable," but narcissistic.

How did thin come to be in?

Historically, views of the "ideal shape" have vacillated considerably. The early Romans placed a high value on thinness and bulimia as an accepted method for achieving it, while the Greeks idealized a body that, while not fat, was substantial. Venus, the goddess of love, is not only decidedly plump, curvaceous and big-hipped, but she is rather flat-chested by today's standards. If translated from marble to flesh, she would probably outweigh any current fashion model by at least 50 percent.[8]

According to Roberta Pollack Seid in her book, *Never Too Thin,* the Gothic nude, as portrayed by van Eyck in his Ghent Altarpiece, is "startlingly slim," while Botticelli's Venus is "sweetly full, round and sensuous." During the Renaissance, the ample women painted by Leonardo da Vinci and Titian coexisted with the slimmer ideals of a painting style known as "Mannerism." Rubens, of course, is the artist cited most often for his paintings of full-figured women—indeed we sometimes refer to this body type as "Rubenesque."

The ideal shape metamorphosed again in the 1800s with the emergence of the hourglass form. While women of this era were permitted to have ample bosoms and hips, these curves were set above and below a tiny waist. As the century drew to a close, the billowy body of Lillian Russell was in vogue and one admirer described her gently rolling curves as "so many sonnets of motion."

During these times, abundant flesh was a sign of success, prosperity, and a clean, temperate life. Thinness was suspect, evidence of a nervous temperament. Even doctors regarded a portly physique and hearty appetite as signs of good health.

Fatness was not generally regarded as an abnormality until the 1920s, when the ideal became almost boylike and women began binding their breasts to flatten their silhouette. The "flapper" look demanded a body with few protrusions. Preferences flip-flopped again in the 1930s, when it was acceptable to look like a mature woman. Seid explains that in a nation gripped by the Depression and then war, with threats of food shortages leading to rationing, overweight was hardly considered a serious problem. *Vogue* magazine, she muses, even ran an article on "how not to be so thin."

Between 1937 and 1945, fewer than two magazine articles a year dealt with weight reduction, notes Charles Schroeder in *Fat Is Not a Four Letter Word*. The count escalated to 54 articles between 1951 and 1953.

Over the last 20 years, television commercials for diet foods and other weight loss products have increased to nearly five percent of all TV ads— up from less than one percent in 1973.[9]

A watershed event occurred in 1951 with publication of the Metropolitan Life Insurance Company's weight/height tables. These tables were, in the opinion of many obesity researchers, flawed from the start because they were based not on a representative sample of the population, but on a select group of men who bought life insurance.

The obsession begins in earnest

Enter Twiggy. The year was 1966. She was five-feet seven-inches tall and weighed 97 pounds. She measured 31-22-32. And things have never been the same. The "ideal" body is shrinking. "There needs to be no body to get in the way of the clothes," remarks Hara Estroff Marano in *Style Is Not a Size*. Even mannequins have become anorexic—during the first half of the century their proportions were more like those of healthy women of normal weight. Since thin has been in, they've had the equivalent of about ten percent body fat.

Investigators found that in the years from 1959 to 1978, there was a significant decrease in the height/weight ratio of Miss America winners.[10] And when this issue was revisited in the year 2000, the *Journal of the American Medical Association* asked, "Is Miss America an undernourished role model?" The researchers for this study compiled data on weight and height of winners of the Miss America pageant from 1922 to 1999. In the 1920s, contestants had BMI's (body mass indexes) in the range now considered normal, which is 20 to 25. But an increasing number of winners since then have had BMI's under 18.5, which is the World Health Organization's standard for malnutrition. The researchers added, "Our finding cannot be explained by the upward trend in stature . . . Pageant winners' height increased less than two percent, whereas body weight decreased by 12 percent."[11]

A similar trend was observed in *Playboy* magazine centerfolds over the same twenty-year period. In fact, *Playboy* centerfolds have grown slimmer every year since the magazine began.

Even every little girl's treasure, the Barbie doll, appears to have an eating disorder. Researchers in Finland, who calculated Barbie's measurements if she were to come to life, concluded she'd be so lean she wouldn't be able to menstruate.[12]

According to Dr. Dean Edell, "This is the only time in history that fat discrimination has ever happened. Look at statues from the Tung Dynasty in China. Their standards of beauty are big, chubby fat faces. Only recently have we become maniacal about thinness."[13]

Fear of fat

Among adults, a University of Minnesota study found in a survey of close to 4,000 adults that 53 percent were currently engaged in some form of "weight control behavior."[19] A body image poll conducted for *People* magazine in 1996 came up with almost the same results—that 50 percent of American women are on a diet at any one time.

Body image expert Thomas Cash found in a national survey that only 15 percent of women were satisfied with all body areas, two out of three high school girls were dieting, and 47 percent of average-weight women viewed themselves as overweight.[14]

The fear starts young. Consider the following:

• Iowa State University investigators found that more than 60 percent of the fourth graders they studied were weighing themselves almost every day, wished they were thinner, and worried about being fat. About 40 percent reported dieting very often or sometimes.[15]

- Eighty-one percent of the 10-year-old girls in a University of California study were dissatisfied with their weight and were already dieting; only six percent of all girls surveyed were satisfied with their weight.[16]

- In a survey of close to 2,000 adolescents for the National Health and Nutrition Examination Survey III, 52 percent of girls who considered themselves overweight were, in fact, normal weight.[17]

- In a national survey of close to 12,000 high school students, the Centers for Disease Control found that more than 43 percent of the girls reported being on a diet—and a quarter of these dieters didn't think they were overweight.[18]

How afraid are women of becoming fat? In a *Glamour* magazine survey, women chose losing 10 to 15 pounds as more important than success in work or being in love. In a similar survey for *Vogue* magazine, the great majority of respondents said they would be willing to give up their spouses, careers and money for an ideal figure. When University of Florida researchers queried formerly fat people who had lost weight after intestinal bypass surgery, virtually all said they would rather be blind or deaf or have a leg amputated than be fat again.[20] Most frightening of all, *Newsweek* magazine in 1990 reported on a survey in which 11 percent of parents said they would abort a child predisposed to obesity.

Some people who come to our group admit they are living their worst nightmare: becoming fat. As I've mentioned, I have always been big, but some people gain weight later in life, as the result of pregnancy, illness or medications. This is what happened to Marion. Medication she needed for an illness had what was, to her, a horrifying side effect—it made her gain weight. She had the courage one evening to say to us: "I have always been repulsed by fat people and now I am one of them."

At a women's conference where I was displaying literature, the much younger woman in the adjacent booth confessed to me that she lived in fear of becoming fat. Rather than be offended, I chose to be curious. "Why?" I asked her. "Because," she replied, "it would signify to the world that I was out of control and had no willpower." I described my lifestyle to her— what I eat on a typical day, my exercise program, and the things I'm doing with my life. "Does that sound like a person who's out of control?" I asked. She admitted that it didn't, and we went on to have what I hope was for her an enlightening discussion about the myths that surround larger people.

Recently I was having lunch with my husband in a restaurant. We sat next to a group of young, attractive women. None would have been considered overweight. I couldn't help overhearing their conversation, which consisted mostly of talk about dieting, body anxieties and how much better their lives would be if they were thinner. I thought of all the more important things they could be talking about, but realized that at their age I would have been having a similar conversation.

That dieting has become "the American way" is illustrated by Schwartz in this observation about the reversal in etiquette: "Dieters in 1937 were advised to fast before a dinner party, then at the party to look as if they were eating. By 1985, a guide to fitness etiquette in *Woman's Day* had more rules for nondieters than for dieters, e.g. nondieters invited to dinner at a dieter's home should not bring their walnut fudge brownies; they should bring flowers."

The costs of dieting

How much do Americans spend trying to lose weight? Using a hypothetical 200-pound person, a group of Boston researchers determined that the cost per pound of weight loss at various commercial weight-loss programs ranged from $10.23 per pound at an individually-focused program to $0.91 per pound at a group program.[21]

Marketdata Enterprises in Tampa, Florida, calculated the size of the U.S. weight-loss market at $31.55 billion in 1999 and estimated that it would grow to $34.58 in the year 2000.[22] This is up from $29.8 billion in 1991. The top two revenue-grabbers are diet soft drinks, which brought in $13.6 billion in 1999, and health clubs, with revenues in 1999 of $10.7 billion. Other highlights from the Marketdata report:

- Sales of diet books, videos, and audio cassettes leaped from $196 million in 1991 to $1.04 billion in 1999.

- In 1999, Weight Watchers was the number one company in terms of actual revenues. They were followed by Slim-Fast Foods, Metabolife International, and Jenny Craig.

Marketdata is forecasting continued growth in all segments of the U.S. weight-loss market through the year 2004, with the strongest growth predicted to occur in the sales of diet books, cassettes, and exercise videos (up 11 percent); health club revenues (up nine percent); medically supervised diet programs, including anti-obesity prescription drugs (up seven percent); and meal replacements and appetite suppressants (also up seven percent).

Has our reward for all the dieting been a thinner population? No. For all the hysteria, the dieting, the frustration, the money spent, the tears shed, the deprivation and all the feelings of failure, Americans are heavier than ever. According to the National Institutes of Health, more than half of U.S. adults are considered overweight and the prevalence of obesity has increased by more than 50 percent since 1960.[23] In its diet industry report, Marketdata stated, "Dieters want quick results and the quick fix. ... They will pay just about anything if they can lose weight by simply taking a pill."

Impossible standards

Society sets impossible standards for women—ideal weights border on anorexia. *Elle* magazine columnist Michelle Stacey notes that "rarely has a society promoted a less attainable ideal shape—a boy's body with breasts."[24]

Yale University obesity expert Kelly Brownell, Ph.D., feels that today's body ideal lies "beyond what many people can achieve with healthy and reasonable levels of dieting and exercise. The percent body fat required for the aesthetic ideal is probably less than half the normal level, so one has to question whether the individual meets biological resistance in pursuit of the ideal."[25] In other words, many of our bodies just don't want to be this thin. When we try to cut our weight, all sorts of physiological barriers get thrown in our way.

The following admonition appeared in a fashion column written by a man: "The new spring clothes are going to produce more rolls than Pillsbury. If you have a few ounces of excess flesh, baring them is a mistake—but a mistake that will be made in large numbers, judging from the blind adherence of women to fashion trends." The sermon ended with the words: "A trim waist has power over the wills of men."

According to this writer, we're not even permitted "a few ounces" of excess flesh, let alone a few pounds. And we certainly should not expose any of this flesh for the world to see. Even more insulting to both men and women is his hypothesis that a trim female waist has power over men. I would like to think that a man is attracted to a woman for reasons that extend far beyond the circumference of her waist.

What madness has gripped this society that women can't even look like women any more? Naomi Wolf has a theory. In her book, *The Beauty Myth,* she argues that by becoming preoccupied with their looks, women have little time left for truly important things. She feels that an unending quest for beauty effectively sidetracks women from any pursuit of real and lasting power.

The authors of a book on women and self-esteem have a similar theory:

> *Devoting ourselves to the pursuit of thinness and beauty may help fulfill the human craving for excellence that in most cases is stunted in women. Men have many areas they are allowed to excel in—athletics, technology, business, wealth, etc. But in general, women are allowed to excel only in very narrow areas, among them being nurturing and being beautiful and thin.*[26]

You may or may not agree with these theories. But one of my goals for this book is to encourage you to dig deep into issues of size and weight, to really look at what's behind these anti-fat messages, to challenge and unmask them. Why is it that fat people are routinely the targets of self-righteous disdain, while people who smoke, drink, clog their arteries with junk food, or do not exercise often can be found leading the attack? Why is it that the research, which clearly shows obesity to have a physiological component, is ignored by everyone except those who conduct it? Why is it acceptable to discriminate against fat people in a society that preaches tolerance and respect for diversity? Decide what *you* think. Find your own truth.

What harm does it do?

So the media continually bombards us with super-thin images. What harm does it really do? Possibly quite a lot. Studies have found:

- Women who looked at fashion magazines preferred to weigh less, were less satisfied with their bodies, were more frustrated about their weight, were more preoccupied with the desire to be thin, and were more afraid of getting fat than were their peers who opted for news magazines.[27]

- Women were more depressed following exposure to pictures of female fashion models.[28]

- Sixty-nine percent of girls reported that pictures in magazines influence their idea of the perfect body shape, and 47 percent reported wanting to lose weight because of these pictures.[29]

- Watching particular types of TV programs, especially music videos and soap operas, caused adolescent girls to dislike their bodies and fueled a desire to be thinner.[30]

Capitalism's contribution

One speaker at a size-acceptance conference challenged the audience to consider how dependent capitalism is on self-rejection. We're too fat, too wrinkled, not well enough endowed. Our chins aren't prominent enough, our lips not full enough, our teeth not straight enough. Even if our weight gets the green light, there's still that wad of "cellulite" on our hips that needs to be subjected to liposuction.

I am not suggesting that we stop paying attention to our appearance, buying cosmetics, highlighting our hair or anything of the kind. But too much of the process is billed as "correcting, camouflaging or covering up." I would rather see beauty products and apparel sold as items that are intended to "accentuate the positive" rather than "eliminate the negative."

Self-acceptance will not spell doom for capitalism. In fact, just the opposite. A large woman who feels good about herself is going to be much more free with her pocketbook than one who has just read an article titled "Hiding Those Unsightly Bumps and Bulges." I spend much more money on clothes, makeup, accessories and hair treatments than I did when hygiene was the only thing that seemed important. I do it because I think I'm worth it, I deserve it, and because it's fun. And so should you!

Women who are made to feel that they should be kept hidden until their bodies are fit for public viewing will not spend much money. Why should they? Everyone has told them it won't matter much what they do until they lose weight. The problem is that many women will be waiting their entire lives for a body that has been genetically out of reach from the moment they were born.

Expanding the definition of beauty

Our society's definition of beauty is badly in need of an overhaul. By the time we exclude the old, the fat, and people with unconventional looks, we have excluded the majority of the population. "Beauty and sexuality come in many more forms than our current values recognize. Unfortunately, these other forms have no place in our narrow and constricted aesthetic spectrum," laments Dale Atrens, Ph.D., author of the book *Don't Diet.*

We need to regard beauty in humans in the same way we regard beauty in nature. If all but one kind of flower suddenly vanished and all but one type of animal became extinct, it would be a tragedy beyond comprehension for our planet. And yet the same eyes that appreciate diversity in nature cannot look at another human being and find a unique beauty in that person's size, shape and color. And why should a tulip aspire to be a rose? Women, however, will do almost anything to mold their shapes to conform to the one and only shape decreed acceptable.

Creating our own ideals

Rarely do we question the warnings of advertising, fashion and the media that if we can pinch more than an inch, we ought to be ashamed of ourselves. Women who have won all kinds of legal, career and domestic victories don't think to challenge a standard of beauty that is restrictive, illogical and largely unattainable.

But *you* don't have to buy into it. You can think for yourself. You can create your own ideal based on your own knowledge and self-discovery. Reject the foolish notion of one culturally-imposed ideal and realize that there can be just as many ideals as there are women.

Allow your beauty to spring from your individuality. Beauty encompasses more than physical characteristics. Let it include your zest for life, your fun-loving spirit, a smile that lights up your face, your compassion for others and perhaps a collection of quirky hats or giant earrings! This comes much closer to the dictionary definition of beauty, which is: "the aggregate of qualities in a person that gives pleasure to the sense or pleasurably exalts the mind or spirit."

Is it getting any better?

Although there are occasional rays of light, Americans seem less content with their bodies than ever. *Psychology Today* conducted body image surveys in 1972, 1985, and 1997. After the 1997 survey, the conclusion was: "Body dissatisfaction is soaring among both women and men—increasing at a faster rate than ever before." Fifteen percent of women respondents and 11 percent of men said they would sacrifice more than five years of their lives to be the weight they want.[31]

According to the American Society of Plastic and Reconstructive Surgeons, the demand for liposuction has increased 389 percent from 1992 to 1999 and grew 34 percent in just one year, from 1998 to 1999. In 1992, there were 47,212 procedures performed. In 1999 there were 230,865. Liposuction is now the most commonly-performed cosmetic procedure in the United States.[32] What's most scary is that in 1992, it was performed on 472 girls age 18 or under. By 1998, the number of girls in this age group receiving this drastic procedure had increased to 1,645.

Nationally, the reported incidence of both anorexia and bulimia has doubled since 1970, according to the American Psychiatric Association.

When *MODE* magazine asked its website visitors in June of 2000, "Do you think the film community has done anything to portray a wider variety of women in movies?", only 30 percent said yes, while 70 percent said no. Said one woman:

> *Hollywood's view of women is still very narrow. Only thin women are desirable. Real-sized women are portrayed as the sassy, single best friend of the more desirable, thinner woman. Time and time again, the larger woman is portrayed as the frightening, man-hungry thing who should be avoided at all costs. Hollywood still has a long way to go.*

I see occasional signs that our "magnificent obsession" with thinness is becoming less magnificent. In 1992 *The New York Times* ran a series called "Fat in America" that dealt thoughtfully and objectively with size discrimination, the failure of dieting, and the connection between genetics and weight. More recently PBS' Frontline produced an excellent program titled *FAT*. The promotional literature said:

> *Despite the appeals of the multi-billion dollar diet and exercise industries, the United States is getting fatter. The media bombards us with*

images of thin models exuding the message that to be thin is to be beautiful. But for many of us, being thin is a difficult, if not impossible, achievement. This program examines how the diet industry is contributing to our frustration over unwanted pounds and asks if one can be healthy, fit, beautiful—and fat. [The video of this program can be ordered by calling 1-800-PLAY-PBS and asking for the Frontline video FAT.]

But such articles and programs end up being drowned out by the continual "din of thin."

While scanning women's magazines in the early- to mid-90s for the first edition of this book, I came across occasional articles with titles like, "Looking Great at Any Weight," "Choosing To Be Big and Healthy," "Good Reasons Not To Diet." I saw no such articles in a recent tour of the newsstand. Instead I saw:

- Drop Five Pounds Fast
- Lose Weight for Good
- Increase Your Metabolism by 25% at Every Meal
- New High-Protein Diet
- Eat More, Weigh Less
- Shrink Your Body in a Week
- Fit into That Dress by Saturday Night
- Get Thin in Three Weeks

The current trend seems to be diets that promote fast, effortless weight loss. High-protein diets, which swept the country in the 60s, are the rage again. They fell out of favor when we all got sick of eating nothing but meat and spending our lives in the bathroom, but they're *baaaack.*

Articles about celebrities and how they maintain their ultra-thin bodies are popular, but also very scary. One female star says she maintains her figure through "strict dietary discipline." For breakfast, she has a fat-free muffin with fruit spread and three ounces of plain yogurt; for lunch, salad with low-fat dressing or pasta with vegetables; and for dinner, salad or pasta with a vegetable soup. Another pop star eats grain pancakes or toast with coffee for breakfast; a protein shake and salad for lunch; and chicken or fish for dinner. Consider that these are the role models young girls are trying to emulate! Could it get any scarier? When I asked a group of middle school girls the question: "Beyond what size would you consider yourself fat?" they responded, "Size 7." When I was in high school a size 12, even a 14, were regarded as "nonfat" sizes.

Herbal supplements have also come on like gangbusters over the past several years. Many promise effortless weight loss without even the need to exercise. At best, they are ineffective. At worst, some of their ingredients pose health risks (more on this in Chapter 13).

On the fashion magazine scene, the messages are mostly about dressing to look as thin as possible. Things like:

- "Look ten pounds thinner for a holiday party: Whenever you wear one color head to toe, especially black, you'll look much slimmer and taller."
- "Drop a size by summer"
- "Dress thin"
- "Figure fixers"
- "Fall's Best Looks: Sleek Shapes, Long Lean Lines"
- "Black and white and thin all over"

I don't need to look ten pounds thinner for a holiday party, and I certainly wouldn't think of wearing all black just for the sake of creating a slightly slimmer illusion, when what I really want to wear is a red sequined dress! I also don't need to dress thin or drop a size by summer (We all know I'd be two sizes bigger again by fall). We act as if clothing were meant as a disguise or a ruse instead of a way to express and enhance yourself. What fun is there in looking for a dress that will make you least likely to stand out in the crowd and most likely to blend in with the furniture? This certainly won't put me in a great party mood. But in my rhinestone-studded emerald green jumpsuit I'm ready to boogie!

We do have a choice. We do *not* have to accept everything we hear, read, and see. We do *not* have to have our thinking done for us by slick ad campaigns or fashion designers who refuse to acknowledge the diversity of the female form. Think for yourself. Don't swallow the messages whole. If you don't like what you're hearing, tune it out.

Until I became "largely positive," I wouldn't have thought to question the premise of an article titled, "How to Camouflage Your Figure Flaws."

But now I look at that phrase and I say: "I don't have any figure flaws. My body is simply a different shape than yours." Yes, some styles may be more flattering to my body than others, but I am not "flawed." And neither are you. Until we can recognize that the flaws are in the messages, not in us, our bodies will not truly belong to us.

So the original question was, "Are things getting any better?" The answer is both yes and no. At least now we have something called a "size acceptance movement," and those involved do a good job of bringing issues to the table for discussion—issues that would probably not have been raised 25 years ago. More and more, these issues are being brought to the public's attention by ardent authors and curious reporters. But, as we will see in a later chapter, size acceptance has had difficulty recruiting members. It's a tough sell in our "never too rich or too thin" society. Movements to stamp out discrimination, ignorance, and intolerance are never easy, but through them our society has achieved some of its grandest moments. We said in the beginning that ideals of beauty are defined by culture. We *are* the culture. If enough of us decide that a redefinition is in order, we can do it!

♥ ♥ ♥ From The Heart ♥ ♥ ♥

A Largely Positive Christmas

M is for magnificent—because that's what you are right now—even if you never lose another pound.

E is for enlightenment. Learn all you can about issues of size and weight so you can separate fact from fiction and absolve yourself from blame and guilt.

R is for relationships. Which ones are helping you grow and which are holding you back? Negative words are toxic to the soul. The antidote is to surround yourself with people who respect and affirm you.

R is for the realization that true beauty lies in diversity, not sameness. Flowers of all colors and shapes are beautiful. Decide which flower you resemble.

Y is for "Yes!" Say yes to life. Decide to do one thing you've been putting on hold and to take the first step before you ring in the New Year.

C is for caring about your self and others. Care enough to banish your internal critic. Donate to others the time you spend obsessing about your weight.

H is for your health. Dedicate the coming year to creating a "healthstyle" that suits you. Make a new health pledge each month and keep a record of what you do to fulfill it.

R is for respect. Demand it.

I is for image. Enhance it with colors you love, a confident stride, and a sparkling smile.

S is for self-acceptance. Accept your body and its biology. Imperfect though it may seem, it's been good to you. It gets you where you want to go. It allows you to touch, to move, to embrace.

T is for today. Life is about change, but begin where you are today and add to it. You already have many attributes. No one starts from zero.

M is for the majesty of the ample form.

A is for attitude. Self-deprecation repels. A positive attitude is magnetic.

S is for the spiritual renewal that comes with the holiday season. Train your mind to function on a grander scale. Focus on what's really important.

4

acceptable discrimination

We must not find size prejudice any more acceptable than any other kind of stereotyping and discrimination. Sizeism is just as repugnant as racism or religious intolerance.

—JANET

What's going on here?

- A large woman is denied employment, despite the fact that she had performed the sought-after job flawlessly several years earlier at essentially the same weight.

- A company docks the paychecks of its larger employees until they lose weight. There is no evidence, however, that they are docking the paychecks of people with high cholesterol, high blood pressure, or other so-called risk factors.

- A man is told by a complete stranger in a fast-food restaurant that watching him eat disgusts her. Her solution? Special restaurants for fat people. (How about special restaurants for cruel, ignorant people?)

- Comedians have a field day with fat people, frequently targeting celebrities with ample silhouettes.

- Bumper stickers warn "No Fat Chicks!"

- A member of Largely Positive is accosted in a grocery store by a woman she doesn't know. The woman tells her she should be ashamed of the way she looks and suggests that she get herself to a diet program.

- Another member, who has a knee problem (and has been told by her doctor she would have the problem even if she lost weight), returned to her car, parked legitimately in a handicapped space, to find a note that read: "Other than morbid obesity, what is your problem?"

- After citing the term "women of size" as the latest symptom of the political correctness virus, *Time* magazine came up with a new term— "women (or men) of solitude" which it defined as "people of size on Saturday nights!"

- Having first said that a 400-pound senior's attendance at graduation would cause an "interruption," the principal of a Chicago high school relented and allowed the student to participate in his class graduation ceremony.[1]

- In Oakland, California, newspapers published letters from people complaining about large women jogging around Lake Merritt.[2]

- And, almost unbelievably, a Michigan woman was shot in the head by her father, who declared it a "mercy killing" because of the mounting medical bills he claimed were due to her weight. She survived. She had just received an award for 1,000 hours of volunteer service to a local hospital and was planning to enroll in college. Hospital employees described her as cheery and happy, and they reported not noticing any severe health problems.[3]

As I asked in the beginning: What's going on here?

It's called weight discrimination, and it may very well be one of the last forms of discrimination regarded as acceptable. Dr. Susan Wooley sums it up in a nutshell: "We're running out of people that we're allowed to hate and feel superior to. Fatness is the one thing left that seems to be a person's fault, which it isn't."[4] Indeed, insulting a person's race, ethnicity or religion has long been deemed unacceptable, and only the cruelest person would make fun of a person with a disability or disfigurement.

Like most forms of discrimination, weight prejudice springs from ignorance and insensitivity. Larger people are assumed to be weak-willed human beings with uncontrollable, voracious appetites. As we have seen, the scientific evidence does not support this view, but the average person doesn't know that. And therein lies the crux of the problem—ignorance. Discrimination of all kinds feeds on ignorance.

Messages and assumptions

Much of the prejudice and discrimination surrounding weight stems from assumptions about large people which are, quite simply, wrong—but which come at us every day and in every way. Some examples:

- Testimonials for weight loss programs generally feature people who "hated" themselves until the appropriate number of pounds were shed. Message: You cannot possibly feel good about yourself while your dimensions remain ample.

- A character on a soap opera, who is pregnant, asks her husband: "Will you still love me when I'm big and fat?" Message: Big women are generally unlovable, and men who do choose to be intimate with them are doing them a big favor.

- The same character, on the same soap opera, about to get married and give birth simultaneously, says her mother found her a dress "that would make even a fat lady look good." Message: It is almost impossible for large women to look good without a supreme effort.

- Talk shows routinely feature programs with titles such as "I Love you, But You're Too Fat." Message: If you really loved me, you'd lose weight.

- Fat people provide comedians with frequent fodder for jokes. Message: It's okay to make fun of fat people because, after all, it's their own fault that they're fat.

- In an episode of the long-running sitcom *Murphy Brown*, Corky tells Murphy about being at a wedding and insisting that her husband, Miles, dance several times with one of the bridesmaids. Her reason: "I felt sorry for the girl—full-figured, you know." Message: Larger women are to be pitied and you will do them a favor by paying some attention to them.

- A famous actress who gained 20 pounds for a TV role said she did it so she would look like "I neglected myself" and to appear "unglamorous and frumpy." Message: All women who are 20 or more pounds overweight are unkempt, unattractive and out of shape.

- A TV commercial poses the question: "Why go to the beach just to get beached?" The image that follows is of two fat people reclining in lounge chairs. The unspoken message, of course, is that the pair looks like beached whales.

- A large lady in a sitcom returns a pair of shoes complaining that they have come apart. The clerk snarls at her that the shoes have a "two-ton weight limit." When the lady threatens to sue, the clerk asks if she'll be represented by the law firm of "Haagen and Dazs." Message: If you're big, you can expect people to be cruel to you.

Men's Health magazine has printed some particularly offensive blurbs. For example:

- About the same as Delta Burke: average pounds of peanuts Delta Airlines uses in one day: 6,000.[5]

- Not counting Linda Ronstadt: Total number of US promotional blimps currently in service: 13.[6]

The March, 2000 issue of this same magazine contained an article titled, "How Not to be Fat, Lazy, or Stupid."

Weight-loss testimonials are particularly distressing. You know—the ones accompanied by "before" and "after" pictures. The "before" picture is someone who was obviously told: "Go home and find the worst possible picture of yourself. Make sure you look as pitiful as possible and that you're wearing the most unflattering outfit you've ever owned." The "after" picture is the antithesis of the "before" picture—glowing smile, attractive clothes, upbeat attitude, confident stance. And the post-weight-loss interview usually goes something like this: "Now that I've lost weight, I feel so much better about myself. I have so much more confidence and self-esteem. My husband loves the new me!"

In one recent testimonial, the woman had gone from a "shameful" size 16 to an 8. (For many women a size 16 is probably a realistic size.) The woman was ecstatic about her four-size drop and exclaimed: "Now I can go out and get any job!" Is the message that size-16 women can't get jobs? Please! If this was the case, I know some doctors, lawyers, congressional representatives and CEOs who should step down from their posts immediately!

There is no reason you can't have all the qualities of the "after" picture *now*. Would we tell a woman with a cholesterol reading of 250 that she is not entitled to possess self-esteem until she reduces the number to 200? Of course not. But isn't this exactly what we do to large people?

Society's never-ending anti-fat assault is rarely called into question. Fat people deserve to be ridiculed. After all, they obviously have no regard for their health, their appearance or their self-respect. I'm reminded of a Ray Charles song titled "You Don't Know Me" because it expresses precisely what I'd like to say to the people who make appearance-based assumptions. Appearance is not an indicator of one's lifestyle.

I asked our members what makes them most angry about the way our culture treats large people. Some of their responses:

- "The view that you're a failure if you can't control your weight. I sometimes think the stigma is worse than that attached to people who break ethical and legal rules."

- "The assumption that if one is overweight, one doesn't 'deserve' to actively participate in social experiences like thin people."

- "Intolerance of other people—not recognizing that we, as part of the human race, are not perfect. People thinking that fat is a handicap and fat people cannot be beautiful."

- "Equating fat with lazy and lack of willpower and assuming we're not fit."

- "The assumption that we *could* be thin if we just didn't 'pig out.'"

- "The idea that large people don't care about themselves."

- "They don't look at what's on the inside, which is what really matters."

- "The fact that large people are looked down upon and not considered as smart as thin people. It has been my experience that many large people have greater intelligence."

- "The blaming, the scapegoating, the heaping of all kinds of negative qualities on people just because of their weight—often by complete strangers who are presumptuous enough to set themselves up as 'judges.'"

- "The condescension of people who were simply lucky enough to inherit 'skinny genes' is as repugnant to me as anyone who would look down his or her nose at other people they consider inferior."

- "People look at your size and think you are lazy, stupid and out of control. They judge you on your size and don't take the time to see what you have to offer—especially in finding employment."

- They treat us like we have no feelings, like we're just big lumps of blubber who don't think and feel like everyone else."

Awhile back, I wrote the following in one of my newsletters:

If we're going to rag on large people because we assume they have poor eating habits, then let's rag on others with nutritional shortcomings. Why not a campaign to make everyone with high cholesterol feel guilty and ashamed? We'll encourage them to have low self-esteem and tell them that the only way to improve it is to reduce their cholesterol to a "goal" level. Then their self-esteem will be based on a number—just like larger people.

Absurd? Yes, but it was meant to be to make the point that a person's physical appearance cannot convey their health status. Many larger people may be quite healthy, while people who look "the picture of health" may be harboring health problems not apparent to the naked eye.

When does the discrimination start?

Discrimination starts very early. In one study, children as young as six years of age labeled silhouettes of heavy youngsters as "lazy, stupid, cheats, liars, and ugly."[7] Even more troublesome is that these judgments were often made by the heavy children themselves. In a similar experiment,[8] children were asked to pick out a picture of a child they would not want to be their friend. Among their choices were pictures of "normal" children, handicapped children, and a fat child. Nineteen of twenty-four children, including those who were fat themselves, picked the fat child as the one they would least like to have as a friend. When the researchers asked one of the fat boys why he didn't want another fat boy as a friend, he replied: "Because he looks like me."

Where do kids get it? Mostly, they get it from adults and from the media. As I walked into a store one day, a little girl, no more than three or four years old, looked at me and said to her mother: "Fat lady, mommy." The mother hushed her but looked amused. Although this was definitely a teachable moment, I'm pretty sure no lesson was taught. Had I been a person of color or in some way disabled, it's likely the little girl would have been told about differences among people and that differences are what makes the world an interesting place.

One young girl speaking at a conference I attended said the most painful thing about being big was not teasing from peers but the attitudes of adults, because, she said, "They should have known better and loved me for me." Remarks by children or even teenagers can be chalked up to the fact that they're immature and still have a lot to learn. But a remark by an adult is not dismissed as easily. As children, we look to adults for answers, for truth, for affirmation of our worth, and to help us make sense of the world around us and the people in it.

An experiment conducted some years ago by researcher Wayne Wooley, Ph.D., of the University of Cincinnati Eating Disorders Clinic, found that some parents are actually ashamed of their fat children. In an address to a NAAFA (National Association for the Advancement of Fat Acceptance) convention, Dr. Wooley told of trying to get pictures of children for a study he was doing:

> We had a brief consent form saying we needed photographs of children
> for a study and asked every parent who passed by to let us photograph

their children. No parent of a thin child ever refused consent. No parent of a fat child ever gave consent. Sometimes parents permitted their thin child to be photographed while hiding their fat child behind them.

Do these parents think that the child doesn't notice their shame? Do they realize that their words and actions can inflict lifelong damage to self-esteem?

Planting positive seeds

One Largely Positive member told me how she deals with curiosity about her size in the children she works with:

Working in child care, I deal with children of all ages. We do everything together—dance, tell jokes, dig in the sandbox—well, all kinds of things. But one thing that almost always occurs is that a bright, curious three-year-old will call to my attention that I am 'fat.' They never 'attack' me with this news, but they are noticing the difference between themselves, their parents, friends, and, of course, myself. I never take offense or become embarrassed. I simply state that isn't it wonderful that everyone is so different and interesting, and what a boring place this world would be if it were any different. Their eyes light up and you can see the excitement in their expressions of newfound knowledge— then my eyes light up as I confirm the planting of some very positive seeds!

What are the effects of weight discrimination?

In September 1993, the *New England Journal of Medicine* published a study comparing the social and economic status of "overweight and non-overweight people," as well as people with other chronic health conditions that limited the work they could perform. The study participants were chosen in 1981 and revisited in 1988. People who remained overweight in 1988 were less likely to be married, had lower incomes, and were more likely to be poor than those in either of the other two groups. It is important to note that the overweight people chosen for the study had no serious health problems that would have restricted their social or economic choices.[9] The researchers felt strongly that discrimination was responsible for their findings, but many others viewed the findings of this study as simply one more reason people ought to lose weight, rather than a wake-up call for putting an end to weight discrimination.

Weight discrimination has also been shown to affect:

- Marriage prospects: Students who were asked to rate various categories of persons for their suitability as a marriage partner chose embezzlers, drug addicts, sexually promiscuous persons, and shoplifters as more suitable spouses than larger individuals.[10]

- College admissions: Students considered overweight are less likely to be accepted into high-ranking colleges despite equivalent high school grades, academic qualifications, and application rates.[11]

- Earnings: A survey of overweight male executives showed that they earned considerably less than those of average weight.[12]

- Housing: Landlords are less likely to rent to overweight persons.[13]

Even children are ashamed of large parents. As reported in *The New York Times*, 77 percent of intestinal bypass surgery patients said their children had asked them not to attend school functions.[14]

You might think that discrimination would be absent from the halls of justice. Think again. It was reported in the *NAAFA Newsletter* (April/May 1994) that a California deputy district attorney rejected a fat man as a potential juror because "obese people don't have the sort of social contact and work-together skills of someone I would like to work on my jury. They tend to be outcasts and unhappy people." Also in California, a large woman was denied employment at a health food collective because of "concerns about your weight." She filed a lawsuit but ultimately lost. One of the state Supreme Court justices who heard the case questioned whether a person "who eats 24 hours a day and becomes 305 pounds" has protection under the law.[15]

Another disturbing trend, sometimes referred to as "lifestyle discrimination," occurs when companies levy some sort of financial penalty against employees they consider too fat—sometimes in the form of docking their paychecks, sometimes charging them more for health insurance. Yet there is no evidence of the same penalties being levied against people who have high cholesterol, who take drugs, drink too much or get no exercise.

The invisibility factor

One of our members and facilitators is a market researcher. Not long ago she received a call from a prospective customer who wanted her firm to assemble five women who eat oatmeal for a videotape discussion. "Of course," the man said to her, "we can't have anyone who is overweight." That was all she needed to hear! Trying to remain professional, she asked, "Why is that?" "Because," he replied, "we want people who are reasonably attractive." "Are you saying that large people aren't attractive?" she shot back. At this point he may be starting to realize he has a large woman on the phone. "Well, no," he said. "But we need people who look fit." Wendy's turn: "Are you saying that large people don't take care of themselves?" He: "Well, not exactly, but isn't that what people think?" Bull's-eye! This is precisely why you hardly ever see a large person in a commercial.

We may be hard to miss in real life, but when it comes to TV, magazines and movies, we barely exist. I call it the "invisibility factor." When we do appear, we're often depicted as comical, pitiful or slothful—which simply reinforces the negative stereotypes. In one recent TV commercial, airline passengers are disgusted to find themselves sitting next to a large man, who is presumed to smell.

Perhaps advertisers assume that since no one wants to look like us, we make poor spokespeople for products. But the fact of the matter is that we *are* one-third of all American women, and we deserve to be represented in the media just like people of color and, increasingly, people with disabilities.

If I never see anyone who looks like me in magazines or on TV, I soon realize that people who look like me are not acceptable for public display. A 1977 unpublished analysis of prime-time television shows discovered that 95 percent of women appearing in lead or continuing roles were thin. The few who were larger were either older or people of color, and their characters almost never had professional jobs. Ken Mayer, author of the book *Real Women Don't Diet*, notes: ". . . the only big women I see on television are the unhappy looking 'befores' on diet commercials and a handful of talented exceptions who are forced to unnecessarily stand beneath the harsh spotlight of self-appointed critics."[16]

A more recent media analysis, conducted by W. Charisse Goodman for her book, *The Invisible Woman*, uncovered the following:

- A survey of 11 mainstream magazines turned up 645 pictures of thin women as opposed to 11 of heavy women.

- The tally after a three-week scrutiny of local newspapers was 221 pictures of thin women and nine of larger women; the advertising inserts contained 228 pictures of thin women and about a dozen heavy women.

- An examination of 160 TV commercials resulted in 120 ads featuring thin women exclusively, 27 depicting heavy males (mostly in a normal or positive light), and all of 12 heavy women, half of whom were either African American, older, or both.[17]

And hardly ever are large women portrayed as the romantic lead. In the movie *Angie*, the supporting actress is a very attractive, jazzy-looking large woman who, although married, is subjected to constant verbal abuse from her husband, mostly about her weight. The movie would not have suffered if she had been portrayed as an attractive large woman with a loving husband—many of us *do* have them!

If visitors from another planet were looking in on our print and electronic media, they'd never know our society included people who wear any size larger than 12! There are some notable exceptions. I've noticed larger women featured in commercials for K-Mart, Wal-Mart, Dawn dishwashing liquid, Cascade dishwasher detergent, Pine Sol cleanser, Dove soap, Chic jeans, and Snapple. So they've finally conceded that we wash dishes, scrub our faces and floors, drink designer iced tea and wear jeans, but there's still no evidence we wear perfume or lipstick!

In a particularly odd explanation, *Glamour* magazine said they cannot show models of different sizes because "we (and most other fashion magazines) shoot our stories at least three months before clothes will be in stores, and we have to use designer samples, which come in just one size, usually 6 or 8 . . . Samples are made by hand and it would be prohibitively expensive to cut them in multiple sizes." *Glamour* also claims that they convened a series of focus groups in which "we asked participants for their reactions to *Glamour* covers featuring size 16 models. The readers, a mix of sizes themselves, rejected every one."[18] (I guess they didn't ask any of us size-positive ladies to be in their focus groups!)

I recently asked our members to name the one thing they would do to improve the way large people are portrayed in the media. Their responses:

- "I'd show them having fun and enjoying life just like thin people—because they do!"

- "Show them walking and playing sports. I walk a lot with my dog, and a lot of my thin friends can't walk as long as I can."

- "Quit always portraying them as "fat and jolly."

- "Portray them as attractive, intelligent, confident, and happy."

- "Create a show that portrays large people in a sexy way."

- "Give them more credible roles."

- "Cease the portrayal of the fat person as being slovenly, ever jovial, putting themselves down, being unattractive to the opposite sex and uninvolved in athletics."

- "Have TV shows and movies portray large people in flattering roles—no fat jokes or derogatory remarks."

- "I would portray heavy people as people with no reference to their weight. Story lines would be exactly the same as they are now with thin people—filled with love, excitement and just normal everyday problems."

- "Large people should be shown in about the same numbers as they actually occur in real life. To look at most forms of the media now, you'd never know society contained any large people!"

- "You wouldn't allow jokes about racism, women, etc. We are human beings—built differently. Just because we don't fit society's norm of beauty (who does?), don't make fun of our differences."

- "Stop cartoons and jokes about large-sized people."

- "Attention newspaper reporters: Some of the unflattering adjectives used to describe us are really not needed!"

- "I would portray us as attractive, energetic, caring people with a lot of talent to give to the world."

The price of fame
(or Mama Cass did not die choking on a ham sandwich)

Why, as a society, do we allow someone's weight to overshadow his or her talents and accomplishments? This is particularly evident in jokes about the size of certain celebrities. When John Candy died in March 1994, I sat back and waited for the attack of the tabloids. It didn't take long before I was standing in the checkout line reading: "How John Candy Ate Himself to Death" and "Tales of John Candy's Wild Food Binges." A large person's untimely death always carries the implication that "it was his own fault." But many thinner people also die early—the 60s crooner Bobby Darin comes to mind—and their deaths do not become tabloid fodder. By the way, someone mentioned to me that John Candy also smoked a pack of cigarettes a day, which could have contributed to his death much more than his weight—not to mention the potentially harmful effects of yo-yo dieting.

People seemed amused—and still do—over the report that Mama Cass Elliott, the soul of the Mamas and Papas, died from choking on a ham sandwich. While preliminary reports did say this, the London coroner announced that the report was false. The actual cause of death was heart failure, but most people remember only the first report. Recently a local newspaper published a list of "some celebrity cookbooks you probably won't see published soon." As you might suspect, the list included "Fabulous Sandwiches" by Mama Cass. I imagine most people laughed. I was sad.

A few years ago after a performance by the sibling music duo Heart, one of our local music critics could not resist pointing out that one of the sisters had gotten a "little thick around the middle." Did it affect her performance? Apparently not, because he went on to praise the show. So why mention it at all?

When Elizabeth Taylor gained weight after her marriage to Senator John Warner and a picture of her appeared in *Women's Wear Daily*, the caption read: "All our lives we have wanted to look like Elizabeth Taylor, and now—God help us—we do."

There is a definite streak of meanness in this country when it comes to issues of size and weight, and it's rarely called into question. The National Organization for Women (NOW) took a step in the right direction several years ago by passing a resolution opposing size and weight discrimination. We need much more of this.

Fat like me

One strategy reporters have employed to illustrate fat discrimination is to don a "fat suit." In one case a magazine reporter suited up so she could see what life was really like for a fat person. Among her experiences: being laughed at by a cab driver as she struggled to get out of the cab—also by a man watching her eat an ice cream cone; enduring scornful looks as she ate in public; having passengers on a bus refusing to sit next to her; having her grocery cart scrutinized by total strangers. Her kids even told her not to pick them up at school looking like that.

In a similar experiment, a TV reporter put on a fat suit and went out onto the city streets. She purposely dropped an armload of packages to see if anyone would come to her aid. No one did. When she repeated the experiment minus the fat suit, people didn't hesitate to help her.

The reactions of the two reporters differed. The magazine writer has become a crusader against weight discrimination and says the way fat people are treated is a disgrace. The TV reporter viewed her experience as confirmation that larger people just need to lose weight. "Thin is in!" the coverage began. What followed was a pitiful account of the humiliations the TV reporter had suffered in her disguise as a fat person. The unspoken message was: If you don't lose weight, you'll get what you deserve. The magazine writer, on the other hand, concluded that it is society's attitudes, not people's weight, that need to change. I applaud her. The TV piece just prolongs the discrimination.

While these experiments are novel, I can't help wondering if the negative outcomes are an example of a self-fulfilling prophecy: the wearers of the fat suits expected to be treated poorly and so they were. In our discussion groups, we often talk about the signals we send, and we are convinced that "what you radiate is what will bounce back to you." People pick up on the vibes you send out via your appearance, demeanor, body language, gait, and facial expression. A person who is unkempt, unsmiling, shuffling along, head held down, emits an entirely different set of signals than the person who looks her best, has a sunny disposition, and struts with an air of confidence.

When Barbara, an animated woman with a mane of gorgeous red hair, receives a compliment on some aspect of her appearance, her usual reply is: "You must need glasses" or some other self-deprecating comeback. In other words, "How could you possibly find something to praise about me when I know how awful I look?" Her self-rejection is an insult not only to herself but also to the giver of the compliment.

I'm not saying weight discrimination will be eliminated if all large people start to smile and act confident. I am not naïve. But it helps. My encounters with strangers usually are pleasant. I get compliments (and I accept them graciously). Men open doors for me. No one seems to notice what I'm eating at a restaurant. Cab drivers don't laugh at me. People don't stare at me. But then again, I don't *expect* these things to happen.

It is not my intent to ignore, minimize, or trivialize incidents of weight discrimination. But this is a book about taking positive charge of your life and becoming proactive rather than reactive. I truly believe that projecting a positive image and attitude can help to *fend off* discrimination.

Battle of the "bulgers"

What can *you* do to fight weight discrimination? One thing is certain. Things won't change if we believe they can't—or if we share the attitude of one talk show host who told a large woman seeking size acceptance: "I know you want people to accept you as you are, but the fact of the matter is that they don't." In other words, it ain't gonna happen, folks, so give it up. I wonder what would have happened if we had said to people of different racial and ethnic backgrounds: "The fact of the matter is that people just don't accept you, so get used to it." This, of course, would be unconscionable. So why should people of size be expected to resign themselves to the same sort of prejudice and intolerance?

The tide propelling discrimination usually begins to turn when the group discriminated against takes the offensive rather than the defensive. We've been on the defensive for so long, it's hard to know how to get the ball back into our court. So how *do* we recapture it? You can begin by heightening your own awareness. Just because you see or hear something in the media does not mean it's true. Start challenging what you hear and read. Find out if there's evidence to support it. But first you have to be able to recognize when discrimination is occurring. "Big is bad" messages are omnipresent, and we have become so accepting of these messages that we don't even think to challenge them. Some examples:

- Clothing catalogs: In a 110-page catalog I received from a major department store, only three pages depicted clothing for the larger woman. Yet we comprise about one-third of the population.

• Fashion reporting: In a 12-page newspaper spread titled "Spring Fashion from New York to Milwaukee," I could not find one picture of a large woman or one reference to a clothing store for large women. I doubt that anyone consciously made a decision to *exclude* large women from the layout, but because we have been "invisible" for so long, no one thinks to *include* us.

• Designer fashion shows: Unless it is one of the few rare fashion shows exclusively for larger women, we are generally absent from the runway when the latest fashions are trotted out.

• Figure flaws: An ever-popular topic in women's magazines is "how to camouflage your figure flaws." For years, I too was eager to find out how to conceal my ugly flab, but I no longer accept the concept of "figure flaws." My figure is not "flawed." It's simply different from yours. Since when does diversity = flawed?

We all agree in principle that human diversity is something to be celebrated, but do we really mean it? For the most part, this is a culture that worships youth and svelteness. It's time we started practicing what we preach.

What can you do to fight weight discrimination once you've trained yourself to recognize when it's occurring?

Complain!

I have written letters of complaint to comedians who tell fat jokes. (Jay Leno even phoned me to discuss a letter I wrote to him.) I wrote to a local department store after receiving a Mother's Day catalog filled with apparel for "that special mom," but not one item for "that special large mom"—although their store carries larger sizes. I have written to mail-order companies that portray their large-size fashions on thin models—I find this insulting and demeaning.

Members of our group wrote to a radio station after a schlocky talk show host referred to his female producer as a "fat pig." You have to do the same. Train yourself to recognize weight discrimination when you see or hear it and complain. Otherwise, people will never realize they've done or said anything to offend you.

Sometimes complaining works. Hallmark cards cancelled production of cards that denigrate fat people in response to complaints from NAAFA and the Fat Activist Task Force. When the "Luann" comic strip contained derogatory comments about a woman who had gained weight since high school, once again NAAFA protested. The strip's creator, Greg Evans, apologized, asked for weight-related educational materials, and said nothing of this sort would happen in his strip again.[19]

Educate

The real answer to weight discrimination is education and enlightenment. There was a time when people thought mental illness was caused by "demons." Later, poor upbringing was the culprit. Scientists have now discovered that diseases like schizophrenia can be linked to biochemical imbalances in the brain. No one is at "fault." A similar scenario is unfolding in the area of obesity as researchers discover how the physiology of larger people differs from that of thinner people. I take every opportunity to educate those around me. I copy scientific articles and give them not only to family and friends but also to the health professionals I encounter both personally and professionally.

Set a positive example

This is a theme I intend to keep reemphasizing. Radiate confidence and self-respect, and you lessen considerably your chances of being treated poorly. A negative self-image attracts disrespect like a magnet. When I walk down the street with confidence and pride, I'm helping to shatter stereotypes about large people.

Teach your children acceptance

As an adult, you can teach your children that it's wrong to make cruel remarks about large people. Teach them that a person's size, like the color of one's skin, is simply another element of the diversity that makes each of us unique, special and interesting. And it's not just the responsibility of parents. Teachers can integrate lessons in size-acceptance into an ongoing dialogue about the importance of respecting human diversity.

Become an ally

If you are not a large person yourself, you can add your voice to the protest against weight discrimination. You can become an "ally." You can cleanse your mind of stereotypes about large people and open your mind to new information—even though it may contradict what you've always believed.

People who work in the media have a special responsibility to make sure large people are not ignored and to portray them in a positive light. Magazine editors can include large women in fashion layouts; movie and TV writers can create positive roles for large people; advertisers can include large people in their commercials; comedians can cut the fat jokes; newspaper reporters can make sure they have accurate information about issues of size and weight; and talk show producers can plan shows that help to educate, dispel myths, and prove that not all large people are out there hating themselves.

Coping with discrimination

What's the best way to cope with weight discrimination and stigmatization at a personal, psychological level? Are some strategies better than others? Researchers set out to answer that exact question in a 1999 study because "there appears to be no systematic study of the strategies used by obese persons to cope with stigmatization." They acknowledged that many books have dealt with these issues and that some (including the first edition of this book by yours truly) set forth coping strategies. But they felt that none of these methods had actually been *tested scientifically*, so they set out to do that by asking larger people about how they handle incidents of discrimination and stigmatization.

Investigators discovered that the stigmatizing situations faced most frequently by larger people were hurtful comments from children, other people making unflattering assumptions about them, and encountering physical barriers (such as too-small chairs). They also learned that the larger people they surveyed reacted to these situations most often by using positive self-statements; attempting to "head off" negative remarks by socially disarming people who might otherwise be critical; and using faith, religion, and prayer for self-consolation. They were then able to sort out the types of reactions that were helpful and those that weren't. The researchers found the following coping strategies to be "maladaptive":

• Negative self-talk, self-criticism.

- Crying, isolating one's self.
- Avoiding or leaving situation.

More successful strategies included:
- Positive self-talk.
- Seeing the situation as the other person's problem.
- Refusing to hide body, being visible.
- Self-love, self-acceptance.[20]

This study confirms what many of us have strongly suspected: project a positive attitude, accept what's uniquely yours, strut your stuff, and don't let your self-esteem be based on the opinions of others!

Weight discrimination on the job

Does job-related weight discrimination really exist or is it just imagined? Esther Rothblum and her colleagues at the University of Vermont decided to find out, so they surveyed members of the National Association to Advance Fat Acceptance about their employment-seeking experiences. Over 40 percent of the men surveyed and 60 percent of the women said they had not been hired for a job because of their weight. Among the reasons given for not hiring them: They would lack energy, they would be bad role models, insurance would not cover them, they would break the new office furniture. More often, however, respondents said they suspected job discrimination but couldn't prove it.

As might be expected, women who weighed at least 50 percent over their "chart weight" were much more likely to be turned down for a job than women with lower weights. The researchers also found that in general, large people held less prestigious jobs, and many felt they were over-qualified for the work they were doing.[21]

Western Michigan University Professor Mark V. Roehling evaluated 29 weight-discrimination studies and interviewed employees who felt they had been victims of weight discrimination.[22] Roehling says many employers he interviewed didn't attempt to hide their prejudice against obese people. One bank manager told him he "would never hire a fat girl."

Among Roehling's findings:

- Despite objective equivalent test performances, overweight applicants were less likely to be hired, and their personality traits were rated more negatively.

- Overweight persons were more likely to be assigned to an undesirable sales territory or not selected at all.

- Size 6 models vs. size 14 models were rated higher in terms of competence, being comfortable to work with, and friendliness.

- There was a strong bias against overweight persons in hire recommendations, especially for female applicants. Bias was greatest among raters who were satisfied with their bodies.

- Overweight male MBAs reported significantly lower starting salaries (averaging $3,000), and salary differences with normal-weight males increased over time.

- Overweight females earned over 12 percent less than their average weight counterparts.

- Forty-four percent of employers considered obesity conditional medical grounds for not employing an applicant.

The assumption is often made that, because of their weight, larger people will be sick or absent a lot. Yet there is evidence that contradicts this view. In a 1981 study by Bjorntorp and Tibblin, it was reported that fat men took no more days of sick leave and were no more likely to collect for disability than those who were not overweight.[23] In yet another study, large men were no more likely to have work-limiting health conditions than thinner men.[24]

Roehling concluded: "Overall, the evidence of consistent, significant discrimination against overweight employees is sobering. Evidence of discrimination is found at virtually every stage of the employment cycle, including selection, placement, compensation, promotion, discipline, and discharge."

One of our members was seeking a promotion that would have required her to greet the public. The promotion was denied because, as management explained: "We don't feel you present the right 'image' at the point of entry to our company." Claire is a very attractive woman, well-dressed, well-groomed and well-spoken. They never actually said: "We can't have you out front because you're fat." But this is what they meant.

Is workplace weight discrimination illegal?

Increasingly, there is legal ammunition people can use when they believe they may have been the victims of weight discrimination, and cases are increasingly being decided in favor of larger plaintiffs. Here is a summary of the legislation that pertains to weight discrimination, followed by some cases where this legislation has been successfully employed:

Federal laws

- **Title VII of the Civil Rights Act of 1964** declares that all persons within the United States have a right to employment free from discrimination based on race, color, religion, sex, or national origin. It has been used in size discrimination cases where weight standards are applied differently to different groups of people, e.g. women and men. For example, in *Gerdom vs. Continental Airlines* (1982), the court determined that the airline's weight restriction program treated employees differently based on sex because it was designed to apply only to females, and "it was not merely slenderness, but slenderness of female employees which the employer considered critical."

- **The Rehabilitation Act of 1973** prohibits discrimination against an otherwise qualified individual with handicaps, solely on the basis of that handicap, in any program which receives federal assistance.

- **The Americans with Disabilities Act (ADA) of 1990** extends the protection against discrimination on the basis of disability to the private sector. In order to establish an actual disability, an employee must be able to prove that he or she is either "morbidly obese" (100 percent over ideal weight) or suffering from obesity that is due to a physiological condition. The majority of larger people who are not considered morbidly obese would have to prove that their weight has a physiological basis to establish an actual disability under these laws. Another hurdle for plaintiffs trying to establish a weight-based disability comes by way of recent Supreme Court rulings that the ADA's definition of disability does not cover conditions that are medically correctable (and the popular belief is that obesity is medically correctable).

State laws

- **State of Michigan:** (Elliot Larsen Civil Rights Act, Act 453 of 1976, Sec. 209), bans discrimination in employment based on race, color, religion, national origin, age, sex, height, weight, or marital status.

Local ordinances

- **Santa Cruz, CA** (July 1992), defines unlawful discrimination as "differential treatment as a result of that person's race, color, creed, religion, national origin, ancestry, disability, marital status, sex gender, sexual orientation, height, weight, or physical characteristic."

- **The District of Columbia,** outlaws discrimination in employment based upon "race, color, religion, national origin, sex, age, marital status, personal appearance, sexual orientation, family responsibilities, physical handicap, matriculation, or political affiliation."

- **San Francisco** (May 2000), makes it illegal to discriminate against a person based on size, in addition to race, religion, color, ancestry, age, sex, sexual orientation, gender identity, disability and place of birth.

Favorable weight discrimination rulings

- The U.S. Circuit Court of Appeals ruled for Bonnie Cook, who was denied employment as an attendant at a Rhode Island home for mentally disabled people, despite the fact that she had worked for the same facility a few years before—at the same weight and with a good work record. The court said that the Rhode Island Department of Mental Health, Retardation and Hospitals had discriminated against Cook when they refused to rehire her. A U.S. district judge upheld the jury's $100,000 award, ordered the state to give Cook the next available job and to award her retroactive seniority (1993).

- In Maryland, a judge ruled that the "perceived handicap of obesity" is protected from discrimination under Maryland state law when he ruled that four women denied employment by the Maryland State Mass Transit Administration were indeed fit to work for the agency. The women weighed between 186 and 205 pounds at the time they were automatically rejected because they exceeded the agency's weight limitations (1990).

- After four years as a security guard with an exemplary record, Jesse Mercado was fired from the *Los Angeles Times* for being too fat. The jury found in Mercado's favor and awarded him almost $500,000 in damages and attorneys fees (1991).
- A New Jersey administrative law judge ruled in favor of Joseph Gimello, who was fired by Agency Rent-a-Car for his weight, even though all previous evaluations had been excellent (1991).

If you feel you have been the victim of weight-related job discrimination and are not sure what steps to take to deal with it, visit the website of the Council on Size and Weight Discrimination (www.cswd.org) and go to their web page, "Dealing with Job Discrimination." (or phone them at 914-679-1209. Fax: 914-679-1206). You may also want to visit the website of the Obesity Law and Advocacy Center (www.obesitylaw.com), a private, full-service law firm established in 1996 to represent larger persons in legal disputes revolving around employment discrimination and the denial of weight-related medical care (you can also phone them at 619-656-5251 or fax at 619-656-5254).

Preventing employment-related weight discrimination

Is there anything *you* can do to reduce the likelihood you'll be a victim of weight discrimination when seeking a job? Some incidents of discrimination, like name calling, can be shrugged off, but a job is different. It's your livelihood. Work is a major vehicle for self-fulfillment and self-expression. You want to feel you've reached a position where you'll be able to use your skills and talents to their greatest potential. And you're entitled to! Chances are you won't be told directly that your weight is the reason you're not being hired or not getting that promotion. Employers are fearful of saying anything that might qualify as discrimination and lead to legal trouble—especially now that some large people have won weight discrimination lawsuits. So the rejection or denial will probably be attributed to other factors.

I often advise people to raise the issue of weight themselves. You know the interviewer has probably made a mental note of it—and probably not a positive note. So why not say something like this:

> *I'm sure you've noticed that I'm a large person and you may be wondering how my weight would affect my ability to do this job. Let me assure you that I'm a healthy person, rarely sick, and my energy level is high. I'm a hard worker and have a good track record, as I'm sure you'll find out if you check my references. I try to take good care of myself by exercising and eating nutritiously. But physiologically I seem destined to be a larger person.*

This opens the door for some honest and positive discussion and gives you the chance to allay any concerns the prospective employer might have about your weight.

You also have a responsibility in this process. Your responsibility is to present yourself in the best possible light. Sometimes I listen to large people complain that they're having a hard time finding a job, and I want to say: "I'm not surprised, given the way you look and the negative attitude you're projecting." Employers are looking for people who are confident, upbeat, motivated—not people who have obviously given themselves a negative self-rating.

Joan Lloyd is a Milwaukee-based organizational-change consultant and author who writes a column for the *Milwaukee Journal*. In her column of January 10, 1993, she discussed the issue of looks and employment. When it comes to prejudice, she says, you can do one of three things: "Do nothing; prove them right; or prove them wrong." Obviously, I would hope you choose the third strategy. But how to do it?

So you've got a job interview. How can you minimize the possibility that your weight will interfere with your chance of being hired?

Emphasize your accomplishments

Make a list of your skills, talents and accomplishments. Internalize them. Tell yourself that these are the things that are important to a prospective employer. Make your statements results-oriented. Say: "I brought in $50,000 in new accounts" or "I designed new computer software that cut processing time in half." If you can convince the prospective employer you have the abilities he or she needs, issues of size and weight will diminish in importance.

Do your homework

Come prepared to show a prospective employer you've taken the time to find out about the company you hope to work for. Learn all you can, and be able to show the interviewer where your talents and abilities can be plugged in. Call and ask for an annual report, brochures or anything else that tells about the company. Know someone who works there? Invite that person to lunch and say you're interested in learning more about the company. Your preparation will be apparent at your interview—and, once again, weight-related concerns may vanish.

Be "interview savvy"

Although you can never anticipate all the questions you'll be asked, some are fairly standard. Come prepared. Early in my job-seeking days I was asked simply: "Tell me about yourself." I felt afterward that a toad would have given a better response. Then I bought a book on interviewing skills and my responses improved considerably, not because I had become any more quick on my toes, but because I knew what to expect and had time to think about how I would respond.

Project confidence

This should be easier if you've followed the preceding advice. A confident demeanor and attitude will almost always neutralize issues of size and weight. Display your confidence in the way you dress, walk, and talk. Enter the interview with your head held high. Don't droop. Smile. Make eye contact. Speak slowly and pleasantly. And *believe* you're the best person they could hire for this job!

Dress well

Contrary to what you may think, your appearance can work in your favor—if you quit buying into the notion that being large equates with being unattractive. No one is more eye-catching than the larger woman—or man—who has taken the time to develop a personal style that projects self-assurance and a sense of being at ease with oneself. Larger fashions have come a long way, baby, and there's no excuse anymore for not looking polished and professional.

Pay attention to grooming

There is no excuse for greasy hair, a stain on your blouse or a run in your stocking. And besides, we have to do everything we can to counteract the stereotype that larger people are sloppy and unkempt.

Regard size as an attribute

I told our support group one evening that we were going to list the advantages of being a larger person. After their skepticism subsided, we actually made quite a long list. One of the women said she has always regarded her size as a plus on the job. "It makes me feel powerful," she said, "and I know it has that impact on others." She feels this is especially true when she is "dressed to kill" in one of her "power suits." The Council on Size and Weight Discrimination suggests pointing out the positive aspects of your weight: "One woman got a job as a counselor on a college campus by telling her interviewer that she thought she could be a role model for the large-size college women who might be having problems."

Believe in yourself

"Not once did I think they wouldn't hire me because of my size." I heard this remark from a lawyer, very attractive and articulate, who spoke at a conference I attended on the subject of weight discrimination on the job. Now, I know we're not all lawyers and that it might be easier for someone in this position to avoid job discrimination, but I also think that it wouldn't be as difficult as it sometimes is if more people adopted her attitude. Tell yourself you are the best person for this job and the company would be lucky to have you. Remember that your weight is not a measure of self-worth or competence. A thinner body would not make you any smarter or more talented. So walk in and make a "largely positive" impression!

Has there been any progress?

What progress has been made in stamping out weight discrimination in the five years since this book first appeared? Actually, quite a bit. Even I was surprised when I compiled the following, which is just the "short list":

- Articles protesting weight discrimination are appearing in highly-respected medical journals. On October 27, 1999, the *Journal of the American Medical Association* ran an article titled, "Effective Health Promotion and Clinical Care for Large People." In 1998 *Weight Control Digest* published, "Health Care Providers' Unhealthy Attitudes Toward Obese People." And on January 1, 1998, the *New England Journal of Medicine* called losing weight, "An Ill-Fated New Year's Resolution" and called upon doctors to "do their part to help end discrimination against overweight people in schools and workplaces."

- Some of the fact-based research is finally getting out to the public. Examples: *Newsweek's* piece, "Does It Matter What You Weigh? The Surprising New Facts About Fat," (April 21, 1997) and the *U.S. News & World Report's* "The New Truth About FAT" (January 12, 1998). The *New York Times* has also done some excellent pieces.

- The *Wall Street Journal* raised questions about the 300,000 annual deaths attributed to obesity in an article titled, "Dire Warnings About Obesity Rest on Slippery Statistics" (February 9, 1998).

- PBS' Frontline series aired a well-researched program called, "Fat and Fit" (November 4, 1998).

- Plus-size actresses continue to emerge and speak out against weight discrimination—people like *The Practice's* Camryn Manheim, soap star Patrika Darbo (*Days of Our Lives*), as well as supermodel Emme who hosts the show *Fashion Emergency*.

- Baywatch was supposedly looking for a "large" actress to appear with the skinny babes.

- Ultra upscale Beverly Hills clothier and perfume maven Bijan created a series of ads using an attractive 450-pound model named Bella. Although some magazines refused the ads, others such as *Vanity Fair, Esquire, Departures* and *Talk* ran them.

- Plus size clothes have been proliferating, and many high-fashion designers are getting into the full-figured act.

- The "Million Pound March" took place in association with NAAFA's 1998 convention and members noted that "coverage was respectful."

- The American Heart Association withdrew an ad they had created depicting a kid snacking after school and morphing into a fat kid, complete with oinking noises. Lynn McAfee of CSWD sent videotapes of the ad to ten leading authorities on childhood obesity and eating disorders, and some wrote brilliant letters opposing the ad. The AHA subsequently withdrew the ad for "further study."

- International No-Diet Days in May are increasingly visible and successful.

I asked William Fabrey of the Council on Size and Weight Discrimination, "What, in your opinion, are the most significant positive and negative trends related to weight discrimination over the last five years?" His response:

The negative:

1. An increasing number of children are said to be on diets and developing malnutrition and eating disorders.

2. An increasing number of adult health professionals bemoan what they believe is an "epidemic" of obesity in children, and appear to be more concerned about fat kids—even putting them on diets—than about thin kids who are obsessed with weight issues.

3. A rise in radical surgical and pharmaceutical experimentation on fat adults is occurring, based on the mistaken premise that any risks are better than being fat. I expect this will give rise to future generations of fat people with severe digestive disorders and other health problems as a direct consequence of those interventions.

The positive:

1. Recent research, which has been gaining acceptance, shows it is possible to remain fat but increase one's fitness level and reduce health problems statistically associated with obesity.

2. There has been an increase in the number of size acceptance activities, including social outlets for large persons such as private

clubs and the Internet, helping to reduce the social isolation felt by so many fat people in the past.

3. The concept seems to be seeping into popular culture that there are all kinds of physical attractiveness, including plus and even super sizes.

The last two trends are very real, to the point that they have been openly criticized by fat phobic commentators, who would prefer that every last citizen be thin, and at any cost.

A collective task

Size discrimination will not be extinguished until it is truly recognized as discrimination and until all people—large, small and in-between—decide that it will not be tolerated. Discrimination in any form taints our society. Almost everyone can do something about size and weight discrimination.

♥ ♥ ♥ From The Heart ♥ ♥ ♥

Is There a Name For This?

- Why did they call me names? I was a nice little girl. Is there a name for this?

- Why do comedians tell jokes about fat women? Do they think we enjoy their comedic cruelty? Is there a name for this?

- Why was I rejected for cheerleading? They said I was one of the best—too chubby, though. Why did they tell me I couldn't be a bridesmaid until I lost weight? Is there a name for this?

- Why do they want to withhold self-esteem from me until I am at a weight that is "ideal?" Do they want me to live a life of self-hatred? Is there a name for this?

- Why do I rarely see anyone who looks like me in women's magazines, on TV, or in the movies? When I do see someone with a body like mine, why are they usually the comic relief? Is there a name for this?

- Why do department stores tick "Women's World" in a drab, remote area of the store? Is there a name for this?

- Why can't all large people go to the theater or ride on a plane in comfort? Is there a name for this?

- Why was a job withheld from a large woman because "we can't have you out front"? Is there a name for this?

Yes, there is a name for this—the name is discrimination. Be sure to call it by its rightful name from now on.

5

creating your own ideals

I basically tell people that God made both St. Bernards and Chihuahuas—that I'm healthy and feel good. (I might also enlighten them about the use of good manners, which they are lacking!)

—DEBBIE

Body acceptance

My friend Kari has often said to me, "I can get to the point where I like and accept myself and I no longer put my life on hold, but I'll be darned if I can honestly say I love and adore my body. Is that okay?"

You'd think that body acceptance and self-esteem would go hand in hand, but this has not been my experience in working with large women. I find that accepting and valuing one's "inner" self usually precedes acceptance and love of the "outer" self. And some women never accomplish the latter, although they are able to disconnect their body dissatisfaction from their self-worth and get on with living their lives.

One night, at a Chinese restaurant, the fortune cookie I got contained this message: "It is better to idealize the real than to realize the ideal." This little pearl of wisdom sums up in a nutshell—in this case a fortune cookie shell—a good philosophy for our relationship with our bodies.

The dictionary provides several definitions for "ideal," including "existing as a mental image or in fancy or imagination only," and "lacking practicality." Let's look at both of these ideas.

- The current "ideal" female body definitely lacks practicality because 99 percent of all women do not possess the genetic material to replicate it. At this point the ideal becomes not an ideal at all, but a burden on the shoulders of womankind.

- I think the majority of women would admit that their ideal bodies, for the most part, have existed "in fancy or imagination only." For years I carried around a mental picture of what my body would look like at its ideal weight. I have now discarded this picture because I know it will never exist outside of my mind.

Bodies have come to represent much more than they should. If a woman has bad feelings about her body, she usually has bad feelings about her entire being. Because of her severely negative body image, one of our members said she was "nothing," "a complete failure." I became alarmed when she said, "I might as well drive my car off a cliff." (Fortunately, she didn't. We worked with her and gradually her self-image improved.) It's almost certain she wouldn't have felt this way if she smoked or had high cholesterol. Why? While smoking and high cholesterol are also regarded as health risks, they can be compartmentalized—isolated from the rest of the person. A person can rationalize: "Yes, it's not good that I smoke, but I'm a pretty good person otherwise."

Noted obesity researcher Albert Stunkard, M.D., would not be surprised by this woman's despair. He has discovered that people with severely negative body images are preoccupied with their bodies, often to the exclusion of any other personal characteristic. "It made no difference whether the person was talented, wealthy or intelligent; his weight was his overriding concern, and he saw the entire world in terms of body weight," Dr. Stunkard has reported.[1] Interestingly, he adds that the people who thought most negatively of their bodies had been big as children or teens. He is also quick to point out that the majority of large people are emotionally healthy and not troubled by their bodies to this degree.

Marcia Hutchinson, who wrote *Transforming Body Image*, agrees. "For women, body image and self-image are much the same thing. We see our inner selves in terms of our outer bodies. We've been taught to emphasize the package (the body) but not the contents (the self)."[2]

The very fact that bodies are visible to the naked eye is another reason women have such a hard time filing their body image away, even for short periods of time. "My body is right out there for everyone to see," said one of our members, "and sometimes I feel like the judgment in their eyes is searing my flesh." We can't put bodies in their proper perspective because we can hardly ever escape society's unrelenting crusade to get us all to fit into the same mold. TV talk shows berate fat people, magazine articles reveal celebrity diet secrets, newspapers admonish Americans for getting bigger, diets are a staple of conversation, fat jokes abound, fat prejudice is widespread. There's no getting away from it!

What is body image?

According to Rita Freedman, author of the book, *BodyLove,* body image can be defined as "an inner view of our outer self."[3] April Fallon adds another dimension: "The way people perceive themselves and, equally important, the way they think others see them."[4] I agree with Fallon on the latter point. One Largely Positive member told me: "Every time I get to a point of accepting my body, someone makes a critical remark about my weight and I am back to square one."

For the most part, our own body appraisal mimics that of society. Disdain for fat is not inborn, as evidenced by societies, both past and present, that admire a larger silhouette. But our American society is unrelenting in its contempt for its larger citizens.

Body image woes are not confined to large women. Even normal weight women think they're overweight, and weight loss carries no guarantee that a negative body image will be shed. Many women who lose weight still harbor negative feelings about their size and shape.

How does body image develop?

Experts have found that there are three major factors that help to determine how you feel about your body:

1. Cultural influences, especially the media.

2. How you felt about your body around the time of puberty.

3. How your family, particularly your mother, reacted to your body as it developed.

Mothers in particular have a major influence on their daughters' body image. In a *Glamour* magazine survey of 33,000 women, daughters who believed their mothers were critical of their bodies had a much poorer body image and were much more likely to engage in excessive dieting behavior. They were also more likely to be bulimic.

Researchers at the University of Michigan found that 25 percent of thirteen- and fourteen-year-old girls were encouraged by their mothers to diet. Women who described themselves as unattractive in a *Family Circle* magazine survey were more than twice as likely to have had critical mothers than women who said their looks were attractive or average. When the National Heart, Lung, and Blood Institute studied more than 2,000 nine- and ten-year-old girls to identify dieting attitudes and practices, they were not surprised to learn that 40 percent had already tried to lose weight. But they were startled by the impact of mothers' attitudes on daughters' behavior. In fact, "a girl was more than twice as likely to be a chronic dieter if her mother told her she was too fat," said lead researcher George Schreiber, D.Sc.[5]

Not saying anything can also be detrimental. Psychotherapist JoAnn Magdoff says that a parent's silence about a daughter's looks can have as profound an impact as overt criticism—especially when a "no-comment" father teams up with a critical mother. "Harsh criticism is the worst," she says, "but silence is terrible, too. A little girl who is never told, 'You're pretty' is going to grow up feeling unattractive."[6] (More on overweight children and self-esteem is in a special section aimed at parents in Chapter 7.)

This brings us to another important determinant of body image— how you felt about your body at about the time you were also discovering PMS, pimples, and peer pressure. Feeling bad about your body at an early age can set the stage for years of blame and shame. I know it was that way for me. At about age 13, I became acutely aware that a bigger-than-average body is a real liability in the teenage world. Your body is repeatedly stamped "unacceptable." The fashion, music, and fitness industries ignore you. Many boys look for svelte "trophy" girlfriends. Your peers may tease you and leave your name off invitation lists for parties. You begin to feel like damaged goods, and the damage can take years to repair.

The impact of the media on body image is fairly obvious, but for young girls it can be especially devastating. I know how I felt when I was a teenager, when I was trying to look like the girls on *American Bandstand*—which wasn't so bad. Some of them were even larger than I was—not like what you see today on MTV. In fact, MTV bodies got me wondering: Is this what girls today think they have to look like?

The only way I knew to find out was to ask some teenage girls, so I made a deal with my friend's daughter: I'd buy the pizza if she and her friends would talk with me about their feelings regarding their bodies. Although none of these girls could have been considered large, they said they had girlfriends who would fit that description. They talked about one girl in particular who is popular and has boyfriends and another who is not so well liked. "What makes the difference?" I asked. The first girl, they said, is "nice and fun to be around," while the other one has a "bad attitude." No one would like her even if she were thin. This surprised me. Attitude is something we "older" women talk about a lot. I didn't know it would be so important a factor in how teens judge their peers. But I was glad to hear it.

"On a scale of one to ten, with one being not important and ten being the most important thing in the world, where would the majority of girls in your school place their weight?" All three felt it would be about an eight or nine.

Even models aren't happy

Many models aren't happy with their looks and admit that maintaining their shape is a tortuous process. Models are almost always required to be 10 to 15 pounds under their natural weight. Recently, some have come forward to confess that the only way they were able to maintain this artificially low weight was by acquiring an eating disorder. In an article on "Fashion's Famished Slaves," the *Boston Globe* reported: "A psychologist who heads the eating disorders unit at a suburban hospital says she hates to look at high fashion ads these days because she almost always sees the telltale swellings at the top of the neck that show the models have achieved their emaciated looks by self-induced vomiting."

Models Carol Alt, Beverly Johnson, and Kim Alexis were interviewed for an article in *People* magazine (January 11, 1993). Said Johnson: "I ate nothing. I mean *nothing*."

Alexis confessed that one night her roommate came home to find her eating a head of lettuce for dinner. "You're eating a whole head of lettuce?" her roommate questioned. Alexis cried and said, "But it's all I've had all day. It's only 50 calories!" Johnson lamented: "In our profession, clothes look better on a hanger, so you have to look like a hanger." She admitted that she had been both bulimic and anorexic. At one point her mother stood her naked in front of a mirror: "I looked like a Biafran. My ribs were poking out, and I started to cry." Alt's commentary on Alexis: "I've known Kim for 13 years. She has been on every cover there is. She's one of the most beautiful women in the world, and I've never seen anyone with lower self-esteem."

Models have become much more than mannequins for clothes. Young American women look to them as the embodiment of the right way to live, love, and look. And yet, for most women, no amount of sweating and starving will result in model proportions. Isn't it time we quit trying to look like someone else and concentrated on looking like ourselves? We spend too much time wishing for what we don't have and not enough making the most of what we do have.

Understanding your body

I wish I had better understood my body at an earlier age. Looking back, though, it is clear to me that my body developed just as it should have, given my genes and physiology. I truly believe that even though my young-adult weight exceeded the chart recommendations by about thirty pounds, I was not overweight for my particular body. When my weight settled at 175 on my five-foot, six-inch body, it felt fine. It suited me. It just didn't seem to suit anyone else.

Jan, a Largely Positive member, explains how she felt once she came to understand her body:

Learning about the genetic link between my weight and that of my relatives did a tremendous amount to relieve the guilt I felt because I hadn't gotten the thin, thin results I wanted from all my dieting and exercise. It took me out of the 'at war with my body' stance to a level of peace, self-esteem and acceptance that I had not known since probably early childhood. I knew for the first time that my weight was not 'my fault' since I was doing all I could—limiting fat intake, exercising regularly and eating healthfully and moderately.

Jan now understands that her body is the product of both her genes and her own unique physiology. Treat it properly and it will find its own equilibrium. I had found mine as a young adult, but just didn't know it. Instead I battered my body for years with strange diets, harsh pills, and a lot of hatred. I wish I'd been advised then to just try to stabilize my weight where it was and not gain any more. I think I could easily have handled that, and it would have taken so much pressure off me. My body had clearly found its "setpoint"; unfortunately, I didn't know it at the time.

Spend some time getting to know your body:

- How does it respond to exercise? Does anything ache or hurt after physical activity? Do you feel energized? Sleep better?

- How much sleep do you need to get through a day without feeling fatigued?

- What are your "hungry" times? Keep a record for a few days and discover your peak hunger periods. Decide how best to respond. I have discovered it's best for me to have four meals instead of three, so I save half my lunch until my peak hunger time of 4 P.M.

- How does stress affect you: Headache? Muscle tightening? Face flushed? What are some things that take it away? My stress relievers are: swimming, going to a movie, going for a stroll (with no thought of achieving my "target heart rate"), looking through catalogs, or laughing with friends. And sometimes it might be an ice cream cone!

Large women often live as heads, ignoring their bodies. Once you get better acquainted with the area below your neck, you'll be able to respond with much more precision to the signals it sends you. You've got to screw your body back onto your head!

Accepting what is uniquely yours

Most large women can get to a point where this all makes brain sense, but they need it to make emotional sense as well. They need to know if there are some specific things they can do to stop being so alienated from their bodies. To get re-acquainted with yours, try the following:

Look for origins

Go back as far as you can remember and trace the evolution of your body image. Who are the people and what are the events that were pivotal?

- How did your parents react to your size and shape as you were growing up? Did they tell you that you were perfect just as you were, or was your size a cause for concern? Were you put on diets at an early age—thus sending the message that there was something wrong with your body that needed to be fixed? Did they tell you boys wouldn't want to date you if you were fat— thus sending the message that you would be hard-pressed to find love and affection at your present size?

- How did other adults react to your size? Were you pronounced "too fat" by insensitive teachers at school? Did the gym teacher embarrass you or, as in my case, break your heart by telling you that you were too chubby to be a cheerleader?

- How were you treated by your friends and peers? Were you excluded from parties because they didn't want the fat girl there? Did you sit on the sidelines at school dances because boys only wanted to dance with the thin girls? Did your classmates make cruel remarks about your weight?

- How was your young body viewed by doctors? When I was a high school sophomore, I got my first prescription for amphetamine diet pills, plus a prescription for thyroid pills (without any tests to see if I actually had a thyroid problem).

- How did it feel to shop for clothes and not be able to find the styles your friends were wearing?

- How did it feel to discover that there was no one who looked like you in the magazines or on TV?

It may help to go through an old photo album as you do this. Take out some pictures of yourself at various ages and try to get back in touch with how you were feeling about your body at the time the pictures were taken. You'll probably discover that your body image has been shaped primarily by other people and outside influences. Once you realize this, you can begin the process of shredding the messages that have clung to you for so many years and replacing them with a new evaluation—your own.

It's extremely important to recognize that most of the negative messages you received about your body as a young person were based on wrong or inaccurate information. Now that you have the facts, it should be easier to discard the old messages as simply the products of faulty thinking and reasoning.

Look below your neck

Start to acknowledge that there really is a body below your neck and care for it in a kind and loving way. Large women tend to be unfamiliar with their bodies, looking at them and touching them as little as possible. But your body *has* been good to you. It's carried you about, hasn't it? Then it's time you returned the favor. Some suggestions:

- Is your skin dry? Caress it with lotions.
- Give your feet a makeover—use creams designed to get rid of rough patches, and polish your toenails.
- Find a scent you like and don't stop at cologne. Buy the accompanying body lotion and powder.
- Do an "elbow check." Are they rough? You may need extra doses of lotion until they no longer feel like sandpaper.
- Check out your hands. A manicure may be in order. If you don't like colored polish, apply clear, or try a French manicure.

Reacquaint yourself with the joy of movement.

Experiment to find out what kind of movement rejuvenates your body and do it regularly. It may be a series of stretching exercises, a dip in the pool, a walk around the block, a game of tennis.

Bodies are designed to move. We knew that instinctively when we were young. We "played" and playing meant moving around. A friend and I recently agreed that as children we romped, ran, wore shorts, played hopscotch, climbed trees, rode our bikes. It didn't much matter what shape or size we were. Then we grew up, came down with the "body image blues," and stopped moving spontaneously for fear someone might laugh at us. We stopped "playing." You'll be a lot happier with your body if you let it play again!

Thank your body for functioning

Start appreciating the functional nature of your body. Even if you don't feel it's perfect, your body is a pretty remarkable thing. You can use it to:

- Walk along the seashore.
- Hug someone.
- Stroll through an art museum.
- Make love.
- Go shopping!

And it can do these things at any shape or size. Aren't these the things that really matter?

Do a body appraisal, but make it positive

What about your body do you like? We are so used to focusing on the so-called "flaws" that we almost never stop to think what we like. Here's my own evaluation:

My legs are shapely—so I wear shorts in the summer. I have graceful hands with long fingers and nicely-shaped fingernails. I keep them manicured. My skin is smooth and relatively free of wrinkles, even though I am in my fifth decade. My lips are full. My bosom is a delight to my husband. I have physical strength and my body seems to resist illness. I don't get sick often, but when I do, I heal quickly. I feel my larger body allows me to wear and carry off more dramatic styles. I like my face. My arms are firm and muscular.

This from my friend Wendy:

What I like about my body? That certainly is a unique concept for a larger woman, but an easy one for me. I like my height and stature. I'm about five feet, seven inches tall and wear a size 24. I stand straight and walk proudly. I'm fairly large busted and really like the way clothes hang on me, because my bust and hips are in proportion. Having been large all my life, I have learned to move in a graceful manner. My size helps to draw attention to me. I like that attention because I am often perceived to be powerful or authoritative, and I command respect due to the way I carry my weight. My body has a softness and voluptuousness that are both attractive and comfortable. I'm proud of who I am and how I look.

Write a letter to your body

I got this idea is from a pamphlet called "Body Image Solutions" developed by the Body Image Task Force of Santa Cruz. The author, Louise Wolfe, acknowledges that the idea "may sound silly, but for many women this has been the first time they ever communicated with their body in a way that didn't involve simply responding to pain." This also allows you, she says, to stop viewing your body as an object that you must control and start seeing it instead as a person with whom you are becoming friends.

Really look at other bodies

Sit in a mall and watch the bodies that pass by. How many of them look like supermodels? These are real people who come in all shapes, sizes, and colors. Let's value diversity, and we'll all be happier.

Find a way to exit weight conversations

Avoid conversations that are dominated by talk of perfect bodies and weight. Try this experiment: Monitor all conversations with others for a few days and note how many times body image woes crop up. If possible, carry a piece of notepaper with you and make a slash mark on it every time the conversation turns to weight complaints. If your friends spend an inordinate amount of time bashing their bodies and the bodies of others, you may want to cultivate some new friends.

Get your priorities in order

Do not connect your major goals to appearance. Some women feel that perfecting their appearance is the most important thing they can do in life. Is this how you want to make your mark? Will anyone remember that you wore a size 8? Will they care? Whittling your body does nothing for your world, your community, or even those around you. Do not, of course, neglect the elements of good health, but do find other areas in which you can succeed.

Find role models

Make a list of large women you admire—perhaps someone famous, a political figure, a friend, a favorite aunt. What have they accomplished? What other traits do you admire in them? Keep reminding yourself that their bodies did not interfere with their achievements.

Whoopi Goldberg told *Family Circle* magazine (September 20, 1994) that she feels good about herself whether her weight is up or down: "Even at my heaviest," she said, "I'm a fairly good-looking chick. Just because you're a big woman doesn't mean you're not sexy and attractive as hell." She advises women with body image blues to "accept your body. If you're okay with yourself internally, I think that's the most important thing in the world."

Pick your century

Take the advice of Jennifer Shute, writing in the September 1994 issue of *New Woman* magazine, and go on the "time travel diet. Instead of contorting yourself to fit the times, why not have the good sense to live in the era that would render you, effortlessly, ideal? . . . Any woman, if she had been born at the right moment in human history, would automatically have been considered a great beauty." Go through some art history books, determine when your body type was in vogue, and tell everyone you have traveled forward in time from the 18th century!

Become more aware of stereotypes

Be keenly aware of the stereotypes of large people in the media as well as the *absence* of any positive images of large people. Notice how large people are portrayed. For the next two months, cut out all pictures of large people you see in magazines, newspapers, and the like. (Be sure to include the before and after pictures in weight-loss ads). Also keep track of comments about large people on TV, in the movies, etc. Then review them and decide whether your collection of images and comments reflect accurate information or stereotypes.

Watch for inaccurate information

Armed with your knowledge of the factors that contribute to size and weight, notice when claims for weight loss programs contradict the research (e.g. any program promising rapid weight loss). Make note of statements that indicate a lack of knowledge.

Give yourself a break

Finally, don't let the quest for complete body acceptance become a burden in itself. Sometimes people feel like failures if they can't achieve total love for their bodies. We've already made people feel like failures if they don't lose weight. Let's not do the same with body acceptance. I don't think you *have* to get to a point where you become enraptured by your naked image in a mirror. You may not feel your body is aesthetically perfect, but it'll get you where you want to go.

And what if, like Kari, you can accept your size and like yourself as a person, but you can't honestly say you love your body? I think that has to be okay. Otherwise, you're putting yet another burden on yourself, and you've got enough to deal with as it is. I think you've done your job if you can accept the body you've got, thank it for functioning, and not allow it to sidetrack your life.

Treating body image disorders

When body image disturbances are serious and accompanied by eating disorders, professional treatment is recommended. Experts have found that body image disorders do not respond well to traditional therapies. Many have had success with a process called "guided imagery," which involves using your imagination to practice attitudes and behaviors you wish to build into your life. "If you can imagine it, you can live it," says Marcia Germaine Hutchinson, Ed.D., in *Transforming Body Image*. She explains further:

> *Body image itself is a special kind of image. When you have a negative body image, your mind's eye sees your body in a distorted manner and your mind's ear hears self-talk saying your body is inadequate, ugly and fat. You are held prisoner, controlled by your perception and sense of self. What better way to gain access to your tyrannical imagination than to turn it around by training your imagination to be your ally so that your body can become your home instead of a battlefield!*[7]

In her 12-week course, Hutchinson asks women to use their imaginations to tap into feelings, images, memories, thoughts, inner voices, sensations, and intuitions. Some of her exercises include using the mirrors in the women's minds to heighten body awareness, replaying childhood scenes with new attitudes, and personifying negative self-talk as inner saboteurs. She also uses a therapeutic type of movement to help women reconnect with their bodies.

Conversation with a body image therapist

Shay Harris is a Milwaukee psychotherapist who has created an approach for treating body image disorders that is based on size acceptance and health. Recently I asked her about the steps she takes with women to improve their body image. She said:

> *The first thing I do is help them unravel how they learned to hate themselves. This can often be traced back to a combination of family and cultural messages. I then have to ask them a real scary question, which is this: 'What if this is the best it gets, and you will never be thinner than you are right now? Can you afford to hate yourself for the rest of your life?'*

Harris then helps her clients become familiar with the research on obesity. The also explore how ideals change over time and across cultures, and challenge biased, stigmatizing media messages and images. It's also important, she said, for clients to forgive and grieve.

Often a woman will have to spend some time grieving the loss of a dream or what "could have been," as well as the time lost postponing life by waiting to be thin. Then Harris and her client are usually ready to start moving ahead with some specific things to help the woman get back in touch with her body and learn to appreciate it rather than hate it.

How, I wondered, does she deal with food issues? She explained:

> *My clients are often struggling with eating and self-esteem issues simultaneously. I usually need to encourage them to eat enough. I work closely with a clinical dietitian who teaches them about normal eating. Most people come to me thinking they're binge eaters, but we often find out this is not the case. They're depriving themselves more often than they're overeating. Restrictive and erratic eating patterns are usually the result of chronic dieting. It is essential to get rid of the diet mentality. Until that happens, body image healing is impossible.*

Harris said she often uses this exercise: Imagine you're an adult, and in walks a child that reminds you of yourself at a young age. Embrace and cherish the child—as you have often wanted to be cherished. Now imagine the child says she is hungry. Will you react harshly and refuse to feed her or will you nurture her lovingly? View yourself as that little child, as an innocent being with valid needs.

Harris feels, as I do, that large women desert their bodies and don't pay attention to physical needs. They often say, "I'm not comfortable in this large body." Then it's time, said Harris, to help them rediscover the joys of pampering their bodies and to start flexing some muscles.

People who say they're uncomfortable may simply need to stop wearing too-tight clothes and get their bodies moving. Sometimes, large people say they're uncomfortable and sweaty in the summer when it's hot, and even in winter when they pile on layers of clothes. I tell them to check to see how people of various sizes are feeling. They find out that they're not the only ones who feel this way—thinner people feel uncomfortable too.

When asked if her clients still want to lose weight, she replied:

Yes, and they think that if they create a new plan for themselves that involves exercise and proper nutrition, this will now become the magic bullet. It may or it may not. I try to help them abandon weight loss as their only goal and start doing things for the comfort, pleasure, and health of their bodies.

Harris also advises her clients to surround themselves with positive, full-figured images, such as paintings and figurines of large women. "I also tell them about your collection of plump little dolls," she said to me. Finally, she has them focus on successful large women as their role models rather than focusing on the "after" pictures in weight-loss ads.

♥ ♥ ♥ **From The Heart** ♥ ♥ ♥

A Letter to Santa

Dear Santa,

I can't help noticing that you're one of the few larger people who doesn't let your weight get in the way. You seem to have a very positive attitude and you're always in a jolly mood. Your laughter reverberates throughout the world every holiday season and just the sight of you makes people happy.

You wear bright colors in stark contrast to the advice often given to larger people to stick to dark colors for a slimming effect. You don't seem to feel the need to hide your size under drab, shapeless garments. Holy cow—you even wear a belt!

You toil all year at a job you love. You didn't say: "After I lose 50 pounds, I'll become Santa Claus and set up a toy shop!" If you had, an awful lot of kids would have been disappointed every Christmas as they waited for you to start your business.

You seem to be very active. You don't let your size stop you from hitching up the sleigh each year and traveling around the world. I bet you weren't even embarrassed to ask that a seat belt extender be added to the sleigh. I've never heard of your going on a diet. And yet you appear healthy.

You and your voluptuous Mrs. Claus have one of the better marriages going. You work as a team and appreciate one another for the qualities that contribute to an enduring marriage—trust, mutual respect, admiration, and sensuality. I hear that Mrs. Claus has a new lacy red teddy she plans to wear for you on Christmas night.

You are a wise and tolerant person. When you noticed that the other reindeer were picking on Rudolph and making fun of him, you showed them all that what appeared to be a negative quality—a big, red nose—could be turned into something positive. We always focus on the negative aspects of being big. We never think there might be advantages. Sometimes it just depends on your perspective.

Mrs. Claus told me she has started cooking healthier meals. She thinks you both need to eat less fat, but she's not going overboard. She still plans treats now and then. And she wouldn't think of asking you to give up your Christmas Eve cookies and milk. She also said she'd like both of you to get a little more exercise. She's having the elves make each of you a pair of walking shoes so you can take after-dinner walks around the North Pole.

You seem to have accepted yourself just as you are. Santa, I think we could all take a lesson from you.

P.S. Please don't forget my diamond earrings.

6

what are you waiting for?

I am what I am. Be it big or small.
I am what I am. Be it short or tall.
And I know that I am, in the very best way . . .
The most wonderful me I can be today!
—Kari

While I was sitting in the food court of a downtown Chicago mall one day, I saw a woman carrying a cloth tote bag bearing the words: "Life is not a dress rehearsal—get out there and enjoy it!" It dawned on me that this sums up the Largely Positive philosophy in a nutshell.

If you're like I was, you're probably an expert at "thin planning"—planning for all the things you'll do when you lose weight. My plans were not necessarily grandiose and I never doubted that I had the skills and abilities to fulfill them—as soon as I got thin. For instance, I used to think I couldn't buy "permanent" clothes until I got down to a size 12, 14 max. Clothes any larger than that were part of my "temporary fat wardrobe," which consisted of duds that were cheap and unspectacular. When I did buy nicer clothes, I'd buy them at least a couple of sizes too small, thinking they would serve as an "incentive" to lose weight. It never occurred to me that I could buy pretty clothes and look attractive at my present size.

One day my husband noticed that he'd never seen me in a lot of the clothes hanging in my closet, and that many garments still had the price tags attached. He thought this odd. I explained to him that these were the clothes I'd be wearing in six months, after I lost 60 pounds, and that they provided visible encouragement for me to stick to my diet. (I refrained from pointing out that the size 12, tie-dyed miniskirt had been there for close to 15 years!)

The logic of this still eluded him (men generally buy clothes they can put right on and wear) and he suggested something radical—going out and buying some clothes that would fit me now. It had never occurred to me to buy clothes that I could instantly button or zip up, but I was willing to try. It didn't take me long to realize that this was definitely more fun than buying outfits that never saw the light of day.

Recently I received a letter from a woman who said: "After years of dieting, my self-esteem is at an all-time low—so low I often feel if I could only be thin, I would be better at everything." How do we get to the point where weight interferes with living? I think it starts very young. Remember my story about not being chosen for cheerleading? The message was: "You can't be a cheerleader now because you're too chubby, but if you lose weight, you'll stand a good chance." Then it was: "Lose weight and the boys will like you." "Lose weight and you'll stand a better chance of being accepted at a good college." "Lose weight and you can buy pretty clothes." It was always "Lose weight and then . . ."

The fact of the matter is that I could have done any of these things with the body I had. I could have been a cheerleader or a majorette. My grades were good enough for any college. I could write and speak well, so any number of careers were possible. But I always thought these goals could be more easily achieved if I were thin.

In some ways I was probably right. We can't deny the existence of weight discrimination. It has been scientifically documented. You may have to work harder than a thin person to achieve your goals. Is this as it should be? Of course not. But a lot of things in life aren't as they should be. We right them by taking a stand, by confronting prejudice, by challenging stereotypes, and by demonstrating that we can do what someone said we couldn't do. Groups that have encountered discrimination have discovered that one of the best ways to fight ignorance, prejudice, and intolerance is to shatter the stereotype by personal example.

At one diet group I attended, we were asked to think of ourselves as caterpillars encased in cocoons. Once we shed the ugly pounds, we could emerge from our "cocoons" as thin, graceful "butterflies." Since my transformation to a "largely positive" woman was already under way, the analogy made me angry. I had no intention of going into hiding until I could fly out thin.

"What have you been putting off because of weight?" I often ask people at workshops. Typical responses are:

- Furthering my education
- Traveling
- Going out socially
- Buying a nice wardrobe
- Seeking a promotion at work

Family Circle magazine surveyed more than 700 women about the affects of appearance and weight on their lives and found that embarrassment caused:

- One in five to refuse social engagements.
- Nine out of 10 to fear wearing a bathing suit.
- One out of three to shun bright colors.
- More than half to avoid wearing slacks or shorts.
- More than one in three to duck athletic activities.
- More than one in 10 to put off seeing friends.

Clothes are an emotionally-charged issue for many large women, perhaps because they are only one step removed from the body and because so many of our goals have been geared toward fitting into a certain size. Clothes do so much more than cover us. They allow us to express our personality, our moods, our feelings about ourselves—even our social and employment status. One of the hardest steps for a large woman to take is to plan her closet around today's reality rather than tomorrow's dreams. One woman said she had been putting off buying clothes for the following reasons:

- She didn't want to waste money on clothes now when she was planning to lose weight.
- Why outfit an ugly body?
- Who notices your clothes when you're fat?

But she has since learned the importance of having great clothes *now,* whether she ever loses weight or not; that her body is not ugly—it's uniquely hers; and that people are going to notice her one way or another, so she might as well look smashing.

One of our members confessed that she had done the same thing until she decided to focus on present, not future, needs:

My closet used to be filled with memories from the past and hopes for the future. What I didn't have were clothes for today. Now, although I confess I still have some too-small favorites in a small part of my closet (she's being honest), I can, for the most part, close my eyes and fit into anything I grab. My closet is filled with happy clothes that get worn with pleasure and pride.

Another member said she put off seeing people socially because she was afraid of what they'd think or say. Now she has decided she doesn't care any more, and that most of them won't be thinking or saying anything about her weight anyway.

Betty said she has already missed two high-school class reunions "because I didn't want to show up at this large size. I felt others' conversations would be humming with talk of 'God, is she big!' or 'Wow! She really let herself go!'" But she decided that the biggest disappointment of all would be her own not participating in the fun and delight of seeing old friends and finding out about their lives. "This summer," she said proudly, "I plan on going to my 20th!"

When I spoke at a diet group about living in the present, a woman came up to me afterward and said: "My husband would like to go away to a motel for a romantic weekend getaway where we could relax, have fun, enjoy the pool . . . but I wouldn't want anyone to see me the way I currently look—especially in a bathing suit." She felt so badly about herself that she refused to spend a weekend away with her husband!

My next question startled her: "What if, God forbid, your husband was hit by a bus and died tomorrow? Wouldn't you regret that you allowed your weight to prevent you from spending a fun, relaxing, intimate weekend together?" She said she had never thought about it that way and would go home and ask him where he would like to go!

Sometimes we get so wrapped up in issues of size and weight that we don't realize we're actually being selfish. Like this woman, we're avoiding opportunities to do things as a couple or a family, things that ultimately bring us closer together and provide lasting memories. When my husband and I grow old, we'll be able to reminisce about:

- The Caribbean cruise we took
- Sunning and swimming in California and Florida
- Weekends in Chicago
- A once-in-a-lifetime trip to Europe

Had I postponed any of these wonderful adventures until I was thin, it's a safe bet they'd never have been part of my life. Even if you are still determined to lose weight, you can live your life along the way. Again, we never know what tomorrow will bring. You could be in the last week of your diet and be struck by lightning. There is no reason to wait. Figure out what you want to do and do it now. There are very few things in life for which being thin is a prerequisite.

If people do notice your weight, it may be because you are calling attention to it. Some of our members have decided to stop doing that and see what happens. Kari said she has stopped apologizing for her weight, and a recent wedding was no exception. There was a time, she said, when she would not have even gone to the wedding, knowing she was bigger than some people remembered her. But this time she didn't hesitate. She put on her "happy dress" and "happy earrings" and made no mention of her weight. Neither did anyone else. She had a grand time.

Veronica decided her weight would no longer be a barrier to career advancement:

I have decided not to wait until I am at my 'ideal' weight (which may never happen) to go after a promotion at work. I know that I am qualified whether I weigh 125 or 225 pounds. My weight has nothing to do with my abilities. I am going to dress myself for success, be confident and let my superiors know that I am eager for more responsibility and have the skills that are needed.

Being thin won't make you any more capable. It won't make you smarter. It won't make you more talented. It won't make you a better person. So what's holding you back? Primarily the negative attitudes we're encouraged as larger people to acquire—and these can be changed. This book is about changing them.

Susan Kano, author of *Making Peace with Food,* says she likes to ask people who complain they're too fat, "Too fat for what? Too fat to walk? Too fat to make love? Too fat to swim or play tennis or run or cycle or hike or dance?" The answer to all these questions, she says, is usually no, and the truth emerges—most people acknowledge that they think they're too fat *to be attractive.*

When you find yourself postponing something because of your weight, ask yourself:

- Is there any real reason I can't do this activity right now?
- What do I stand to gain by waiting?
- What do I stand to lose by waiting?
- What if I never get thin—or "thin enough"?

I think, if you're honest, you'll find that putting your life on hold doesn't make any sense. You're denying yourself a life filled with interesting activities, you're denying others the pleasure of your company, and you're denying the world the benefit of what you could contribute.

Sometimes things we put on hold truly cannot be recaptured. Listen to Barbara:

Unfortunately, the one thing that I put off, that I doubt will now come to fruition, is having another child. I'm reaching an age now where I don't believe that having a child would be right for me. I do regret, however, feeling that I had to wait until I lost weight to have another child. Today I have decided to live life the way I want to live it and surround myself with people who appreciate and love me for everything that I have to give. I don't have to accept people's prejudices and I don't have to remain associated with them just because I feel that I deserve no better.

"Staying in the present moment is grounding," writes Carrie Hemenway in the NAAFA workbook. As long as we're worrying and fretting, we accomplish little. As long as we're daydreaming about what we'd like to do, but not actually doing it, we're not helping our self-esteem any . . . Instead of saying, "If only I knew how to sing," start singing! Instead of saying, "I wish I had a computer," go to the computer store and ask the salesperson to demonstrate one.

Sometimes women use negative feelings about their bodies as an excuse for not participating in activities they really wouldn't want to do at any weight. There's no law that says you must want to participate in every experience life has to offer, and it's important to understand that this is okay. Just be clear about what you're putting on hold because of your weight and what you're avoiding simply because the activity doesn't mesh with your temperament and personality.

A "full plate" of life actually will help you manage your weight better. If you don't think you can live your life until you lose weight, there isn't a whole lot for you to do in the present, except for the mundane activities of daily living, one of which is eating. No wonder people become preoccupied with food when it's all they have to think about. If, on the other hand, you're out doing things you enjoy, you'll have little time to be bored, lonely or depressed.

Listen to what Janet said one night when we were making "largely positive" New Year's resolutions:

I resolve to get out more. I am going to find some volunteer work to occupy the time that I now spend sitting home, thinking about food and diets. I thought that when I lost weight, I would go out and participate in more community activities. I now see that I have it backwards. I will focus less on what I'm eating or not eating if I'm involved in thinking about others, rather than sitting home thinking about my weight.

Bathing suits and swimming are especially difficult, but Sue finally conquered her fear and here's what she had to say:

I was waiting until I lost weight to go swimming, but decided that if I continued to wait, I would probably never go swimming again. So I 'took the plunge.' I noticed that when I went out and had fun and didn't worry about others and what they thought, I actually didn't care what they thought and enjoyed myself.

What are Largely Positive women doing with their lives?

Many of our members have rich, full lives. Some are single. Some are married. Some work inside the home. Some work outside the home at varied and interesting careers. Some do community volunteer work. But they're *all* out there. They're out there living their lives this moment, not waiting for the scales to announce: "You're thin enough. You can go out now."

Are some of them still trying to lose weight? Of course they are. We've never said they shouldn't. But they are no longer allowing their weight to prevent them from living their lives and they are no longer putting their lives on hold.

Here are just some of the jobs Largely Positive members are currently performing: market researcher, attorney practicing family law, manager of a clothing store, artist, psychotherapist, computer technician, water aerobics instructor, optician, cardiologist, pediatrician, college professor, high school guidance counselor, hospital lab technician, hospital administrator, grade school teacher, Catholic nun.

To get yourself out of the future and back into the present, try the following:

Make a list of things you've been postponing

Taking dance lessons? Going canoeing? Traveling to Europe? Enrolling in a computer class? Ask yourself why you can't do these things right now. Be honest. "Because I'm too fat" is not a valid reason. Write down the first step you could take toward achieving each goal. Take one of those first steps tomorrow. Maybe it's calling for information. Or filling out an application. Whatever it is, just do it. Then decide on a second step and so on until you're on your way to achieving your dreams.

Do something unexpected every day

I remember reading that one of the reasons it's hard for people to make changes is because they try to change too many things all at once. If you start with smaller changes, bigger ones will eventually be easier to make. If you do something a little differently each day, pretty soon you will welcome rather than resist change. It may start with something as simple as altering the route you take to work. Or trying a new vegetable.

Or walking around the block. Or combing your hair a different way. The important thing is altering your routine in some way every day.

Do a closet "purge"

Try everything on. If it's too small, it goes to charity, into a rummage sale, or to someone who could wear it right now. Here is your new rule: Nothing comes home from the store unless you can put it right on and wear it. There will be no more waiting-to-be-thin clothes.

Plan a trip

Avoiding travel is common among larger people. No more! Go to a travel agency and collect brochures. Pick a destination that suits your budget and book it. Afraid the plane seats will be too small? See our tips on "fitting in" in Chapter 13.

Get your body moving

Unfortunately, one of the things larger people put on hold is exercise. You don't have to wait until you lose weight to begin an exercise program! As a matter of fact, studies show that you can be more fit even if you don't lose weight. Studies also show that women who exercise have better self-esteem. Pick an activity you like and find out where you can do it. Can't find anything? Call your local YMCA and ask them to start a Plus-Size Exercise class.

Champion a cause

What beliefs do you hold dear? Find an organization that champions those beliefs and volunteer. They'll be glad for your help, and, believe me, they won't care what you weigh.

Get out beyond the "four walls"

Plan at least one social event a week. Go out to dinner with friends, go to a concert or a movie, stroll through craft fairs. Your life will be as full or as empty as *you* decide to make it.

Stop your thin daydreaming

Finally, stop daydreaming that you're thin. I once read the phrase "To dream of the person you would like to be is to waste the person you are," and it stuck with me. Is there a movie constantly playing in your mind with you as the star, but in a thin body? I had a movie like that. You must yank that reel of film. Begin producing a new movie with all the same dreams, but starring the current you. Then go out and make your dreams a reality!

Summertime blues

Do you have the "hiding-from-summer" syndrome? Symptoms include:

- Wearing a trench coat when it's 90 degrees
- Refusing to bare anything but your hands and face
- Going to the beach in an outfit more suited to ski trails
- Trying to get a tan through pantyhose

I hope you're not a victim of this syndrome, but if you are, I understand. I used to suffer from it myself. Many large women feel most comfortable when they can cover up their bodies with layers of clothing. They're relieved when the weather becomes cool enough to truly require a jacket.

I was always looking forward to "next summer" because by then I'd be thin and could participate in all the fun-in-the-sun activities in skimpy little frocks. But, of course, the "thin summer" never came for me (although I do recall squeezing into some size 14 hot pants for one week during the summer of 1966).

Summer is such a glorious, carefree time. Don't let it be something else you put on hold while you're waiting to be thin. Get out there and enjoy those sunny days and starry nights! And to those of you who wear coats in summer, I know how exposed and self-conscious you feel without them. But trust me. The coat isn't fooling people into thinking you're a size 10. On the contrary, it's probably just calling more attention to you because it looks so silly in the sweltering heat. I'm not suggesting you go out and buy a bikini, but here are some suggestions that may help you enjoy a coatless summer:

- Buy a bathing suit that has a matching skirt. I have a black maillot that I pair with a long black gauze skirt. It suits my poolside modesty level. And I didn't buy black to look thinner.

I bought it because it looked sharp and up-to-date. I also have a bright purple suit with a gold sunburst in front!

- Let your legs see the light of day in an easy-fitting skort or loose-fitting short that comes to the knee. Top it with a loose, V-necked tee.

- Look breezy in a gauzy, loose-fitting sundress. Try one of the brighter colors, such as orange, turquoise, lime green or fuchsia. Accessorize it with a colorful necklace and big earrings. Add a big-brimmed hat.

- Pair some slouchy white pants with a tank or tube top and top it off with a big shirt. Roll up the sleeves. Paint your toenails and show off your feet in metallic sandals.

- Tight clothing is uncomfortable and a constant irritant in hot weather. Think "light, loose-fitting" and you'll be sure to have fun in the sun!

Don't let summer slip by unnoticed because it means shedding a few layers of clothes. You have just as much right as anyone to catch some rays!

Holidays and special occasions

Holidays and special occasions should be times of fun, togetherness, spiritual renewal and relaxation. But they can also be uneasy times for large people who worry what others may think or say about their weight. It goes something like this: "Last Christmas I announced at the family dinner that by next Christmas I'd be into single-digit dress sizes. And I did lose some weight, but now I've gained it all back and I think I'm even heavier than I was last year. I don't want to have to explain all this. I have nothing to wear and I don't want to go."

Or perhaps you're nervous about accompanying your husband to a company function, or going to a wedding where you'll see people you haven't seen in years, or attending what for many large people is at the top of their list of dreaded events—the class reunion! As the event draws closer, we become very creative in concocting excuses to stay home:

- "I have a plumber who only works on Saturday evenings."
- "I have an appointment with the eye doctor that day and I won't be able to see after he puts the drops in my eyes."
- "It's my great-aunt Tillie's 100th birthday and I have to be there."
- "It's my night to monitor the weather radio for severe weather alerts."

At one time I could probably have written a book of excuses. We have to find a remedy for this I'm-big-and-I-don't-want-anyone-to-see-me virus. Once again, you're the only one who really suffers. Once they make note of your absence, everyone else will be having a good time, while you're home feeling blue.

Let's take some more bad excuses one by one:

"I have nothing to wear."

This one is easily remedied. Go buy something! There is no longer any excuse for large women not to be able to look smashing—and in any price range. What with the department store sections for large sizes, specialty stores, dozens of catalogs, home shopping channels and the worldwide web, the options have mushroomed in recent years.

"People will notice I've gained weight."

Maybe they will. Maybe they won't. But if they do, it'll only be for a split second and then they'll be more interested in what you've been doing since they last saw you. I'm sure that you also notice physical changes in other people, but you quickly move on to more important things in their lives. I've said it before, but I'll say it again: If *you* don't call attention to your weight or apologize for it, chances are it'll never be mentioned. If your demeanor suggests to others that you feel good about who you are, *that* is what they'll notice and remember about you.

"My husband will be ashamed of me."

If he's enlightened about issues of size and weight, there's no reason he should be. And if you accompany him proudly, looking your best, knowing you're not inferior to anyone and you have just as much right to be there as anyone else, why should there be any shame involved? One Largely Positive member was afraid of just such a situation, but she went and tried to enjoy herself. After she and her husband had returned home, she said to him: "They all said how fat I was, didn't they?" He replied, "No, they said you were a lot of fun and they enjoyed talking to you."

I frequently include tips for enjoying the Christmas holidays in my winter newsletter. Here are a few that could apply to almost any holiday or special occasion:

Be snazzy

Toss out that drab old outfit you've been wearing to every event because "it doesn't really matter what I wear while I'm still big." It *does* matter. It matters because you'll feel a lot better about yourself if you think you look good. Decorate yourself with the same care you give to your tree—with color, sparkle and pizzazz. This is not the time to avoid buying clothes because you're waiting until you get thin. Buy something smashing in a bright, festive color, and *make sure it fits and is comfortable right now*. Wear a glittery barrette in your hair, put on holly berry lipstick, paint your nails red. Feeling that you look your best is a great self-esteem booster! Even a very basic outfit can be glitzed up with dramatic accessories, such as a metallic scarf, bold jewelry, hair ornaments, a rhinestone clip on your shoes!

Decide to sparkle!

People react to the attitude you project. If you stride confidently into a room with a smile on your face, knowing you look your best, knowing you're a fine person just as you are, that's what people will notice. Talk about the interesting things you've been doing. Be animated!

Put things in perspective

So you aren't as thin as you thought you might be by now. So what? In the grand scheme of things, it's not very important. Everyone has *something* he or she didn't achieve during the past year. Chalk it up to being human. Think of all the things you *did* achieve. Rather than dwelling on the few things you didn't do, make a list of all the positive things you did do this past year—the many ways in which you nurtured your family, the good deed you did for a neighbor, the extra time you put in at work to help your boss, continued your education, worked for a charity, started an exercise program.

Eliminate weight from the conversation

Don't apologize for your weight or call people's attention to it. Apologies are used to right a wrong, and you haven't done anything wrong. It's nobody's business and it's not a very interesting topic of conversation. If someone should comment, use it as an opportunity to educate. Instead of being hurt or becoming defensive, use it as an opportunity to tell them what you've learned about weight issues. Explain that you now know there are many physiological factors involved in determining a person's weight. Tell them you now realize your weight is not a measure of your self-worth, you've decided to stop blaming yourself for it, and you're now focusing on developing a healthy, positive lifestyle. Then change the subject.

Get busy

Get into the holiday spirit and take the focus off your weight by attending some of the festive events that abound at this time of year—concerts, religious activities, plays, ballet, and the like. And, once again, don't just deck the halls. Deck yourself out!

Think of others

Focus on others instead of your weight. Start writing your cards early and compose a personalized note to friends and relatives you seldom see. Let them know what's interesting in your life. (Don't mention your weight!) Make a list of the people for whom you intend to buy gifts. Beside each name list the person's hobbies and interests. Then plan an extra-special gift. Decide to do at least one thing for those less fortunate. Call a homeless shelter, find out what they need, pack a box, and take it to them. Make the holidays brighter for a less fortunate family or an elderly person in a nursing home. Make yourself feel special by helping others to feel special.

Take care of yourself

Be good to your body through the holidays. Regular exercise is very important. Take a walk and enjoy the neighborhood decorations. Be especially mindful of meal planning so you won't always be eating on the run. Spend some time each weekend planning meals for the upcoming week. Cook meals ahead and freeze them. Get the crock pot out of mothballs—it's the perfect item for busy days.

Throw your own party

If you still don't relish going to places you feel obligated to go, throw your own party and have fun planning it. If you're still concerned about overindulging, make sure you include other activities such as caroling through the neighborhood, games, card playing, contests, trimming the tree. Enjoy the goodies you like, but when the party's over, consider sending leftovers home with the guests on holiday plates tied with a pretty bow. Include some low-fat, but tasty goodies along with traditional treats. Fruit and vegetable plates with low-fat dips are always welcome. As a gift to yourself, buy a health-supportive cookbook and experiment with recipes.

Enjoy the goodies

Don't deprive yourself of foods you like or you'll end up on a rum ball binge. Unless there is a medical reason, enjoy your favorite holiday foods in moderation.

Remember what the season is all about

Love, joy, peace, sense of purpose, connectedness, human potential and reverence for living . . . Next to all this, a number on the scale is not all that important. Take the focus off yourself and your weight and put it on things that really matter. Your family is important. Doing something for someone else is important. Loving yourself "just the way you are," as the song says, is important.

So don't hold yourself back from being a full participant in the holiday season. Get out there, and in the words of a popular holiday tune, "Have a holly, jolly Christmas!"

Reunion jitters

Your 20th class reunion is now two months away and you're wondering if there isn't some way of losing 40 pounds in the next eight weeks—perhaps through a combination of fasting, liposuction, and step aerobics. You begin to worry that no one will recognize you and those that do will try their best not to look too horrified. You've decided that a root canal would be a more pleasant event.

But deep down inside you know you really want to go. You know it will be fun to see people you haven't seen since high school, to catch up with their lives, to see your old boyfriend, perhaps to see some of your old teachers. So what do you do about this dilemma? You go!

There are lots of reasons you may not recognize someone you haven't seen in years. At my last reunion, a man approached me with a big smile on his face yelling "Carol!" I turned and hadn't a clue as to who he was. He had to tell me. I had known him very well. His size hadn't changed a bit, but his hair was completely gray. It gave him a different look and I just didn't recognize him.

Although I was heavy in high school, I'm heavier now—and yes, I had some pre-reunion jitters. But everyone still recognized me and greeted me enthusiastically. The high point of my evening came when a young boy who had accompanied his parents glanced at the high school graduation picture on my name tag, then studied my face and said, "Gosh, you don't look one bit different now than you did then." Larger women often retain a youthful look. I tell people, "I really do have wrinkles, but they're all plumped up!"

You have to stop worrying about what may or may not be in other people's minds and concentrate on creating a positive environment in your own mind. Remember:

- All eyes will *not* be on you. You will be one of many. While people will certainly notice you and want to get reacquainted, they'll be trying to do the same thing with many others.

- Everyone else will be fretting about the same things you're fretting about: how they look, what kind of impression they'll make after 20 years, whether former classmates will be sufficiently impressed with their careers and accomplishments.

- You see these people maybe once every five or ten years, so what difference does it really make what they think or don't think? Even if some particularly catty person does notice your size, what impact will this have on your life as a whole?

- People who have been your friends all along will still be your friends.

So now, aren't you ready to put on a jazzy dress and go have fun? The bottom line here is: Stop putting things off until later. Later is now!

♥ ♥ ♥ From The Heart ♥ ♥ ♥

Twelve Things I Wish Someone Had Told Me 25 Years Ago

1. It's not your fault you're a bigger girl. Your weight is governed by a variety of physiological factors, including genetics. It's the same process that determines the color of your eyes and hair.

2. It's no crime to be big. There are a lot worse things you could be, such as cruel, uncaring, or selfish.

3. Nobody's perfect. Everyone is doing *something* that isn't good for them. Lots of thin people aren't eating in a healthy manner or exercising regularly.

4. We live in a culture obsessed with thinness, and this is society's problem, not yours. Like human beings, societies are imperfect and are not always right. Society's preoccupation with "perfect" bodies is causing a lot of damage in the form of eating and body-image disorders.

5. You are not your weight. The essence of who you are is not defined by your weight but by all the talents, qualities and accomplishments that, when mixed together, make you the wonderfully unique person you are.

6. Count your blessings. You may think that having a bigger-than-average body is the worst thing in the world, but there are people who are starving, ill, or without necessities. They are in far worse situations.

7. When it comes down to it, your weight is not that important. Turn your attention to activities that will improve your school, your community, your world.

8. Dieting is often the problem, not the solution. Concentrate on health, not weight loss, and your body will find its right weight. Stabilizing your weight may be the best option.

9. Physical activity is the real key to weight management. Instead of worrying so much about what you eat, get your body moving regularly.

10. You *can* look good. Clothing manufacturers have wisened up. Plus-size clothes are fashionable and attractive. Create your own

personal style and make your outer image a reflection of your inner self-esteem.

11. Don't put your life on hold waiting to be thin. You can do everything you want to do right now! Don't wait years to discover that.

12. Self-esteem comes in all sizes. Your weight is *not* a measure of your self-worth.

7

self-esteem comes in all sizes

Largely Positive has changed my attitude about myself. I'm O.K. I'm not a second-class citizen. I can now make a list of positives about myself, which I could not do in the past.
—NANCY

- Is your day ruined if the scales do not reward you with a lower weight?
- Do you feel that you would be a "better" person if you were thinner?
- Do you feel that you must "settle" for leftovers when it comes to romance and companionship?

If you answered yes to any of these questions, you are typical of many large women who have handcuffed their self-esteem to their size. This is illustrated most clearly in the testimonials of people who have lost weight, which usually go something like this:

SPOKESPERSON FOR WEIGHT LOSS PROGRAM/PRODUCT: How did you feel about yourself before you lost the weight?

SHE (On the verge of tears): I didn't like myself. I had no self-esteem or self-respect. I didn't want to go out of the house. I was out of control.

SPOKESPERSON: And how do you feel now?

SHE: Now that I'm a size 8, I can finally look in the mirror and like who I see. I'm happy, my husband is happy, and I'm enjoying life.

Now, what happens if this woman eventually joins the 95 percent of people who regain the weight they lost? Should she be divested of her self-esteem until she sheds the pounds once again? And failing that, should she be sentenced to a lifetime of self-loathing and self-rebuke?

When I ask people why they came to Largely Positive, the answer I'm given most often is, "Because I want to learn to feel good about myself." And yet, they wonder if this is possible. Most have spent years believing that the only way they could truly feel good about themselves would be to achieve their "ideal weight." I can see the skepticism in their faces and hear it in their voices.

I wish I had a magic self-esteem potion that I could give everyone who walks in—or a pill taken before bedtime that would produce self-esteem upon awakening. Like the Wizard of Oz gave courage to the lion, a brain to the scarecrow, and a heart to the tin man, I wish I could give self-esteem to all the larger people who say they don't have enough of it.

The fact of the matter is, much as I'd like to, I can't "give" you self-esteem. You have to give it to yourself. Be patient. It takes a little time and effort, but you're worth it!

What is self-esteem?

We certainly hear a lot about it, but what exactly is self-esteem? According to Nathaniel Branden, who has written extensively on the subject and could be considered the "guru of self-esteem," it is "the sum of self-confidence and self-respect. It reflects your implicit judgment of your ability to cope with the challenges of your life (to understand and master your problems) and of your right to be happy (to respect and stand up for your interests and needs)."[1] Healthy self-esteem, says Branden, is based on six practices:

1. Living consciously: having respect for facts, being open to information, seeking to understand both the world outside as well as our inner world.

2. Self-acceptance: taking responsibility for your thoughts, feelings, and actions; the virtue of realism applied to oneself.

3. Self-responsibility: realizing we are the authors of our choices and actions. The question is not "Who's to blame?" but always "What needs to be done?"

4. Self-assertiveness: being authentic, refusing to "fake" the reality of who we are or what we value to avoid disapproval.

5. Living purposefully: identifying short- and long-term goals and how we will attain them—and going back to the drawing board if necessary.

6. Personal integrity: living in harmony with what we know, what we profess, and what we do, i.e. telling the truth.[2]

You can see that these six principles have nothing to do with how much you've accomplished or accumulated, with how many awards you've won, how many degrees you have, or with fitting into a pair of size 6 jeans! Branden cautions that self-esteem is not based on the acclaim of others, nor does it depend on "knowledge, skill, material possessions, marriage, parenthood, charitable endeavors, sexual conquests, or face lifts."[3] The root of self-esteem, he says, is not our achievements but those internally-generated practices or values that make it possible for us to achieve. It's living your life in a way that allows you to respect yourself and others.

Self-esteem should be a constant, no matter what your size. It should not yo-yo along with your weight. But this is what our society teaches. You can't get through a day without catching the message from a talk show, a weight loss ad, or a magazine article that extra pounds make you an inferior person.

The downward slide in self-esteem begins at a very early age. The minute little girls are able to turn on a TV set or look at a magazine, they start getting the message that they're unacceptable unless their shape "conforms to the norm." I picked up a magazine that featured prom gowns, curious to see what girls would be wearing this spring. There was not one large size in the whole magazine, but there are lots of large young girls, and they're just as entitled to pretty party dresses as thinner girls.

When things like this keep happening to plus-size young girls, the message is pretty clear: you don't "fit in"—quite literally. We don't make clothes for bodies like yours. Either shape up or stay home simply because you have bloomed more fully than the other girls. And once that message is received, the downward slide in self-esteem is in full swing.

Dieting and self-esteem

The more you diet, the more your self-esteem suffers.[4] Here are some of the things women have said to me about the impact of dieting on their self-esteem:

- "I have tried every diet product and machine that I've been able to get my hands on. At each failure, I was left with a deeper feeling of depression and a greater loss of my self-esteem."

- "I'm tired of being overweight, feeling worse than a second-class citizen, and, worst of all, not liking myself because of the vicious cycle."

- "By way of very strict dieting, I am able to keep weight off, but after six years of constant dieting, I started to fall off and regain weight. Unfortunately, as the pounds have gone up, the self-esteem has gone down."

- "After years of dieting, my self-esteem is at an all-time low, so low I often feel if I could only be thin, I would be better at everything."

For some, even a few pounds in the plus column can spell self-esteem disaster:

- "I am presently in therapy and could really use some help in dealing with my weight problem. I am presently 20 pounds overweight and have very poor self-esteem."

Some spend years in a tug-of-war between weight and self-esteem:

- "I have struggled 20 years with my weight up and down. No matter what size I was, I never had body confidence. I now weigh 210 and am sick of dieting, gaining and losing, mostly gaining."

Some, however, are beginning to realize that weight and self-esteem are not really close relatives:

- "I am one of those who has, many times in my life, made losing weight a prerequisite for liking myself. What a wonderful feeling to know my self-worth does not depend on my size."

- "I have been heavy since my teens and have fought all these years to be thin, to no avail. I was always trying to live up to someone else's expectations. My life is great, except that I was always trying to come up with the magic way to be thin. Thanks for your inspiration and help in taking the first steps in learning not to beat myself up and that I'm okay in the body that I have."

One evening I asked our group members why weight should have any bearing on self-esteem. "Because," one woman said, "people view you as being not able to control yourself." "Because," said another, "people view you as unattractive and undesirable." As we continued, it became obvious that erosion of self-esteem is mostly due to external messages, to judgments by other people. It is important to recognize this because at some point you are going to have to repair your self-esteem from the inside out. As another member wisely noted: "Self-esteem by definition comes from the self—it has to come from within."

It would follow that the larger a woman becomes, the lower her self-esteem, but at least one study of female nursing students shows this not the case. Women who considered themselves fat, but were of "normal" weight, scored lower on measures of self-esteem than women who were really large.[5] The researcher does not offer an explanation for this, but I will try. Fear of becoming fat may produce more anxiety than the undeniable conclusion that one is *indeed* fat.

Women who can still shop in the misses' department have told me their worst fear is that they will someday have to shop in plus-size stores. Then you're officially fat. For many women fatness is an "unknown." They don't know what to expect. Once you know you're fat, the uncertainty vanishes and you deal with it—and you find out it's not the end of the world. You still have friends. People still love you. You still go to work. People still value your opinions. The plus-size stores carry attractive, up-to-date fashions. The fear does not match the reality.

Acceptance skeptics

Self-esteem and a plus-size body—peacefully co-existing. How is that possible? Newcomers to our group often register disbelief when told they can feel good, look good, and be good in the larger state. It's not surprising. Our society doesn't want you to feel good about yourself while displaying an abundant physique. A large woman is acceptable only if she's dieting or preparing to diet. To be content with oneself while your tummy still protrudes is risky business. Many people won't even believe you. Poor dear, they'll whisper—she's just deluding herself.

Accepting oneself "as is" is baffling and suspect to most people. I recently saw a talk show about being big and beautiful—although only one of the women met these criteria. The other two were thin women. One had lost weight and gotten married. The other had formerly been an anorexic and was now simply thin. The title of the show became confusing as the thin women dominated the conversation and the large woman was made to feel that she was faking her self-acceptance.

I saw the skepticism again yesterday—three absolutely stunning, competent, articulate large women who felt great about themselves forced to defend their positive attitudes and debate a woman who refused to believe them. The disbeliever had lost 90 pounds, although she admitted she had regained some of it. (She said she planned to lose it again.) "You can't tell me you feel good about yourself at that size," she said to the more abundant women. I was delighted when one of them said, with a decidedly British accent, "Honey, when I take off this bra at night, it's as though I've opened a gift package for the man in my life!"

Size-acceptance activist Pat Lyons agrees: "When fat people accept themselves and are happy, they are accused of lying, and when they decide to make health changes, such as walking more or eating less fat, it is assumed that their sole motivation is to lose weight."[6]

Our member, Phyllis, says it angers her that people can "express their feelings about our size being unacceptable, *but will not accept how we feel about ourselves.*"

I for one am not delusional! On the contrary, I'm finally "sizing up" this whole weight thing in a rational manner and realizing that it makes no sense to base your self-worth on the size of your assorted body parts. I am an intelligent woman. I have a master's degree. I graduated magna cum laude. I know my own mind. I do not have to accept the dictates of society. If I say I feel good, then I feel good. Don't tell me that I really don't feel good or how you think I feel. I will accept as genuine your self-disclosure. Please have the courtesy to do the same for me.

I am my weight

Women especially can get to a point where weight rules their lives. The anxiety it breeds can fill the mind to overflowing and wash away any ambition that is not related to "losing." After awhile, weight becomes their sole defining characteristic.

Listen to Nina talk about how weight became the ruler of her life:

During the period between 14 and 25, I was constantly preoccupied with food and my weight. Every pound gained threw me into a downward spiral of depression, and I could barely think of anything else all day. In my early anorexic days I would weigh myself several times a day, and even packed the bathroom scale in my suitcase when I went out of town! It makes me want to cry to think of the number of hours most women spend thinking about what they are or aren't eating. I am filled with sadness when I look at the thin arms of some of the college women I see and watch them obsessively exercise. Think about all we women could do if we harnessed that energy! Since I stopped dieting, I have had the emotional stamina to go into business for myself and to help other people do the same.

I was a lot like Nina during the same period. It seems ridiculous now to think that the number representing my weight had such power over me. Would I have let the number that represents my blood pressure dictate my worthiness as a person? Of course not. Why, then, do we allow weight to control our destinies?

You must stop endowing thinness with the power to solve all of life's problems. How often have you encountered difficulties at work, a crisis at home, a relationship gone sour, jeans that no longer button, only to convince yourself that life would be so much easier with tight buns and a flat stomach? "Being thin," you tell yourself, "will make me so happy that nothing else will matter." But people who always have been thin and people who have become thin tell us it is not the elixir they imagined. Their problems are not diminished, and the rigors of trying to stay thin can sap the energy they need to deal with those problems.

We've got it all backward

Conventional thinking has been: Lose weight and then you can have self-esteem. But if I can't have any self-esteem until I lose weight, I have no reason to take care of myself. The motivation to do that cannot be eked out of self-hatred; it springs from valuing yourself and having compassion for your body. Self-esteem provides a much sturdier and lasting foundation for building a healthy lifestyle than a foundation of self-loathing, which crumbles easily.

A doctor was asked during a radio interview what he considered to be the nation's number-one health problem. His reply: Lack of self-esteem. Asked why, he said that people with low self-esteem don't think they're worth taking care of. He's right. I see it all the time—larger people who think they can't be healthy until they're thin, so they don't bother doing the things that are good for them. Many get to a point where they don't want to do anything or see anyone. They don't want anyone to see them. They feel they are complete failures and have little interest in doing anything that would be good for them. So they often turn to the very thing they're trying to avoid—food.

If, on the other hand, I *like* the "me" that exists today, I will want to treat myself well and create a healthy lifestyle. I'll want to eat nutritious food and get some exercise because I like who I am and I believe that my body is worth nurturing. The more I care about myself and my body, the more I care about what goes in it and how I take care of it. If that results in weight loss, fine. If it doesn't, that's fine too—because I will know I'm doing all that I can to live a happy, healthy life.

If weight loss is the only route to self-esteem, then we have automatically doomed one-third of the female population to a lifetime of feeling rotten about themselves. Think what a power surge there would be if the negative energy fueling body hatred were suddenly converted to positive activity!

Reclaiming your self-esteem

What's the secret to self-esteem at any size? Where's the recipe? I'm going to try to give you the basic ingredients, but you'll have to stir them up. You may decide to add some ingredients of your own. And don't try to hurry the cooking process. It takes awhile to bake!

In her wonderful book, *Making Peace With Food*, Susan Kano says that when we lack self-confidence, we have three choices: (1) to flounder around in a state of indecision and inaction; (2) to develop self-confidence; or (3) to act according to others' judgments and expectations regardless of our own needs and desires.[7] The last alternative, she feels, is the easiest and most common course. But not the best one. Let's choose (2)!

What does the research say?

There has actually been very little scientific research on how larger people can improve their self-esteem—probably because it is generally believed that if they would just lose weight, they would have better self-esteem. So why bother doing any research on the topic?

The ideal solution, of course, would be to eliminate weight prejudice, but as one observer of weight discrimination points out: "Research on the stigmatized may be criticized for focusing too much on what to change about the stigmatized and not enough on how to change the culture. Although we would like to see the culture changed such that being above average weight and feeling above average weight is no longer stigmatizing, there is little evidence that our culture is moving in that direction."[8]

For now, it will be mostly up to larger people themselves to bolster their self-esteem, but there is a small body of research that may help. You will be on the road to better self-esteem if you:

1. Do not view yourself or other larger people with dislike or disgust. Research on "anti-fat attitudes" shows that weight prejudice is not confined to the thinner population. Larger people often harbor negative attitudes toward *other* larger people. Disliking overweight people when one is a member of the group seems risky for self-esteem, especially given the actual difficulty of ever leaving the group![9]

2. Do not base your self-regard on others' approval. People whose self-esteem is highly dependent on receiving praise and approval from others are vulnerable to low self-esteem when they sense disapproval or fail to win praise.[10]

3. Realize that not all outcomes are deserved and not all things (including weight) are under personal control.[11] In one study, larger children who attributed their weight to factors they could not completely control, such as genetics or biology, had much better self-esteem than the children who believed that they alone were responsible for their above-average weight because they just ate too much or didn't exercise enough.[12]

4. Reject or ignore society's dictates about acceptable body weight. Studies show that African American and European American women have very different opinions of the larger figure. When shown photos of both average and above-average weight women, African American women did not denigrate the larger women, but the European American women did. Black women consider themselves attractive even if they feel dissatisfied with their body size. When asked what constitutes attractiveness, young African American girls thought that things like personal style and presentation were just as important as weight.[13-15]

5. Blame the bias and prejudice of critics rather than yourself. Thus a larger person who fails to get a job might conclude that the potential employer is prejudiced against fat people rather than that he or she did not interview well.[16-17]

Baby steps

Do not expect your self-esteem to be revived overnight. That's not how it happened for me or for other members of Largely Positive. Unfortunately, this is a society of instant gratification. We want everything fast. Fast weight loss. Fast food. Oil changes in ten minutes. Fast fixes for whatever ails us. I didn't suddenly become "largely positive." I took a few steps forward, sometimes a step backward, and sometimes stood still for awhile.

I like the attitude of a woman who wrote to me after reading an article about Largely Positive: "Learning these new behaviors and thought processes will take some time," she said, "but not nearly as long as I have been mad at myself and dieting." And the advice of Nathaniel Branden: "In the arena of raising self-esteem, we evolve, not by dreaming of giant steps, but by committing ourselves in action to little ones, moving step by relentless step to an ever-expanding field of vision."[18] "Accepting yourself totally won't come overnight, so it's helpful to decide which areas you want to deal with first, and leave others on the back burner," advise the authors of *Women and Self-Esteem*.[19]

Size-acceptance advocate Cheri Erdman, Ed.D, agreed with this in her dissertation about large women who have achieved self-acceptance. All in all, the process tends to be slow and gradual, she said. She added that there can be more than one avenue: "My conclusion about the process which women go through toward size acceptance is that there is not just one, but many. It is a complex construct, and it appears we can share our experiences with each other, but ultimately we will have to live our own way through it."

One of our facilitators advises people who are new to the "largely positive" philosophy to take baby steps. No, you won't wake up tomorrow morning and suddenly throw away your scales, toss out all your "waiting-to-get-thin" clothes, enroll in a tap-dancing class, and confront everyone who has ever been critical about your weight. You can decide to do one thing each day to advance your cause, which is to feel good about yourself in the body you have right now and to live your life the way you think you would if you were thin.

Get up each morning and write down one thing you will do that day toward achieving your "largely positive" attitude. It can be a health-related step like taking a walk or writing a letter to a comedian who made a nasty fat joke. It might be advising your mother that your weight will no longer be a topic of discussion.

I know this is not easy. It's not easy to walk down the street and be the target of a stranger's cruel remark about your size. It's not easy to make a confident entrance at a party for which you swore you'd be thin. It's not easy to be told by your doctor that the pain in your elbow would subside if you lost weight—and to have the courage to stand up for yourself. And it's not easy to tell your well-meaning friend that you're not interested in the diet she clipped from a magazine for you because you've learned that diets rarely work. But if you don't start, you run the risk of living life on the sidelines and wondering what might have been—if you had only been thin.

Start with self-acceptance

The first step in uncoupling weight from self-worth is to arrive at a point of self-acceptance. It helps, I believe, to distinguish self-acceptance from self-esteem. I got to a point around age 40 where I had to ask myself the question: "What if you never get thin?" Initially, it was a scary question, and not one I necessarily wanted to answer. But I had to face reality. I had never once been thin in my life (unless we count that one day back in 1966 after a bout with amphetamine diet pills). I had, however, spent the better part of my life *planning* to be thin, which means lots of things got put on hold. I realized this had to stop. I didn't want to live in the future any more; I wanted to live in the present.

Nathaniel Branden also makes the distinction between self-acceptance and self-esteem. "Accepting," he says, "does not mean we cannot wish for changes. It means accepting that the face and the body in the mirror are your face and body, and that they are what they are."[20] Even though you may not like everything you see in the mirror, you are still able to say: "Right now, that's me. I accept it. This is the body I currently have and it gets me where I want to go. Because of differences in physiology and genetics, it is a larger body. This does not mean it is a bad body." You must do this without self-blame or self-recrimination.

This is kind of like preparing the canvas for a painting. You don't have to love it at this point. After all, you don't even know yet what you're going to paint. But your canvas has to be clean and free from preconceived ideas.

Writing in *Full Lives*, Avis Rumney says: "Now I can stand before a mirror and own that this is my body—not perfect, but mine. There are aspects I like better than others, and this seems natural . . . but now I accept all these parts. And, most importantly, I know now that these physical aspects are only the external expression of my whole self."[21]

Acceptance does not mean giving up, although sometimes people think that it does. Maybe it does in one way. I have given up on the idea that my body will conform to society's narrow definition of beauty, but in every other way I am taking charge: of my health, of my mind and body, of my life and the way I choose to live it.

It may be helpful to listen to the words of my good friend Wendy, one of the facilitators of our group, as she describes her first step:

The first time I went to a Largely Positive meeting and walked into a room filled with large women, I thought to myself: What on earth could these fat people have to tell me? I sat through the meeting swinging my foot and thinking: 'If these people think they are going to convince me that I should be happy as a fat person, they are sadly mistaken.' I had seen shows on TV with large people talking about how they liked themselves and their bodies and I thought they must be nuts or they have just given up. For some reason, I kept going to the meetings and I realized that these wonderful, beautiful people did like themselves well enough to dress well, be happy, have fun, and engage in all sorts of activities that many large people never do, like swimming, dancing, biking, walking, exercising, even public speaking. One day I got it: Why shouldn't I like myself? I'm just one of the great varieties of people in this world. People come in the flavors of short, tall, in-between, thin, medium, big, blonde, brunette, redhead, black, brown, red, white, yellow. Diversity is what this world is about; we all belong and deserve to be happy and lead fulfilling lives.

Wendy is quick to add: "This does not, I repeat *does not*, suggest complacency. We do not just sit back and sigh. We take action to make ourselves healthy and attractive."

Education as the key to acceptance

Self-acceptance became much easier for me when I began to *truly* understand the factors that contribute to a person's size and weight. I did this by reading books like *The Dieter's Dilemma* and by familiarizing myself with the research related to obesity. Realizing that my view of myself had been based on faulty information paved the way for self-acceptance. *The Dieter's Dilemma* author, William Bennett, would agree. Referencing people who view themselves as "diet failures," he says: "The failure . . . does not lie in your weak will. It lies in the misconceptions about weight and weight control that dominate our belief system."

I now have a better understanding of my body and why it's the way it is—and I can accept that. I can accept that researchers don't have a complete understanding of obesity. I can accept that they're still searching for a permanent cure. And I can accept that they may not discover it in my lifetime. I can accept all that and get on with my life.

Psychologist Debby Burgard surveyed over 100 women weighing at least 200 pounds and found that:

- It *is* possible to accept your body size regardless of weight. About half the women felt their bodies were acceptable "as is."
- Higher self-esteem is associated with giving up dieting. Women who said they no longer dieted scored higher on almost all the personality and self-esteem measures.
- Women with the greatest degree of self-esteem were able to separate a failed diet from personal failure. They had educated themselves to recognize that diets fail "not because of excess emotionality or lack of self-control, but because of a combination of normal physiological and psychological reactions to caloric deprivation."[22]

It could be worse

I once wrote an article for Largely Positive's newsletter titled: "There are a lot Worse Things I Could Be than Big." Here's some of what I wrote:

There are a lot worse things I could be than big. I could be a mean, vindictive person. I could be deceitful. I could be selfish and unfeeling. I could be unmoved by the atrocities that occur in the world or by the plight of those less fortunate. I could be an untrustworthy friend. I could be an abusive parent. I have committed no crime. I'm just big.

Sometimes it seems as though we place more importance on molding our bodies than on molding our characters. Being a large person is not the crime of the century. It's not even a misdemeanor! Your body is just bigger than average. Why, then, do we treat being large as a crime? Does the obsessive pursuit of thinness result in a more just, humane world? How often have you seen an obituary that read: "She/He excelled at being thin"?

Blueprint for self-esteem

Now we come to the question I'm asked most often. "How can I improve my self-esteem?" This is the central question for people who come to Largely Positive. Who are these people? Generally they're people who have spent years on the diet merry-go-round, losing, gaining, losing, gaining—but never getting the brass ring marked "thin." They're people who have been beaten down by the relentless din of messages that thin is in and fat is not where it's at. Often they're people with friends and family members who badger them about their weight. (For more on this subject, see Chapter 9.) Many have put their lives on hold waiting to be thin.

They're people who feel deceived and betrayed by the diet industry. Many have spent thousands of dollars on various weight-loss remedies that, over the long term, have left them not thinner but fatter. Nevertheless, many still blame themselves. Some are close to drowning in feelings of inferiority and worthlessness.

But they're also kind, fun, interesting, generous, resilient, attractive people. They're some of the nicest people I've ever met, and the world is certainly a better place with them in it.

So what advice do we give those who come seeking to heal their self-esteem? Read on.

Create a positive portfolio

Begin to create a "positive portfolio." To do this, you need to buy a loose-leaf notebook. You may also want to purchase some dividers. Clip blame-absolving articles on obesity. Cut out articles on self-acceptance. Jot down memorable quotes. Save pictures of attractive large women. Keep a running tally of all the positive things you are and do. Note when you've done something well, when someone compliments you, when you've done a good deed for someone, when you've done something positive for your health, when you have been assertive—and, most importantly, the moments you have allowed your inner integrity to shine. Over time, you'll have a very positive self-digest! Pull it out when negative thoughts invade and they won't stand a chance.

You're in charge now

It's very important that you make a conscious decision to be in charge of your own life. Your mother is not in charge. Your husband is not in charge. Your boss is not in charge. *You* are in charge. The decisions you make from now on will be *your* decisions. You cannot depend on others for your health and happiness, and you cannot base your self-perception on the opinions of others.

Everything that follows is based on the assumption that you have decided to be captain of your own ship. That ship is your body. You are at the helm. You control the direction, the speed, the destination. Others may want to chart you a different course. Don't allow it or you'll end up someplace you didn't really want to go.

The only master your body has ever known or will ever know is you. Knowing you're in charge is a marvelous feeling. Sure, the weather may get rough from time to time, but that's when you grip the wheel more firmly. Sail your ship with pride and determination and no one will ever be able to capsize you again!

Get the facts, ma'am

As I said before, it's critical to do all you can to educate yourself about issues of size and weight. Learning about the physiology of size and weight, learning that I wasn't to blame, learning that large people are not universally scorned—all this paved the way for me to continue down the road to self-acceptance. Start reading books that contain accurate information about issues of size and weight. (See the "recommended reading" at the end of this book.) Once you chuck the self-blame, you can get on with the business of becoming "largely positive!"

Take inventory

Janet Wolfe, Ph.D., a psychologist specializing in the field of women's self-acceptance, explains in the June 1994 issue of *Self* how she gives patients a pie chart and asks them to label the slices—body size and shape, friendship skills, work competence, artistic abilities. This helps to show them that they only hurt themselves when they base their entire worth on one slice of the pie—such as body size.

Another way to put your weight in its proper perspective is to divide a sheet of paper into two columns. At the top of the first column write your weight (or your best estimate—I know how you've come to hate the scale). In the next column, start to list everything about you that is positive and good. Your list should include personal attributes—things like kindness, generosity, tolerance. It should include skills and talents. Do you play the piano, paint, write, make jewelry? It should reflect the support you give to your family and friends, as well as time spent in community activities. It can include career accomplishments, recognition, awards. This may be difficult at first. Sometimes when I ask women to state something positive about themselves, it's hard for them to think of even one thing. They've given their inner critic free reign for so long. But stick with it. Start the list. You don't have to finish it right away. Put it aside and add to it as you think of things. Pretty soon your weight will appear as one tiny blip at the start of pages filled with all the terrific things that you are and that you do. The things you do that are good and positive far outnumber the not-so-great stuff. Your list will help to frequently remind you of this. One caution: I ask you to do this because it is helpful in illustrating all that is good about you, but your self-worth is not dependent on your accomplishments. You were a worthwhile person the day you were born and started your life on this earth. Your worth lies in being, not in doing.

Be sure your list includes courage

Every time we walk out the door we face the possibility of being assailed by both cruel and well-intentioned remarks about our weight. It takes a lot of courage to keep going out there and forging ahead despite the anti-fat messages that bombard us continually, the affronts by complete strangers, the fat jokes, the stern lectures from health professionals, the "tsk-tsk's" should we dare to eat an ice cream cone, public accommodations that are not kind to our hips, and mates who monitor our plates "for our own good." I commend you—and you should commend yourself—for surviving all that and emerging as a bright, competent, well adjusted, kind, caring, fun-loving, attractive woman—one fantastic lady!

Nina, who would not be considered fat, but has battled an eating disorder, says: "I know that women who weigh more than I ever did get a lot of negative feedback from the outside world . . . That means that people who are truly fat should be even prouder of themselves when they learn to ignore the crazy societal messages we get about having to be thin to be okay."

Spotlight your skills

I think it's very important to find something you do well and capitalize on it. Everyone needs to feel that they are good at something. It's human nature and good medicine for your self-esteem. When I was quite young, my mother realized I could play the piano by ear. She offered me further instruction so I could develop my talent. In high school I entertained at assemblies, playing hit tunes from that period. I enjoyed the applause.

In high school I also discovered that I had a talent for writing and journalism. Now I am often the person summoned to "take all this information and make some sense out of it." My end product usually wins praise. I like praise. I'm sure you like praise.

Despite all your perceived "shortcomings," there are things that you do very well and things that you know you could do even better. If you know you have a talent for art, why not take some classes in drawing or painting? If your cooking always leaves people wanting your recipes, take some cooking classes. If you're always called upon to lead the Christmas caroling, why not treat yourself to singing lessons? If you often find yourself weaving thoughts into a poem, how about a poetry course? The more you concentrate on nurturing your God-given talents, the less time you'll have to fidget about your weight.

What's important here is that you *recognize* your natural talents and do not bemoan activities that don't seem to lie in your personal talent reservoir. It's probably a good thing that I didn't aspire to be a ballerina, for instance, because I had neither the physique nor the coordination. It would have brought me heartache and disappointment. Thank goodness we're all good at different things. Otherwise the world wouldn't work very well!

Don't make comparisons

Stop comparing yourself with others. There's a reason no two people on this planet are alike—so each of us could be unique and special in our own right. The world works because we all have different skills. Constantly comparing yourself to others drains energy that is better spent on activities that please *you*.

Count your blessings

It's time to make another list—this time of all the good things in your life—a job you like, friends you enjoy, a nice home, a loving family, the knowledge you've acquired, a sunny day—even things like shoes or a coat. Many people don't have these things. A mind that counts blessings has no room for self-pity.

Become preoccupied with the world, not dieting

When we're constantly dieting, weighing, measuring, counting calories, calculating fat grams, writing in food diaries, and generally agonizing over what to eat and what not to eat, we have little time left for what's going on in the rest of the world.

Body image expert Marcia Germaine Hutchinson often advises women to calculate the amount of time they spend obsessing about their appearance by estimating how much time each day they spend worrying about what they look like or what others think of their looks and multiplying this amount by 365 days in a year. "At my workshops," she says in the book *Full Lives*, "I ask women to consider that, by some measures, as many as 75 percent of American women are similarly wasting their time and energy."[23] Adds Dr. Hutchinson:

We are so busy obsessing over what is wrong with us—whether it's our weight, misproportion, wrinkles, pimples, excess hair, or functional limitations—that we fail to develop our potential as human beings. If we could harness a tiny fraction of the energy and attention wasted in body hate and use it as fuel for creativity and self-development, just think how far we could go toward our life goals.

I read an article by novelist Marge Piercy about some friends who got together for a dinner party. The hostess asked one of the women to stand up and exclaimed: "Nancy has lost 20 pounds. Isn't that fabulous?" Piercy said she was shocked:

First, the woman in question had recently had a show of her paintings at a prestigious gallery. No one in the group clapped for that accomplishment. I had finished a novel that took me seven years of research, and a doctor who was present had built a house with his own hands, but we were not cheered. Having caused part of her body to disappear seemed to everyone else in the room an act of such singular merit it overwhelmed the merely artistic or commercial success. ("My, Haven't You Lost Weight," Woman's Day, October 25, 1988)

The scales can truly be an instrument of terror. Recently I received a letter from a woman who works as a leader in a group diet program, although she's regained some weight and fears she may be terminated. She told me she was at a management seminar when it was announced that everyone would be weighed the next morning:

In the few moments it took for her announcement, I saw a room full of confident, intelligent, motivated businesswomen turn into paranoid, self-conscious, nervous ninnies! No one could eat their dinner—people went swimming, running, exercising for the rest of the evening. They ran to the drugstore for laxatives—anything to get their weight down by morning. Everyone panicked—except me. I knew that I was over goal, so what difference would one night make? I took a walk with a friend and fellow manager. We discussed our anger, humiliation and sense of betrayal at the fact that a weigh-in was 'sprung' on us, and then went out for fat-free yogurt!

The next time you're part of a conversation that veers toward dieting, grab the wheel and turn it in a different direction. Say: "Seen any good movies?" Or: "Tell me about your trip to Mexico." Or: "Let me tell you about my new project at work."

Sometimes I advise women to "contemplate the cosmos." Go outside and gaze up at the night sky. Think about the universe. Does it ever end? How many other galaxies are out there? Does life exist elsewhere? How far is it to the stars you see? Are they even there any more? What really lies out there? Does your waist measurement have any significance compared to these questions?

I think you'll find that as you become more involved in activities with a focus beyond your body, weight management will be easier. Because you'll be busy with other interests, you're more likely to forget about food until your body sends you a signal that it's time to eat. What does dieting really signify anyway? That for a few weeks you were able to resist mocha fudge ice cream and fettuccine Alfredo? I would rather hear that you worked at a homeless shelter or took a fund-raising walk for AIDS or signed up to be a big sister. These sorts of things are the true measures of character.

When you start scolding yourself for losing control and eating a macadamia nut brownie, think of these words spoken by Hilde Bruch, one of the foremost authorities on eating disorders: "There is a great deal of talk about the weakness and self indulgence of overweight people who eat 'too much.' Very little is said about the selfishness and self indulgence involved in a life which makes one's appearance the center of all values."

Make someone happy

"Make someone happy, make just one someone happy," goes the song. Making someone else feel better is one of the best ways for making yourself feel better. Do something unexpected for a friend or family member. Think about volunteering. It's good for your health. Scientists are discovering that people with a strong community-service orientation are healthier than those who tend to isolate themselves. In one study, women who regularly helped others through volunteer work reported a strong sense of satisfaction, even exhilaration, an increased sense of self-worth, less depression, and fewer aches and pains.[24] In the words of Charles Dickens: "No one is useless in this world who lightens the burden of another."

List the advantages of being big

I often bring a flip chart to workshops and write the word "advantages" at the top of the first sheet of paper. "Let's list," I say, "the advantages of being a larger person." Dead silence. Perplexed expressions. People looking at me as if I were a few slices short of a loaf.

Okay, I say, we'll start with disadvantages. People have no trouble with that. I don't let them off the hook though. We return to the search for advantages. Part of the problem is that we never ever think that there could be anything good about being big. The cultural messages have all been negative. Even after I get their thinking aimed in the direction of advantages, some of the things they come up with aren't exactly what I have in mind:

- "Men won't bother with you."
- "People in cars can see you easier."

We usually settle into a more positive groove, and as we gain momentum, the list starts to grow. Here are some of the items from these lists over the years:

- "As a larger person, I have become more tolerant and compassionate of anyone who is different in some way."
- "I seem to ward off diseases better and am not sick nearly as often as some of my thin colleagues."
- "I feel I can carry off a more bold, dramatic style than a smaller person."
- "I have learned a great deal about nutrition."
- "It forced me to really look beneath the exterior for self-definition. I feel more substance of body has led to more substance of character."

- "My size gives me a feeling of power and competence on the job. When I am dressed in my power suit and present my ideas articulately, I know people take me very seriously."
- Large women tend to be more "amply endowed."
- Large women look younger. Not that there's anything wrong with looking older—this is another obsession we have—but if looking youthful is important, then many large women are blessed with smooth, wrinkle-free skin that subtracts years from their age.

Being big can even confer certain health benefits, although no one really wants you to know that. Researcher Paul Ernsberger, Ph.D, has found a reduced incidence of certain forms of cancer in large people, as well as enhanced survival rates. Large people, he says, also exhibit more resistance to infection, are less likely to die of lung disease, and are less likely to develop osteoporosis, anemia, and peptic ulcers.[25] One study found that obesity may help protect against pain,[26] and it was reported in the December 1993 issue of *Working Woman* that large women suffer fewer hot flashes during menopause!

Without realizing it, being large may have allowed you to blossom in a way you never would have otherwise. Writing in *Radiance* magazine, New York therapist Barbara Altman Bruno says:

> *If I had been a slim child, I might never have had the opportunities that being a chubby outsider gave me. I might have succeeded at fitting in and not discovered that I had anything unique and valuable to offer. Being 'overweight,' with all its negative connotations, required me to look beneath the surface and beyond the stereotypes, to use more than my eyes to see what was there, to appreciate individuality, to seek health instead of pathology, to trust my own experience.[27]*

"Fat," says Angela Barron McBride in *Overcoming Fear of Fat*, "does not just conjure up society's negative images, but calls to mind fecundity, prosperity, expansiveness. To be 'large' is to be great, substantial, extensive, benevolent, strong."[28]

Thank your body for what it does for you

People often confess to me: "I can get to the point where I feel good about myself as a person, but I'm not sure I can truthfully say that I love my physical body. Is that okay?" I say sure. Studies show that very few women, including thin ones, are truly satisfied with their bodies.

So instead of feeling frustrated that your hard-won self-acceptance is incomplete without totally embracing your body, try this: thank your body for what it does for you. Thank your legs for carrying you around, your arms for being able to hug someone, your eyes for enabling you to see the beauty of nature, your ears for being a pathway for music. This will allow you to feel affection for your body even if you can't view it as perfect.

Another strategy is to neutralize your body parts. Instead of saying: "My hips are so fat and ugly," simply say "My hips are big." Do not be judgmental. Just state it as a fact. Remember, you do not have figure flaws; you have a shape that is unique and contributes to the diversity of the human race.

No one is perfect

I'm not sure I like this argument, but I'll offer it up. Saying "no one is perfect" assumes that my size is an imperfection, and that negates everything we've just said. But it still may help you to remember that everyone has faults and imperfections. Most of the time these faults and imperfections are not visible to the naked eye, so you wouldn't really know at a glance what someone's less-than-perfect qualities are. Most bad habits don't show. There are also no physical markings to let me know whether a person is abusive, bigoted, or apathetic.

Charles Roy Schroeder, Ph.D., in his book *Fat Is Not a Four Letter Word*, believes that "it is the height of arrogance for a person to badger fat people to lose weight simply because he or she considers fatness an imperfection." When you are harassed about your weight, he suggests: "Instead of defending that which needs no defense, respond by asking, 'Pardon me, are you perfect?'"[29]

Look good, feel good

I worked on my self-esteem both from the inside out and the outside in—and pretty soon the two merged. Realizing I was just fine at my current size made me want to look my best, and looking my best made me feel better about myself internally. Looking your best will make the "inner work" easier. You'll like what you see in the mirror, you'll be getting compliments from others, and this will add to the proof that good things come in *all* size packages!

We talk in more detail about personal style in Chapter 8, but I need at least to mention it here because it's an important ingredient in my recipe for self-esteem. Personal style is an outward expression of your individuality, personality, and creativity. It's about clothes and makeup, yes, but it's just as much an attitude and an aura of confidence and self-respect.

Discover your own personal style. Look at catalogs and magazines for large women. Visit plus-size stores. Find out what feels right for you. While you're at it, experiment with makeup, with hairstyles. Get a manicure.

Fake it

Wendy often advises new members: "If you're not there yet, fake it!" The "inner work" usually takes more time than the "outer work." So while you're working toward inner acceptance, send out positive vibes. Even if you don't feel totally confident, act as if you do. You can stand tall, smile, and stride with pride even if your self-esteem is still a little wobbly. And before you know it, the inside will catch up with the outside. One day you'll suddenly realize you aren't faking anymore. What the world sees will be a reflection of how you truly feel about yourself.

Watch out for the "shoulds"

Do you often come down with a case of the "shoulds?" "I should be making more money." "I should be jogging every day." "I should lose weight." The next time the "shoulds" attack, ask yourself, "Why should I?" If you can't come up with an answer that satisfies you, maybe you don't need to do it. What you *should* do is to be good to yourself by doing things that please you and that contribute to your health and well-being.

Let's try applying the above advice to the statement "I should lose weight." Now ask, "Why should I?" If your answer is about pleasing your mother or if it's about getting thin for your class reunion, this is not about you. It's about other people. If your reason is "to be healthier," then focus on your health. Studies show that women who exercise regularly have better self-esteem than those who don't. If your answer is "to look better," then look better now. I look better today than I did ten years ago, but I haven't lost weight. What I *did* do: bought attractive clothes, got a new hairstyle, donned bold jewelry, and got a new attitude.

The "shoulds" often leads to a quest for perfection, and perfectionism is a killer. Notes Susan Kano, in *Making Peace with Food*: "A search for perfection is always a search for fault because no matter how much merit we find, perfection exists only where fault does not."[30]

Get your priorities in order

Do you take care of everyone else's needs first, and if there's time left over, then maybe you'll take care of your own? Not a good idea. What happens is that you often have very little energy left over for what *you* need. Start telling others that you've decided to set some priorities, starting with yourself. Learn to say no. I know I said earlier to "make someone happy," but you have to achieve a balance between your own needs and the needs of other people.

If that's too difficult, cut yourself some slack. When someone asks you to do something, tell them you'll have to think about it. Then decide whether you have the time, whether you have the physical and emotional energy, whether it's important to you. Then get back to the person and say, "I'm sorry, my schedule's filled for the next few weeks. If it's something you'd like to do, but just not now, you always can add, "Ask me again another time."

You have to stop trying to please everyone else and start to pay attention to the things that please you. This doesn't mean your needs should always take precedence. It simply means finding a balance between what you need and what everyone else around you needs. For many women, the scales are tipped almost completely in the "other" direction. In the long run, that's not fair to you *or* to them. You can't give your best to others unless you can give it to yourself first.

Build your self-esteem from the inside out, not the outside in

This may be the most critical step in building healthy self-esteem. You have to stop looking to others for validation, and you have to stop living your life trying to please everyone else. The gift of lasting self-esteem has to be given from within. Oh yes, praise from others helps, but it's fleeting, and soon you're looking for the next compliment or approving glance to validate yourself. Inner validation is constant, and no one can take it away from you. Again, Nathaniel Branden: We may get a very pleasant "hit" from someone's compliment, and we may tell ourselves that when we win people's approval we have self-esteem, but we may also notice that the pleasant feeling fades rather quickly"[31] and we go looking for more.

Thoreau once said: "Public opinion is a weak tyrant compared with our own private opinion. What a man thinks of himself, that is what determines, or rather, indicates his fate." If you are secure in your own self-opinion, it will not matter what others think.

In a discussion of self-acceptance in our support group one evening, a woman said: "It's not so much what I think. It's what other people think and say about me." My response was threefold:

- You can't look to others for self-validation—because there will always be someone who doesn't "validate." The only approval that's truly important is self-approval.

- There are lots of people who *do* accept you as you are—or would be willing to if you gave them the chance.

- If you allow other people's opinions to define who you are, you'll never get to a point of knowing yourself.

I find that large people often want to be liked by everyone—usually as a result of having suffered deep and repeated wounds to their self-esteem—and so they strive to be pleasing in every way other than weight: "If I can't be the weight everyone wants me to be, I'll be perfect at everything else and then they'll all like me." Give it up. Trying to "make up for" your weight by being perfect at everything else won't make you feel any better in the long run—and the internal anger it creates can be suffocating.

"It finally dawned on me," said Sharlene, "that the only times I really overate were the times when I allowed myself to be put down by other people. When I started telling them that I had learned to accept myself and they would have to do the same, my eating habits changed. I found I was eating my rage rather than letting it out. I don't know if I'll lose weight, but I do know that I like myself better for not letting people walk all over me."

Dr. Dean Edell has this suggestion: "Rather than wait for the world to change—because the world changes slowly—learn from the lessons of other minority groups. First develop your own self-esteem based on your own beliefs and your own knowledge system."[32]

You may have to develop a bit of a thick skin. I caught this remark on TV the other night, and while it wasn't related to weight, I think it applies: "You have to develop a tough hide to protect the soft interior." If you allow yourself to be bruised continually by the opinions and remarks of others, you may never know to what heights you could have soared—which brings us to the next piece of advice.

Take risks

Risk-taking is scary for most people, but especially so for large people. Risks can increase their vulnerability to rejection, hurtful remarks, and discrimination. But without risks, life takes on a dull sameness that may actually have more to do with producing unhappiness than size ever did.

Bodies dubbed too big prevent women from doing many things—going to the beach, dancing, sailing, hiking. You don't have to start out skydiving. You can make small changes, and each time you try something new, the risk you take will add to your confidence and pave the way for other adventures.

If you never take a risk, or say anything controversial, or disagree with anyone, or support the underdog, your overall approval rating from others will probably be pretty high. But your own self-approval rating will suffer.

Surround yourself with positive people and influences

Associate with positive, upbeat people. Stay away from those who put you down or who refuse to accept you as you are. There is no rule that says you have to be around people like that. In fact, you can choose not to.

This is easier with friends than with family because you can change your friends. While you can't change your family, they can be educated and enlightened. Show them this book. Tell them you've decided to accept yourself in the present and if they can't do that, you'll be spending more time around people who can. For more advice on dealing with other people, see Chapter 9.

Putting positive images of large people where you can see them on a regular basis also can be very helpful. I have several prints of large women by the artist Botero hanging in my office; I also have a collection of fat dolls. Additionally, I subscribe to *Radiance, BBW,* and *MODE,* magazines for large women that are always upbeat and inspiring. I recently came across some greeting cards with pictures of large women being bold, brazen and beautiful. And I'll have to get another box to send, because I framed all the cards from the first box I ordered! I'm constantly on the lookout for resources that depict large women in a positive light. I like being surrounded by them.

Remember that societies are like human beings— they're not perfect

Just because we have a cultural obsession with thinness doesn't make it right. An obsession is no healthier for a society than it is for an individual. People with "obsessive" disorders are referred for therapy. Maybe our society needs therapy!

Like human beings, societies are imperfect and make mistakes. Historically, there are many examples of societies that have inflicted grave injustices on groups of people. You now have some accurate information about size and weight. Ask yourself: Is society's idolatry of thinness based on sound research or is it based on myth, prejudice, and intolerance? Chances are you'll start to recognize, as I did, that popular beliefs about size and weight bear little resemblance to the facts. It's just that society keeps sweeping these facts under the carpet. If we join forces, we can yank that carpet up and let the truth out!

Eject the negative tapes

Does your mind constantly play negative tapes: "I'm so fat," "I'm no good," "No one likes me," "I'm such a failure"? When these tapes start playing, you must learn to pop them out and insert some positive lyrics. "Cognitive distortions" is a term mental health professionals often use to describe thought processes that greatly magnify your perceived faults and diminish your far more numerous positive qualities.

Betty felt she was "such a failure;" yet she had a job she liked, a supportive husband, a family that loved her, and friends who sought her company. "Why do you think you're a failure?" I asked. "Because," she said, "I can't ever seem to do anything right." I asked her to keep a list for a week of the things she "didn't do right." At the end of the week she had five things on her list, ranging from forgetting to return a friend's phone call to eating a candy bar when she felt she shouldn't have. I said: "Since you surely did many more than five things this week, the majority of things you did must have gone just fine." She agreed that most things did go well and that the things that didn't were really relatively minor.

Even if you do make a major mistake, you're still not a "failure." No one fails at everything. The next time something goes wrong at work, instead of labeling yourself a "failure," say: "That project didn't turn out as I would have liked, but I've had many other successful projects. This one was a good learning experience, and what I learned will allow me to be more successful in the future." Marilyn Sorensen, author of *Breaking the Chain of Low Self-Esteem*, agrees: "People with healthy self-esteem do not obsessively review their behavior, nor are they highly critical of their daily performance when they do look back on it . . . Even when they occasionally wish they had done or said something differently, they do not beat on themselves; instead, they devise a plan to correct the problem or think of how they will respond differently next time. They do not continue to dwell on the problem endlessly."[33] Or in the words of Kobi Yamada: "Never let yesterday use up too much of today."

I also like the attitude of Janet Simons of the University of Iowa School of Social Work, who tells people in stress management workshops to incorporate the "Twenty Percent Mess-Up Factor" into their lives. The basic principle is that you don't get upset with anyone, including yourself, unless you mess up more than 20 percent of the time. Once this rule is in place, you come to realize how the world, your colleagues, your family, and even you, yourself almost always get at least 80 percent of things correct.[34]

Many experts recommend that, when your mind starts playing a negative tape, you say to yourself: "Stop!" Or "Shut up!" Or "Stop this nonsense!" Sometimes it helps to personify your inner critic. Then you can talk back and forth. For instance, you might say: "Your constant disapproval is not very helpful to me. It frustrates me and prevents me from living fully. You are constantly ignoring all the good things I do. Until you have some positive things to say, you are not welcome in my mind."

Here's another neat idea from Sunny Stout, a management trainer who runs CareerTrack workshops:

> One way to counter your inner critic is to assemble your own 'self-confidence first aid kit.' Cover a corkboard with reminders of all the things that make you feel good, such as photographs of your friends or family, appreciative notes, cartoons—and use it to boost your confidence whenever you feel a little shaky.

The price you pay for negative thinking may be a steep one, indeed, if it prevents you from taking risks and being a full participant in life. Think about what it's costing you and you may decide it's a real drain on the account labeled "my life."

Don't use "all-or-nothing" thinking

Many of us, through years of dieting and listening to society's messages, have fallen into the trap of all-or-nothing thinking, which is characterized by a belief that "only a perfect outcome will do":

- If I can't lose 100 pounds and wear a size 8, I might as well forget it.
- If I eat a piece of candy, I've ruined everything and I might as well go on eating it all.
- If I can't walk for three miles, I might as well skip it.

If we can't remake ourselves overnight, we feel we've failed. Part of the problem is our need for "instant gratification." We want everything now. We can't wait. And part of it can be traced to the promises of quick weight loss that bombard us constantly. The fact is that small improvements in lifestyle can often make a significant difference.

We try to do too much all at once. To illustrate this, it's helpful to distinguish between goals and objectives. A goal is an ideal state we've decided to work toward. Objectives are small, manageable steps toward that goal. The goal may never be reached completely, but important and worthwhile progress is made by meeting objectives along the way.

Instead of setting objectives, we try to go for the goal all at once. We read a diet book or attend a diet group and try to alter our eating and exercise habits radically overnight. We'd be better off doing it in increments, deciding, for instance, to take a walk around the block several nights after dinner.

Consciously decide to do just one thing each day that is good for you. Write it down each evening before you go to bed. You will, of course, unconsciously be doing many things that are good for you, but try to pay particular attention each day to just one of these things. Single it out and say "I did that for myself today because I like myself and I want to treat myself well."

Doing one thing each day will have a cumulative effect on improving your self-esteem. What will you do tomorrow? You might decide to try a low-fat recipe, substitute vegetable juice for sugar-laden beverages, practice relaxation techniques, sign up for golf lessons. Maybe you'll take a very special walk—perhaps in an area where flowers are blooming, or at the zoo, or by a lake. Perhaps a local nightclub that plays disco tunes once a week. What fun and what a good workout!

Who do you admire?

Who are the people that you most admire, both historically and currently? Who are the people who have had the greatest impact on your life? What do they look like? Are they all thin? Chances are your list will contain people of all shapes, sizes and colors; and you put them there, in all likelihood, not because of physical appearance, but because of their intelligence, wisdom, benevolence, individuality and creativity. I once had an English teacher who was shaped like a redwood tree trunk, but she taught me to write and would accept nothing less than my very best. Her beauty was in her dedication to teaching and to her students.

Now think of several women who would be considered beautiful by society's standards. Have they all led charmed lives? Probably not. And no, I'm not suggesting that all beautiful women are unhappy or that they can't be admired for attributes other than their looks—just that conventional beauty does not guarantee happiness and that lasting impressions are often made by people who wear over a size 12.

Laugh

We tend to be very serious when what we really need to do is not take ourselves too seriously. It has been scientifically proven that your mood will improve if you simply try to smile.

Liz Curtis Higgs, author, speaker and self-anointed "encourager," feels that laughter brings empowerment. Says Liz: "I cried for 30 plus years and through 300 plus diets. I do not intend to shed one more tear over this body. I believe that laughing at life, at myself, and even at my own ample flesh, is part of the healing process."

I totally agree. I sometimes poke fun at my own size. "That chair won't make my hips too happy!" I've been known to say, without any hint of shame or embarrassment. My humor about my body is playful, never self-deprecating. It often puts other people at ease—and shows them that I'm perfectly at ease with my ampleness.

Create your own personal affirmations

Find a poster or a quote that speaks to you and put it where you'll see it daily. You might even try writing your own affirmations and repeating them frequently. Studies have shown that, repeated often enough, affirmations do become self-fulfilling prophecies.

Create your affirmation using positive language, and as if the desired state of mind were present now. "I will try to love my ugly body" is not likely to work, but "My body is uniquely beautiful just as it is" will start to take root if repeated often enough. Someone once told me that affirmations are like seeds. You plant them, can't see them for awhile, but pretty soon they poke through the ground and sprout into wonderfully unique flowers and plants.

Your decisions have been good ones

We generally make the best decisions we can with the information we have on hand and the circumstances that exist at the time. You've tried, over and over, to make good decisions about your body. You may not have known about the biological and physiological factors that contribute to size and weight. You didn't know that diets would betray you. You tried very hard. You should commend, not condemn, yourself!

Now sing your praises!

I love this story from the book *The Ten Commandments of Self-Esteem* by Catherine Cardinal. She says:

> *During the time the movie '10' was popular, I was watching a TV special in which three actresses were being interviewed, one of whom was Bette Midler. Each actress was asked if she thought she rated a '10.' The first actress (who was an international sex symbol) replied, 'I guess I'm at least an 8.' The second (who was both an actress and a model) answered, 'I suppose I'm a 7 or an 8.' Bette Midler responded without a moment's hesitation: '10! Are you kidding? I'm a 57!'* [35]

You can do it—we can all do it!

You must not become discouraged. None of us has achieved instant acceptance, and some times are easier than others. When I told Joe McVoy, Ph.D., head of the former size-acceptance organization AHELP (Association for the Health Enrichment of Large People) about this book, he couldn't resist a little good-natured teasing: "You may be on talk shows—golly, you'll have to lose weight!" My reply: "I know you're joking, but the thought actually crossed my mind until my better judgment chased it away."

We live in America—land of the free, home of the brave, and culture of the svelte. Size acceptance is foreign. It will take time for us to get to know it, assimilate it, and learn the language. But we'll be glad we made room for it when we realize how much further it's advanced us in our search for inner peace and outer harmony.

Happiness, confidence, and self-esteem are not prizes waiting to be claimed behind a door marked "weight loss." They're rightfully yours at any size. Don't let anyone withhold them from you.

Self-esteem and larger children

It should come as no surprise that children labeled overweight learn very early that this is not a good thing to be. Studies show that children as young as third grade are already concerned about their weight and shape.[36] When researchers asked nine-year-old kids what they thought of silhouettes of thin and heavy children, they were quite derogatory in their comments about the heavier figures.[37] And when first graders did a similar exercise, the majority said they would not want to befriend someone who looked like the larger shapes.[38] The researchers concluded that the children were simply "echoing the prejudices against overweight voiced by society."

What about larger kids themselves? Do they have poor self-esteem? The few studies that have been done are interesting. The central question is whether being considered overweight affects a child's entire sense of self-worth or just the aspect of self-worth that pertains to appearance. While some studies have found that being big sends a wallop to children's self-esteem in general,[39] others suggest that big children, at least while they are younger, may feel poorly about their bodies, but not about their overall self-worth.[40-42] However, by early adolescence, this ability to "compartmentalize" disappears and weight becomes, for many, the absolute ruler of all aspects of self-esteem.[43]

Youngsters who are teased and ridiculed about their weight have scars that can last a lifetime. Not too surprising is the evidence that kids who are teased about their weight grow up to dislike their bodies.[44] The heaviest children suffer the most. Studies show that the heavier the child, the poorer his or her self-esteem.[45]

Self-blame and self-esteem

Children who believe their above-average weight is their own fault have lower self-esteem than those who are able to attribute it to an external cause.[46] The most vulnerable children are those who believe they are totally responsible for what they weigh because they are overeating and not active enough. Larger children who understand that their weight results from a combination of factors, some of which they cannot control (e.g. genetics and physiological factors), have better self-esteem. At least one study has demonstrated that children can be taught, and that they do understand, the many aspects of obesity that cannot be controlled.[47] What was most interesting about this study is that while the children grasped that obesity has biological and physiological underpinnings, this knowledge did not do much to reduce their negative stereotypes of larger people already in place.

Like mother, like daughter

Mothers need to choose their words very carefully. In a government study of nearly 2,400 nine- and ten-year-old girls, researchers were startled at how big an impact mothers' attitudes had on their daughters' behaviors. They found girls were more than twice as likely to be chronic dieters if mothers told them they were too fat. They advised parents "not to be judgmental, but to help young girls acquire a relaxed attitude about food so they are less likely to develop eating-disordered behavior." Even more troubling is evidence that mothers who curb what their daughters eat, badger them to diet and exercise in order to lose weight, and perceive them as "overweight" may be contributing to the development of an eating disorder.[48-50]

I have found in my workshops that women who feel the best about themselves and their bodies are those from homes where they were loved and accepted unconditionally, no matter what their weight, and where thinness was not viewed as a prerequisite to a full and happy life. This is especially true of African American women, who are often surprised to think that a mother would criticize her daughter's weight. The words of one voluptuous African American woman stick in my mind: "My mama told me I was beautiful every day of my life!" These same women have far fewer self-esteem problems as adults, and I told a group of predominantly African American women who had come to hear me speak about self-esteem, "It's apparent you don't need me. You could be teaching the class yourselves!" Their upbeat attitudes and feelings about their bodies were clearly shaped by positive familial messages they heard while growing up. These are not just anecdotal observations. Many studies have demonstrated that larger African American girls have better self-esteem than white girls, including a recent study of more than 2,000 multi-racial girls.[51]

So what's a parent to do? Here are some dos and don'ts I often send or hand out to parents and professionals.

DOs:

- Do love and accept your child unconditionally. This will help them love and accept themselves.

- Do treat size and weight as a characteristic that contributes to your children's uniqueness. Teach them that diversity is what makes the world so interesting. Nature provides many examples. Flowers, for instance, come in all shapes, colors and sizes—and yet all are beautiful.

- Do examine your own biases and ask yourself whether your concern is for yourself or your child. A larger child may make some parents feel embarrassed, and some may feel that having an "above-average-weight" child somehow signals a family's lack of self-discipline. As with most forms of prejudice, these feelings stem from myths and misinformation.

- Do educate yourself about what causes some people to be larger than others so you can separate myths from facts. Then educate your children. Have a discussion about heredity. Explain that body size is an inherited characteristic, like hair and eye color. When children understand they are not to blame for their weight, research shows they feel better about themselves.

- Do emphasize your child's positive attributes and talents and teach them that these are the things that count. Help them to develop the things they're good at.

- Do make an extra effort to help them find clothes similar to what their friends are wearing. It's real important at this age to "blend in."

- Do arm your children for dealing with the outside world and our culture's obsession with thinness. Tell them that many groups of people have suffered discrimination and prejudice, and that larger people are one of these groups. Help them plan how they would react to negative comments about their weight. Do some role-playing.

- Do make your home and family a safe haven for them where

they can always count on your support and encouragement. They'll have enough to deal with outside the home in our fat phobic society.

- Do be a good role model. Don't criticize your own body. You're the most important person in your child's life. If they see that you like your body, they'll find it easier to like theirs. Research has clearly shown that how a mother feels about her own body will have a significant impact on her daughter's body image.

- Do provide examples for them of attractive and successful larger people, both current and historical. Also give them an anthropology lesson and inform them that many other cultures value and desire bodies of ample proportions.

- Do help your larger child to unravel the "thin is in" media hype. There are about 400 top fashion models, and less than one percent of the female population has the genetic potential to look like them. Attractive people come in assorted shapes, sizes and colors. One mother took her daughter to a mall and a nursing home, where she pointed out various types and shapes of women. She told her daughter that every one of them was a unique and worthwhile individual, and followed up with a talk about self-worth.

DON'Ts

- Don't *ever* say or imply that your child's weight makes him/her less attractive or less acceptable in any way. Studies show that "direct parental comments" hurt the most and do the most damage.[52] There is NO connection between weight and self-worth and you are responsible for helping your child realize this. Shaming or teasing a child about his/her weight or body will backfire and make them hate their bodies even more. And for heaven's sake, don't tell your child she has "such a pretty face" —if only she'd lose weight.

- Don't tell your child that no one will want to date them unless they're thin. First of all, it's not true. Plenty of plus-size girls have boyfriends. Tell your child that lasting affection looks beneath the surface and is not bound by narrow definitions of beauty.

- Don't put your child on a traditional "diet." Most reputable dietitians now agree that this is not the way to help them manage their weight. Continual dieting may cause them to be heavier in the long run. Focus instead on development of a healthy lifestyle—for the whole family. Make physical activity a family affair. Go for walks together, buy family swimming passes to a community pool, have a family "dance party," go biking.

- Don't become the "food police." Nagging your child about what he/she is eating will surely backfire. Children can always find ways of getting "forbidden" foods. Studies confirm that when children are denied foods they like, they will end up craving them and eating more.[53] In the worst-case scenario, you could be contributing to development of an eating disorder such as anorexia or bulimia. Besides, foods should not be categorized as "good" or "bad." All food has a place in normal eating.

One last word: Despite your child's very best efforts, your child may never be thin. This is not the worst thing that could happen. Many heavy children become heavy adults and still live satisfying, fulfilling lives. Researchers will tell you that there is much to learn yet about obesity and its causes, and that there is no permanent cure for most people. Teach your child that a rich, rewarding life has nothing to do with their weight and everything to do with their own attitude and self-image.

Resources for Parents, Professionals, and Larger Children

In-service training kit for professionals

Children and Weight: What Health Professionals Can Do: A kit containing materials to conduct in-service training for physicians, nurses, dietitians, and other health professionals on diagnosing, assessing, and treating pediatric obesity. For more information, call 1-800-994-8849.

Books and pamphlets

- *If My Child Is Overweight, What Should I Do About It?* by Joanne Ikeda. Call 1-800-994-8849.

- *Am I Fat: Helping Young Children Accept Differences in Body Size* by Joanne Ikeda. Order from Gürze Books at 1-800-756-7533 or www.gurze.com

- Ellyn Satter, *How to Get Your Kid to Eat But Not Too Much*, Bull Publishing, 1987 (available at amazon.com)

- Jane Hirschmann, *Preventing Childhood Eating Problems*. Order from Gürze Books at 1-800-756-7533 or www.gurze.com

- For more books pertaining to larger children, go to the NAAFA website at www.naafa.org and the Gürze website at www.gurze.com. You can also call Gürze for a catalog at 1-800-756-7533.

Online resources

Radiance Kids Project. www.radiancemagazine.com

Body Positive: Children and Weight. www.bodypositive.com/childwt.htm

SizeWise. www.sizewise.com. Click on "Kid Stuff."

Curricula for school-based programs

School-based self-esteem education programs have been found to significantly improve the self-esteem and body image of young adolescents.[54] Some resources available are:

- Kids' Curriculum and Outreach Project, sponsored by the Council on Size and Weight Discrimination. At www.cswd.org or call project manager Cathi Rodgveller at 206-323-9354.

- *Healthy Body Image: Teaching Kids to Eat and Love Their Bodies Too*, by Kathy Kater, LICSW. Available from Gürze Books at 1-800-756-7533 or www.gurze.com

- "Working with Fat Children in Schools" by Michael Loewy, Ph.D. Read at Radiance Kids Project at www.radiancemagazine.com

- NAAFA Kids Project—speakers and curriculum materials on the issue of body image. www.naafa.org/kids.html or call NAAFA at 1-916-558-6880.

Magazines for plus-size teens

- *Extra Hip* Magazine: An online "Ezine" dedicated solely to the millions of young, plus-size women in America. At www.extrahip.com or subscribe to snail-mail delivered magazine by calling 1-888-928-9447.
- *New Moon* Magazine: At www.newmoon.org or: 1-800-381-4743

Plus-size girls' clothes

Check out:
- www.blessingsindresses.com Phone: 1-800-422-7465
- www.jcpenney.com Request a catalog at 1-800-222-6161
- www.connieskids.com/Half-Size.html Phone: 1-800-547-6933
- www.olivetreegirl.com or 1-213-385-9970
- www.bcoole.com/designs/kids.html or 1-800-992-8924
- I have also been told that Sears, Target, and K-Mart carry plus-size kids clothes.

Wide width kids' shoes

- www.kidsnshoes.com/widewidth/default.htm or 1-888-540-6223

Plus-size teen clothes

Check out:
- Benina and Lu www.beninaandlu.com or 1-888-992-9899
- Girlfriends LA www.gfla.com or 1-800-617-4352
- SoWhatIf www.sowhatif.com Website only. No phone number listed.
- IGIGI Curves www.igigi.com No phone number listed. Fax: 1-707-462-9603.

♥ ♥ ♥ From The Heart ♥ ♥ ♥

Do-It-Yourself Self-Esteem Repair

If you feel your self-esteem is on the fritz, here's a "self-esteem repair kit" you can use to help get it back in good working condition. Follow the instructions carefully!

1. Do not use your weight to measure your self-worth. What does weight have to do with it? Self-worth is the sum of everything that makes you special and unique—not just your thigh and waist measurements! Add up your assets, talents, accomplishments, how you treat others, how you treat yourself, the contributions you make to your family, friends and community. Now you have self-worth.

2. Count your blessings. You have a lot of things to be thankful for—a home, a loving family, friends you enjoy, a job, a sunny day, the knowledge you've acquired—even things like shoes, a coat. Many people don't have these things. A mind that counts blessings has no room for self-pity. So you don't wear a size 2? Neither did Eleanor Roosevelt!

3. Are you continually playing negative tapes in your mind? Eject them and insert new tapes! You may have to make a conscious effort. When the critical tape starts playing, picture yourself hitting the "stop" button and insert a new, positive tape.

4. Don't use "all-or-nothing" thinking. No one is a "total" failure. Most things you do right. Just because you sometimes make a mistake or take a wrong path does not make you a "total" failure. It makes you human. Besides, the president of CBS was recently asked for his secret to success. His answer: failures—because how else would we learn?

5. Let go of perfectionism, particularly in terms of food. You probably eat healthfully a lot of the time. Improvements can always be made, but consider the glass half full, not half-empty!

6. Strut your stuff! Shine! Show the world your talents. We all have them. Capitalize on whatever you do well. I'll never dance Swan Lake, but then again, I bet that ballerina doesn't play a

mean piano like I do!

7. Give thanks to your body for what it does for you. Appreciate its functional nature. It's a pretty remarkable machine. You can use it to take a walk along the beach, hug someone, listen to a concerto, make love—or go shopping! And it can do all of these things no matter what shape or size it is.

8. Educate yourself (and those around you) about issues of size and weight. Learn what's fact and what's fiction. What the research really says and what most people believe are two different things. Reputable researchers will tell you that obesity is still a complex, poorly understood condition that has very little to do with lack of willpower and a whole lot to do with biology and physiology. Most importantly—especially for those who are considered "overweight"—stop blaming yourself. It's not your fault. The research continues to show this over and over.

9. Become preoccupied with the world, not dieting. When we're constantly dieting, weighing, measuring, counting calories, calculating fat grams, recording our thoughts in food diaries and agonizing over what to eat and what not to eat, we have little time left for what's going on in the rest of the world. And it's such an interesting place!

10. Put nothing on hold as a reward for weight loss. A Largely Positive member recently suggested: "The best advice I ever got was to make a list of the things I would do differently once I was thin—then pick the top one and do it right now. The item at the top of my list was to take flying lessons and now I'm a single-engine land pilot!"

11. Develop a personal style that announces you. Find some signature pieces. Never put off buying attractive clothes until you lose weight—you don't have to wear a 10 to be a 10! Don't buy into the silly notion that you can only wear dark colors because they're more "slimming." At best, dark colors shave off five pounds. Big deal! If I have a choice between looking five pounds thinner or wearing lime green, I'm going for the lime green!

12. And, Women of America: We do not have "figure flaws," despite what many of the magazines tell us. Each of us is simply shaped differently. It's called diversity.

13. Surround yourself with positive, supportive people. Tell weight critics that your size and shape are no longer topics on the conversational buffet table! Eliminate negative people from your life. Surely you have enough supportive people in your circle of family and friends that you'll never miss the "nay-sayers."

14. Look into your past for sources of low self-esteem. Retrieve critical comments that were made to you, especially as a child. You will probably discover that your body image was shaped by other people and outside influences. You are an adult now. You have better information. Refute these old messages and from now on, shape your own body image.

15. Concentrate on developing a healthy lifestyle rather than losing weight. Developing a healthy lifestyle is positive and can be measured in lots of ways. Losing weight has only one measure of success: the scale.

16. Slow down! If we can't remake ourselves overnight, we feel we've failed. We need instant gratification. The truth is, slow weight loss is the only kind that will ever last (haven't you noticed the fine print in ads for quick weight loss products that says, "Results not typical"?) Stop setting weight loss deadlines: for the class reunion, the wedding, the party. Make weight management an ongoing part of your "healthstyle."

17. You've heard of PMS? Trying having PMA—Positive Mental Attitude! How you feel about yourself is how others will feel about you. Your attitude is always reflected back to you. I guarantee it!

18. Remember that society is not always right about things. Just because we have a cultural obsession with thinness doesn't make it right. Society has a long list of injustices and intolerance. Like human beings, societies are imperfect and make mistakes.

19. Recognize and fight size prejudice. Size prejudice is often called "the last acceptable prejudice." One thing we can all do is stop laughing at fat jokes. There is nothing funny about comedy that inflicts pain. As a little girl, I took every fat joke personally. Maybe big girls don't cry, but little girls do.

20. Remember, in the final analysis—it's the size of your heart that counts, not the size of your body.

8

creating personal style—in a big way

I wear clothes with brighter colors. I wear "wild" earrings.
The nicest thing I've discovered is that I smile more. Maybe
it's because I've discovered I'm a pretty nice person to know!
—KATHY

Like it or not, first impressions count. Psychologists estimate that impressions are formed in about 30 seconds and mostly on the basis of physical appearance. I thought I had to wait to get thin to be glamorous—then I decided to be glamorous while I waited. I didn't get thin, but I got the glamour!

This morning, before I even got to work, I had already received two compliments—both from strangers. At the post office, the woman behind me in line wanted to know what fragrance I was wearing. She said she found it very pleasant. At the grocery store bread counter, another woman admired my earrings—very bold and dangly. I told her where I had bought them.

Compliments are not the exclusive province of the reedlike among us. Big women can get them too—and often!

One of our members told of being out for Easter breakfast in a dress splashed with bright colors and earrings to match. The waitress, she said, took time from her very busy morning to pause and compliment her on her outfit and bright, cheerful demeanor.

While riding up to my office in the elevator recently, a woman said to me: "I just love your hair." And after I arrived at the office, a male colleague surveyed my attire and remarked: "That's a really good looking outfit!" It was a good-looking outfit—a knit cardigan and matching tank in bright turquoise with orange, yellow and silver beadwork in a southwestern design.

Do you know what happens when you present a positive image? People don't really notice your size, or if they do, it no longer stands out as a negative quality. A couple of years ago I spoke at a women's conference. During the question/answer segment, a woman said to me: "I know you're a large woman, but it's not what I notice about you. As you were speaking, I noticed how attractively you present yourself—what a lovely outfit you have on, how nice your hair looks, what a nice smile you have, and how confidently you speak. And although the largeness is there, it's not offensive in any way. It's just part of all the qualities that blend together to make you a very attractive person."

I am used to compliments now. I get them often. I don't say this to brag. It wasn't always that way—only since I decided that attractiveness does not stop at size 12. If I can't be an attractive size 12 woman, I will be an attractive size 24 woman. And so can you.

Sometimes at workshops women say to me: "It shouldn't matter what I look like. People should like me for what's inside." I heartily agree with the second sentence. The defiant contention that appearance is unimportant is often a front for low self-esteem, rather than a true disinterest in appearance. Large women sometimes feel that it doesn't matter how they look because, after all, they're fat and nothing is going to hide that fact. But why should it have to be concealed? Instead of trying to conceal my size, I have decided to flaunt it, to use it as an attribute. A large figure is a good foundation upon which to build an attractive image.

Many times, when women who profess no interest in image start to experiment with clothes, makeup, and new hairstyles, they find they enjoy it and feel better, and other people start paying them compliments. Nancy Roberts, author of *Breaking All the Rules*, said, "I'm not the only one who's impressed with the powerful looking, well dressed big woman I see on the street. She demands a different kind of attention, better treatment than does the embarrassed looking, shy, sadly-dressed woman in the navy tent."[1]

There's another reason to be cautious of the "it's-what's-inside-that-counts" defense. The implication is that there's something wrong with the outside. Of course your inner attributes are important, and more important than how you look. But when I hear large women say, "They should like me for what's inside," they may be tacitly agreeing that their exterior is defective. There's no need for this. Large women are not defective, they're simply deluxe editions. We have to stop apologizing for our size, and when we say "It's what on the inside that counts," this is in essence what we're doing. Yes, the inside counts, but my outside is just fine too, thank you!

Says Roz Thurner, a Milwaukee plus-size image consultant: "You have to think of yourself as a delectable meal. All good chefs know how important presentation is. If they slopped it in front of you, no matter how delicious, you would be turned off. But when artfully and tastefully presented, you can't wait to eat it!"

A tool for self-esteem

When I first started to pay more attention to my image, doing so was simply another tool to help me improve my self-esteem. But now I do it because I feel good about myself, and I use my image as one way of expressing those good feelings.

It's not that I neglected my appearance before, but I bought into all of the "rules" about how large women should dress and not dress. These rules don't leave much room for a lime-green palazzo pantsuit or a fuchsia jumpsuit. Once I realized that the rules themselves were based on the prejudiced view that there's something wrong with being big, I began to judge clothes not by their fat-camouflaging potential, but by their potential to create some excitement and magic.

Now my image is visible proof of the value I place on myself. It shows I care enough about myself to spend a little time trimming the package. It's *because* I care about what's inside that I do it. You wouldn't wrap a gift you lovingly chose for someone in a brown paper bag. You'd choose pretty paper and ribbon and maybe some other type of adornment. Place the same value on yourself.

Trying harder

In order to counteract the stereotypes of large women as lazy, sloppy, unclean, and lacking in pride, we have to try harder to look good. Is that fair? No, but it's reality. I feel a responsibility to help shatter the myths about large people, and so I pay attention to my grooming and appearance every time I step out the door.

I don't ever want anyone to look at me and feel sorry for that pathetic-looking large woman with greasy, stringy hair dressed in a dirty sweatshirt and too-tight polyester pants. I want them to look at me and say, "Wow! There goes a confident, attractive woman!" And if they say a "confident, attractive *large* woman," so much the better.

I sometimes refer to myself as an "ambassador-at-large!" If I can help to change some attitudes as I move through life, I am making it easier for other large people. Won't you join me? We need all the "ambassadors" we can get!

The elements of personal style

One of the more fun things to do in this oh-so-serious world is to express your personality and individuality through your choice of hairstyle, makeup, clothing, jewelry and other accessories. Personal style knows no size. It reflects your personality, individuality, and moods—perhaps your astrological sign or whether your spirit leans more toward "yin" than "yang." Your style can be playful, whimsical, glamorous, sexy, romantic, powerful—and can change to reflect your moods and purposes.

Personal style is much more than clothes and makeup. It's also the mirth in your voice, the sparkle in your eye, a confident stride, the radiance of your smile, body language that is magnetic and self-assured. Personal style is about expectations that others will respect you, admire you, love you, choose to be with you, value your opinions, and enjoy your company. It shows you know you have something to offer and lets that knowledge shine through. Your style creates an aura that says, "I'm worth knowing; I'm worth loving."

Remember that style and fashion are two different things. I once heard that fashion is when everyone tries to look the same, but style is about uniqueness—standing out in the crowd, making a statement—your statement. The "fashion police" are known to issue "rules" on how large women should dress. But just as there's no one way for slim women to look, there's no one way for large women to present themselves. We're big in different ways, and something that looks great on you may not do a thing for me.

Large women often think that style is just another thing lying dormant until that thin person buried inside comes out of hibernation. But I am not harboring a thin person. I find that notion insulting. It implies that the me you see is not good enough and is just a sorrowful facade waiting to crumble and let the real me—the thin me—out.

The only "real me" I have ever known is "big me." I was "big me" as a baby, "big me" as a child, "big me" as a teenager and "big me" as an adult. "Big me" is who I am. And "big me" is pretty darn good. The reality is that the essence of who I am will not change even if my dimensions do. The gift inside remains the same no matter how it's wrapped. But back to the wrapping!

Attitude is everything

Your image begins with your attitude. "A woman who projects admirable traits finds admiration reflected back from those who look at her," says Rita Freedman in *Bodylove*.[2]

How you feel about yourself is evident to others from your posture, your gait, your body language, your voice, and your eyes.

- Do you stand straight and proud, or do you slouch?
- Do you stride assuredly, or do you shuffle along with your eyes glued to the pavement?
- Is your body language welcoming, or does it signal to others that you have closed yourself off?
- Do you speak confidently, or tentatively and apologetically?
- Do you look people in the eye when you speak, or are you afraid to let your eyes make the connection?

These aspects of image are just as important as your hairstyle, makeup, and style of dress. They signal to others that you know and like who you are, and expect others to treat you with respect. Move with poise and grace. Carry yourself proudly. A larger body does not spell clumsiness. I have seen large women dancing, and they are often among the most graceful dancers on the floor.

I have a book at home—bought many years ago—on how to dress to look thinner. The authors suggest that if you feel and move like a "slim, sensual, elegant and sexy woman," you'll be one. I advocate that you move like a *large*, sensual, elegant and sexy woman—and you'll be one!

The next time you go out your door I want your head held high, your shoulders back, your chest forward, a brisk stride, and a smile on your face. These are the physical manifestations of a positive attitude. But as we all know, attitude is mostly mental. It's believing that the you that exists right now is a terrific you. It's knowing that you're a person who has something to offer. It's expecting that you'll be treated well by those you meet. It's saying to yourself, "Yes, I'm a large person, but I will not allow that to deter me from looking my best, feeling my best, and expecting the best from others."

I never expect to be treated poorly because of my size, and I rarely am. I firmly believe that's because I convey with my carriage, my voice, my face, my attire—indeed, with my entire being—that I'm comfortable and content with who I am. People don't comment about my weight. People don't give me weight-loss advice. And they don't shoot me looks of pity or scorn. My image invites none of this.

Your size is a prize

My size is part of my image. I don't try to hide it. You must start to think of your size as a prize! I know this sounds crazy, but do it anyway. What's crazy to me now is that we assail large bodies with almost every negative adjective imaginable. Finding positive traits among the rubble is almost impossible. But they're there and it's worth the search.

"I used to think if I just blended in and tried to be inconspicuous, I'd be better off than if I tried to draw attention to myself. I now realize how destructive that attitude can be," says plus-size image consultant Ruthanne Olds in *Big & Beautiful*.[3] For many large women, personal style amounts to figuring out the best strategies to draw attention *away* from themselves. They view their larger bodies as shameful, as something to be hidden. This is wrong.

Some canvases are small. Some are medium. Some are big. No matter what size the canvas, though, the artist can paint a beautiful picture on it. You're fortunate. Your canvas is big. Your picture can be bigger—and just as beautiful!

Because of my larger size, I can do things in a big way and carry it off. My jewelry can be bigger without seeming overwhelming. My clothes can be more dramatic, flamboyant, and flowing without engulfing me. My accessories can be grander without overpowering me.

I like the words of journalist Gloria Emerson, who wrote in the April 1994 issue of *Allure* magazine about being tall:

Although I felt unspeakable sorrow at the age of 14 when I reached the startling height of 5 feet 11 inches, it has been an uncommon blessing to be so tall. It has made me bolder, more reckless and resolute, than I might have been if 5 feet 2 inches was all I reached.

I could say much the same about my weight. I, too, felt "unspeakable sorrow" in the eighth grade when I reached the "startling" weight of 175 pounds. I weighed more, for heaven's sake, than most of the boys! And I certainly didn't view it as any kind of blessing at the time. But, in retrospect, I believe it has made me stronger, more aware of life's challenges, more appreciative of diversity in people, and more courageous. When I spoke recently to the staff of a fitness club, the owner commended me for my "courage" in appearing before them. I hadn't really thought about it in that way, but I do think that as large people bulldoze their way through society, with all the obstacles and detours set in their way, they acquire a durable, rugged spirit—in more ways than they know.

The thesaurus in my computer lists the following synonyms for the word "big": grand, great, important, major, vital, towering, lofty, substantial, generous, lavish, mature. Let's not just let these words sit in the thesaurus. Let's apply them to ourselves!

Rosalind Russell once said, "Taking joy in life is a woman's best cosmetic." If you're soaking up the world around you, living with verve and vitality, exuding confidence, you *will* make a positive impression at any size. If, on the other hand, you move through life looking like a "before" picture for a weight-loss ad, you invite pity—and the only thing people can think to do for you is to give you a copy of the latest diet.

So stop regarding your size as something shameful and start viewing it as a good, strong foundation for your new "largely positive" image.

Don't large women deserve makeovers?

"Makeovers" are a staple of many women's magazines. The only problem is that I rarely see large women as candidates for makeovers unless they involve weight loss. This is another example of what I referred to earlier as the "invisibility factor" when it comes to the media. We're acceptable only if we've dieted and lost weight, or, sometimes, if we're embarking on a diet (so there can be a "before" and "after" picture). It's often assumed that we have no interest in looking good until we lose weight, but it's time for those assumptions to cease. We *want* to look good, *can* look good, and *deserve* to look good!

A makeover can be a real self-esteem booster, and there's no reason why large women shouldn't be just as entitled to them as thinner women. I look forward to the day when magazines will routinely feature large women in makeover features.

The world of plus-size clothing

If I had written this about 15 years ago, this section would have been short indeed—probably no more than a paragraph, and the news would have been mostly bad. This has all changed. Manufacturers have discovered:

- Close to 40 million American women, or one-third of the female population, wear a size 14 or over. The average woman in America wears a 12 to a 14. At least 10 percent of the plus-sized market is supersize (over a size 24).

- There are as many women in this country who wear a size 18 as wear a size 8.

- We have money and we're willing to spend it.

- We want to look good.

- We lead multi-faceted lives, have careers, and need clothes for a variety of occasions.

According to the *Wall Street Journal* and the NPD Group, a market research firm, plus-size clothing sales jumped 10 percent in 1999, totaling $26.1 billion. Growth from 1993-1999 has averaged 9.7 percent per year. Compare this to women's apparel sales overall, growing only 3.7 percent in 1999. Marketdata, a Tampa-based market research organization, estimated that the plus-size market would grow by about 11 percent in the year 2000, to more than $29 billion.

Large women know all too well how fashions—or the lack of them— can affect their confidence. For years, our choices were sadly limited to such styles as:

- Double-knit polyester pants with a sewn-in crease down the front
- Polyester overblouses in big floral prints
- Muumuus, tent dresses, and caftans. (Roz Ryan, one of the big, beautiful, feisty sisters from the former TV sitcom *Amen*, liked to say: "I've helped bring big women out of the caftans . . . I believe in slinging it!")

The choices implied that we did not work, did not go out in the evening, and had no sex lives. If we ordered from a catalog, we had no way of knowing what the clothes would look like on us because they were (still are in many cases) shown on thin women—the assumption being, I guess, that it would be too depressing to see what they would really look like on a model whose size more closely resembled our own. There was no fun, nothing to uplift our spirits, in the world of plus-size fashion.

For a long time I had no idea what size I wore. By the time women surpassed a size 18, they were assumed not to exist anymore. Something called "half sizes" existed, but they were always too short-waisted for me. (Another assumption manufacturers made for a long time was that all large women were short.) I never knew where to look for clothes. I usually ended up buying the half sizes even though they were ill-fitting, matronly, and not very well constructed.

This has all changed. Clothing manufacturers and retailers have discovered that the earlier assumptions are myths. Large women have multi-faceted lives—they work, they play, they go to parties, they relax, they even have sex! They have also realized that we have money and we are willing to spend it on things that make us feel good about ourselves, and one of those things is attractive clothing.

Most department stores have plus-size clothing sections—although they are often hidden away in the store's most undesirable space which is often too small. I once complained to a local department store that the merchandise in their plus-size department was crammed together so tightly, I could barely walk between the racks. It's as if they are grudgingly acknowledging that we exist, but are sending us the unspoken message, "Damned if we'll allow you any more space than is absolutely necessary, and certainly not any of our prime space!" And I wish they'd get rid of that worn-out designation, "Women's World." What does this mean anyway? We're all women.

Even the more upscale stores, such as Saks, Nordstrom, and Bloomingdale's, have discovered their plus-size customers. And I've noticed that Neiman Marcus has gradually been increasing the number of items in its mail order catalog that are offered in a spectrum of sizes. Bloomingdale's By Mail routinely sends out a catalog devoted to sizes 14-24.

The number of stores that cater exclusively to the plus-size woman continues to increase. Some tend to be expensive, but many carry more moderately-priced items. Add to that the explosion in plus-size mail order catalogs, plus-size websites, and the television shopping channels that now regularly offer plus-sizes and you have a fashion scene for the large woman that is vastly different from the one that existed ten to fifteen years ago. (See the resource section for a list of plus-size catalogs and websites.)

Having said all this, I would like to point out that shopping for clothes is not too much of a problem as long as you are size 24 or under. Clothes in sizes above 24, sometimes referred to as "supersizes," are not nearly as plentiful, even though 10 percent of the plus-size market—about 4 million women—falls into this category. Stores rarely carry sizes above 26, so women who wear supersizes must rely mostly on mail order.

Snubbed by high fashion

Although our fashion options continue to proliferate, many high-fashion designers continue to snub the plus-size woman. Their designs are for the toned and taut. However, some designers, such as Harve Bernard, Geoffrey Beene, Liz Claiborne, Gianfranco Ferre, Givenchy, Adrienne Vittadini, and Andrea Jovine, have added plus-size lines. I would like to think they did this because of their conviction that large women are attractive in their own right and as deserving of beautiful and alluring fashions as thin women. But my practical side tells me it had just as much to do with the discovery that large women have checkbooks and charge accounts!

I've discovered that I'm not the only one who feels left out of the fashion mainstream. An executive director colleague of mine, who is slim, says she feels most of the styles paraded down the runway are ridiculous and unprofessional, while my mother says there is nothing fit for an older woman. Says Molly Haskell in the April 1994 issue of *Self*:

> *Even the magazines are getting defensive about the outrageousness of the styles being promulgated in their pages. 'Get real,' cry the texts, as models disport themselves in see-through business suits, pierced body parts, S&M halters, baby doll dresses and filmy streetwear that our mothers would have been shy about wearing to bed on their honeymoon.*

She adds: "At its worst, the fashion industry infantilizes women, making us feel bad about what we can't wear, thus eroding, instead of buttressing, our confidence."

I know that large women will probably never walk down the fashion runways of New York, Paris, or Milan in my lifetime, but there's no reason why they shouldn't. In a perfect world I would hear the commentator say: "And now let's see what the stylish large woman will be wearing this fall."

Chuck the "rules"

Most of the rules that dictate what large women should and shouldn't wear are based on what the clothes conceal and camouflage. I abandoned these rules long ago. This does not mean that I no longer pay attention to what is flattering and comfortable. It does mean that I know I'm going to be perceived as a large woman whether I wear black or shocking pink, so if I like shocking pink, why not wear it?

The words "rule" and "personal style" are not compatible. Rules are generally rigid and the same for everyone, while personal style is about individuality and originality. I think you should wear what makes you feel good and what makes you feel special. Wear the colors you like. Wear the fabrics that feel good against your skin. Wear the styles that express your personality.

If I obeyed all the rules in my book about dressing to look thinner, I would never be able to wear:

- round necklines
- a v-neck with ruffles
- anything sleeveless
- dirndl skirts, gathered skirts, straight skirts, circle skirts or skirts with all around pleats
- harem pants
- tapered pants
- bulky sweaters
- double-breasted jackets
- short jackets
- furs or fake furs
- a white sweater with a white shirt
- horizontal lines
- large plaids
- shoulder bags that hang at hip level
- short necklaces
- wide belts

If I wear a dress, I am advised to stick primarily to princess styles, and I am to wear a dress belted only if the belt is narrow. If I wear light colors, I should confine them to the "inside" of my outfit and surround them on the outside with a dark color!

Now I may not choose to wear some of these "forbidden" items, but the key word here is "choose." I may decide certain styles and colors do not flatter me, but I also may find that because I am well proportioned, a wide belt looks just fine, or that because I have nice legs, tapered pants are a good look for me. Actually, one of my best looks is a long, loose tunic with leggings or stirrup pants.

Just as small bodies come in a variety of shapes, so do large bodies. Those who give advice to large women on how to dress seem to assume that because we're big, we're shaped identically. But we're not. You have to decide which styles flatter your individual shape and which are better left for someone else. Short jackets, for instance, are not good on me; I look better if the jacket extends past my hips. But I have seen large women, shaped differently than me, who look great in short jackets.

Back to my how-to-dress-thin book. In many respects, it is a very good book. I'm sorry to have to pick on it. The authors advocate carrying yourself proudly, looking great, feeling good about yourself. They bemoan our obsession with thinness and point out that "the world is full of healthy, good looking women who have flesh in abundance." If only they'd take out the part about dressing to look thin and replace it with dressing to look good—at any size.

It's time to remove some of the old rules from the books. Let's not feel we have to:

- Buy to "hide" or "camouflage:" This is silly. Hiding is for things you're ashamed of or don't want anyone to find. You're going to quit being ashamed of your body and you're going to hope everyone finds out what a wonderful, beautiful person you are. You have nothing to hide. I have now gone to the opposite extreme. I call attention to my size by wearing bright colors, bold jewelry, dramatic styles.

   Buying to hide also leads some large women to conclude that the only garments they dare wear are tents and floats. Hara Estroff Marano in her book, *Style Is Not a Size,* says she overheard a plus-size fashion designer say: "Tents are for campgrounds and floats are for parades." This is not to say that there can't be a place in your wardrobe for an occasional tent dress, but if tents are all you're buying and you're buying them for the express purpose of hiding your body, start to consider some other styles.

- Stick to dark colors: I once heard Carole Shaw, former editor of *BBW* magazine, say dark colors, at most, shave five pounds from your weight. Ruthanne Olds feels much the same: "Ten pounds is about all you can cover up with clothing styles and color." Even if I were still trying to create an optical illusion, why would I forego a favorite color for the sake of five measly pounds? Wearing bright colors will elevate your spirits and send out positive vibes. The pleasure you will reap from wearing bright, sunny colors is infinitely more important than looking five pounds thinner.

- Avoid horizontal stripes: I know—they're supposed to "widen" you in the eyes of the beholder. Even if that's true, so what? Remember—we no longer consider big to be bad. I have several outfits that feature stripes going in the "no-no" direction and I have not stopped traffic in them, nor have I engendered any sort of public outcry. Again, wear your stripes any way you like. You've earned them!

- Refrain from tucking your blouse in: Some blouses, such as big shirts, are meant to be worn out, but don't think you always have to wear your blouse out. Blouses that are not made to be worn out often look sloppy worn that way and tend to pull apart toward the bottom. Try tucking yours in and see if it doesn't look neater.

- Shun belts: I love Carole Shaw's story of the woman who said she couldn't wear a belt because she had no waist. Carole replied: "Sweetheart, everyone has a waistline. Just bend over— wherever you crack, that's your waistline!" A belt is often just the accessory needed to give your outfit a chic, pulled-together look.

New "guidelines"

Just because I am no longer a slave to the ancient rules of "fat lady dressing" does not mean I live in a state of fashion anarchy. I think there are still some basic guidelines that large women should heed in choosing apparel. Consider the following:

Comfort and fit

There is nothing worse than a garment that's not comfortable. You can't move freely; you feel constricted; you may even develop a stomach ache! Eventually, too-tight clothing distracts you from everything else you're doing and all you can think about is getting home, ripping them off, and getting into something "comfortable." I often find that when large women say their weight causes them discomfort, the truth is that their clothes are too tight.

Buying clothes that fit and are comfortable is the most important guideline of all. It will make a world of difference in your mental outlook, physical comfort, and how you look to others. It sounds so simple. Why would anyone buy something that doesn't fit? Basically, to fool herself into thinking she wears a smaller size. But no one is fooled. You're not fooled. You know you're uncomfortable. Others aren't fooled. They can see your blouse is ready to pop. And snug clothes do not make you look slimmer. They usually have the opposite effect.

I didn't want to have to shop in the plus-size department either, so I squeezed into 16s and 18s for as long as I could. But once I gave in and admitted that "Women's World" is where I really belonged, I felt liberated. No more tugging and pulling. No more stomach aches from too-tight pants. Just the freedom to move my body with ease, comfort, and grace. Until then, I never knew I could wear clothes and feel comfortable at the same time!

Tight clothes are a constant reminder that you don't look the way you think you should. When something is too tight, you can never really forget it and focus on living. When I go out the door in the morning, I want to know I look good, but then I want to be able to forget it and go about the business of living.

Beware the sales clerk who exclaims, "That looks wonderful!" just to make a sale. I recently watched a clerk gush to a woman about how great she looked in an outfit that was clearly too tight. Better to bring along someone you know will be objective than to rely on the clerk's judgment. In my case, my husband will always tell me the truth.

One more word of advice: If you buy something that needs altering, do it. Because of my body shape, skirts are usually shorter in the back on me. If I don't have them altered, I end up with an uneven hemline.

Before you buy something, ask yourself:

- Can I button it? I used to think it didn't matter if a blazer didn't button because I didn't plan to wear it buttoned anyway. But it does matter because if you can't button it, it won't hang properly.

- Does it cling or pull? Are the buttons of your blouse pulling? Do they create a peephole to your bra? Do your T-shirts cling to every roll of flesh or are they roomy? If creating room requires buying a size or two larger, grit your teeth and do it. I know it's hard at first to buy a size you vowed you would never wear, but the feeling of comfort will be worth it. A size is only a number.

And if it bothers you that much, cut out the size label. The road to self-acceptance may require some compromises.

• Does it make red lines on your skin? If you remove your bra and see red lines on your skin, it's too tight! Likewise for the waistbands of pants or skirts.

• Is it too big? Sometimes large women go to the opposite extreme and buy clothes that are actually too big. The result is usually a sloppy look, which is just as unflattering as the "ready to explode" look.

Determine your body type

Spiegel, as part of the company's previous *For You* catalog for plus-size women, came up with some good guidelines to help the full-figured woman determine her body type. "While we all have different body proportions," the advice went, "it is possible to group women's shapes into three different silhouettes—high, low and balanced."

The high silhouette is sometimes referred to as an "apple" shape and is characterized by an ample bosom, broad shoulders, narrower hips, and slim, shapely legs. In general, your figure appears larger above the waist than below.

Low silhouettes are sometimes called a "pear" shape. With this figure type, your bust and shoulders appear smaller than the rest of your body, your waist is clearly defined, your lower hip is as big or bigger than your high hip, and your legs are average or plus-size.

With a balanced silhouette or "hourglass" shape, your shoulders and hips/thighs are about the same width, the low hip is wider than the high hip, and your legs are slim or average while your thighs are more curvy. From the profile, your waist curves inward.

Women with high silhouettes are advised to look for styles that create strong vertical lines. Look for:

• Skirts: slim and shorter with elastic waists

• Dresses: wedge-shaped, shirtwaist dresses with padded shoulders, and coat dresses

• Tops: deep V-necks, and fuller tops or long blousons

• Jackets: straight, unfitted

• Big sweaters over slim pants

High silhouettes should avoid jackets that stop at the waist, clothes with ruffles or details that emphasize roundness, and turtlenecks.

Women who have low silhouettes should aim to add width to the shoulder area. Shoulder pads are recommended. Try:

- Skirts: with softly pleated fronts in fluid fabrics, longer lengths, and bell shapes. All-around pleated styles should have a draped yoke.
- Dresses: A-line and trapeze styles
- Tops: styles with epaulets/flanges, cap sleeves, tapered wrists, or cowl necks
- Jackets: shorter, cropped
- Pants: with soft pleats, or leggings with long, lean tops

Looks to avoid for this silhouette are tops with dropped shoulders or raglan sleeves, jackets that fall at hip line, slim knit skirts.

Finally, women with balanced silhouettes may want to try:

- Skirts: softly pleated or trumpet styles
- Dresses: simple lines, semifitted shapes, coat dresses, or styles with a gently dropped waist
- Tops: tunic styles
- Jackets: long, slim, over slim skirts
- Belts: narrow- or medium-width cummerbunds

Looks to avoid include fussy ruffles, full or circle skirts, boxy jackets, blouses with details that overemphasize the bust. [Note: Information from the Spiegel *For You* catalog is reprinted with permission.]

One of the reasons I like Spiegel's "Guide to Good Fit" is that it makes no mention of dressing to look thinner or to conceal flaws—just how to dress to flatter your particular body type. I have no problem with this concept. Some styles really do not look good on me. My goal is not to dress thin, but to dress in a manner that is flattering.

Think "fluid" and "drapey"

Clothes that have a fluid line and drape loosely work well on many larger figures. They provide an unbroken line that is flattering and allows for ease of movement.

Knits, if they fit, are good at meeting these criteria. I am very fond of knits—for a lot of reasons. They travel well. They can span the seasons. And they're super-comfortable. But, once again, a proper fit is essential. Knits can look great if they fit well, but they can look awful if they're too tight. Make sure your knit outfits are loose and flowing. Jersey knits are usually best.

Beware of the "hodge podge closet"

This is something I have to guard against myself. Now that they're making so many snazzy fashions in plus-sizes, I've become the proverbial "little kid in a candy store." I want it all! What ends up happening when you take this hit-or-miss approach is that you accumulate a lot of clothes but sometimes wonder what to wear. This is because your wardrobe is not really integrated; it's made up of isolated pieces that don't relate very well to one another.

Rule number one in building a successful wardrobe, according to Hara Estroff Marano, is to start with a core of classics. "Believe it or not," she says, "there are only eight basic pieces you need as the foundation of a great wardrobe, sometimes referred to as a capsule wardrobe." These are:

- a black slim skirt
- a cardigan sweater
- a suit
- a pair of jeans or khaki slacks
- a classic silk shirt
- a white tee shirt
- a large shawl
- a signature scent[4]

She also recommends buying your basic pieces in just one or two neutral colors. You can then update your wardrobe each year by adding accessories or a T-shirt in the season's trendiest colors. Neutrals generally include black, beige, navy, gray, or white.

Roz Thurner doesn't believe in one basic wardrobe for everyone. As she points out:

There's no use recommending that you buy a pair of basic black trousers if you don't wear pants, or a white sweater if you never wear sweaters because they're too hot. And a core wardrobe for someone who works at home won't be the same as for a woman who works in a law firm. I base my recommendations on personal preferences and lifestyle. I also have to know what you aready have to know what you may need to add.

Discover your "true colors"

Ever since I found out I was a "summer," I became one of those annoying customers who refuse to try on clothes that didn't match my color swatches. (I have since loosened up a little! Tangerine, for instance, is nowhere to be found in my "palette," but I like an occasional shot of it in my wardrobe. Often I combine it with turquoise or lavender, colors that are part of my "season.")

You too may want to invest in a color analysis. Variations in skin tone can mean that some colors will look better on you than others. It's a fun thing to do, a good starting point for your new image, and a great way to give yourself a treat.

Here's another color tip someone gave me: Have you ever been on an impromptu shopping excursion when you spotted a pair of purple shoes at 75 percent off that you think might match your purple pants, but your purple pants were at home and you just were not sure? Match paint chip samples to items in your wardrobe, label the chips, and carry them with you. This will help you avoid return trips when you spot a bargain.

Don't buy it just because it's there

It used to be you had to do this. There were so few choices for large women that you were grateful to find anything that fit, even if it was a polyester tent dress peppered with huge zinnias. Occasionally I am still tempted to buy something simply because it zips—even if I'm not particularly fond of it. I have to stop and say to myself: "You don't have to settle for something mediocre. There are other stores—other catalogs. With a little patience, you'll find just the right thing."

Grab it if you love it

On the flip side of the coin, if you find something that's "love at first sight," try to find a way to buy it. What if it's something a little off-beat?

That's okay. If you've established a good basic wardrobe, you can usually always find a way to wear it. When I was in Washington, D.C. recently, I found a marvelous white, gauzy big shirt with a huge yellow sunflower on it. I had to have it. It looks great with my basic white cotton slacks. Likewise for my gold Lurex tank top that adds pizzazz to a basic black jacket and skirt. These are the items that help to create your personal style—the ones that make you feel special when you wear them.

There are other times you should probably grab something if you see it, you like it, and it fits:

- When you see an item you don't need right now, but know you're going to need within the next few months—such as a coat.
- When you happen upon something you always have trouble finding, such as a particular style and make of bra.
- When you spot a classic, such as a crisp white blouse that is timeless.

In keeping with the theme of being good to yourself, why not establish a "mad money" account that you contribute to regularly for impromptu purchases?

Find out where to shop

You will need to spend some time finding out where to shop for plus-size fashions. There are several alternatives: stores, catalogs, TV shopping channels, and the Internet. Locate stores near you that carry plus-size fashions (look in the yellow pages) and allocate a day or two to explore them all in order to find which ones best suit your taste and your budget. This could be an amusing excursion for you and a friend. If you're not sure whether certain establishments, such as department stores, carry larger sizes, let your fingers do the walking before you waste your time and gas.

Another option is catalog shopping—something I've become quite good at! Currently there are a multitude of plus-size catalogs. I've listed the toll-free numbers of the major mail order companies in the Resource section of this book. Plus-size magazines, such as *Radiance, BBW,* and *MODE,* contain information on mail-order companies in ads as well as in their classified sections. You could also purchase a plus-size directory that contains information on plus-size shopping (several of these are listed in the Resource Section). Once you start ordering from plus-size catalogs, you'll be amazed how many more start showing up in your mailbox.

The home shopping TV channels, especially QVC, regularly feature apparel in plus-sizes. Many items come in both misses and plus-sizes. And for all of you Internet-savvy gals, the worldwide web is blossoming with websites catering to plus-size apparel. Doing a search for "plus-sizes" will generate many options.

Look in places you wouldn't normally look

I was in a mall in downtown Chicago and walked into a store that had very trendy, unusual jewelry and accessories. It also had some great-looking clothes, but I wasn't bothering to look at any of them. Since it wasn't a plus-size store, I assumed nothing would fit me. One of the clerks watched me for a few minutes and then came up and said, quite gently, "I don't mean to offend you, but I notice you're not looking at any of our clothes. You may be thinking nothing will fit you, but I'm sure we have things that you could wear." As it turned out, many of their pieces were cut very generously and "oversized." I ended up buying a fabulous jacket, which looks as though it has been painted with purple, pink, and gold watercolors. I love it and get many compliments on it. Check out the merchandise in boutiques such as this. You may be surprised, as I was.

One of our members regularly checks out men's departments and says she sometimes finds shirts and sweaters there!

Try different combinations

Don't be too rigid about what colors go together or think that your shoes and purse have to match, or that you can't wear white after Labor Day. A pair of white jeans worn with a hot pink sweater is a great way to jazz up a drab winter day.

I love to mix bright colors, such as turquoise and lime green, melon and fuchsia, mint green and iced chambray, purple and jade. Experiment with mixing fabrics and textures. Add something unexpected—I have a turquoise sequined baseball cap that's really an attention getter!

Keep it simple

Don't create too much visual "noise." Less is usually best. Generally, one or two major accessories are enough. If I am wearing a pair of bold, dangly earrings, I often stop right there. I'm not saying you couldn't add a scarf or a pendant, but earrings swinging to and fro, a tangle of chains, chunky bracelets, rings on every other finger and a jeweled barrette is probably too much. The most classy looks are usually the simplest ones.

Find a "signature" item

Find something that's uniquely you, that people will come to identify with you. For me, it's big, unusual earrings. For you it might be a collection of long elegant scarves, pendants amassed from different travel destinations, colorful fish pins, a piece of jewelry for each season or holiday, a signature "scent," an assortment of chunky bracelets, a stash of hats. How about button covers? I have them for Halloween, Christmas, and the Fourth of July. Another idea might be interesting hair ornaments. You will have fun assembling your signature pieces, and they will add another dimension to your personal style.

You know your style is well defined when others see an item and instantly associate it with you. A friend bought me a pair of earrings because she knew the moment she saw them that they were "Carol earrings."

Keeping your options open

A fashion consultant once told me of the importance of "options." I had asked her what "looks" large women carry off better than smaller women—my own feeling being that we are well suited to bold accessories. She told me she's careful not to throw big earrings on every large woman: "I used to think that all large women should wear bold accessories, but I have found that while some like a dramatic look, others may never be comfortable doing that. There have to be options, just like there are for smaller women. Not everything should look like a tent, have a waist, cost $29 or cost $400." You are the creator of your own personal style. Only you can decide what feels right and looks right on you.

Cosmetics

Cosmetics can enhance your image as well as boost your self-esteem. "Few can confidently get away without any makeup at all and still feel attractive," says body image expert Thomas Cash.[5] It's valuable both psychologically and socially to put some effort into self-adornment—but not too much. Cash also found that women who wore heavy makeup were more self-conscious than those who opted for a more natural look.

I've had women say to me, "I don't wear makeup. People will have to take me as I am." While some may feel makeup is superficial and frivolous, and that women who wear cosmetics are shallow, I find, once again, that this is often a smokescreen for feelings of inadequacy and unworthiness.

Makeup, if used properly, is not about creating an artificial look. It's about enhancing your image and caring about yourself enough to want to present yourself to the world in the best possible light. It's yet another way of communicating outwardly that you're a person of beauty and value.

This is not the same as being so self-absorbed that it takes you a half hour each morning to "paint" your face. The result of this process often looks artificial and garish. My makeup routine takes me about five minutes and includes foundation, loose powder, lipstick, eyeliner, and mascara. I don't try to "slim" my face with elaborate contouring. If I touch up during the day, it's just a stroke of lipstick and a dab of powder.

Rick Teal, a top New York makeup artist, says: "A lot of people have fancy theories about contouring the face to make it look thinner, but I think it just looks silly and freakish and calls more attention to what you're trying to hide." His philosophy of makeup for the plus-sized woman: "I don't do anything different for larger women. I make them as pretty as other women."[6]

Spend a little time "browsing" in the cosmetics department. See what each line has to offer in terms of colors and products. Many offer free makeovers. You might even want to have several (on different days, of course!) to find out whose products you like the best.

Hair

What about hair? Personally, I think the biggest mistake some large women make is cutting their hair too short, which makes their heads appear out of proportion with the rest of their bodies. While I have seen short "dos" on large women that look chic, I have also seen short, cropped hair that is clearly making the statement: "Minimal upkeep is all I need." Think again! A flattering hairstyle can do wonders for your self-esteem. I spend more time on my hair than anything else and I enjoy it. I go to a top stylist. I like trendy hairstyles. I want to stand out, not fade away, and I make sure my stylist knows that.

In an article on "Looking Great at Any Weight" in the May 9, 1994 issue of *First* magazine, the word on hairstyles was this:

> *Big women need a hairstyle with some volume to balance their figures. But contrary to popular belief, long hair will not create a slenderizing line. It tends to flatten on top and can make you look shorter and wide. A close-cropped cut is equally risky, since the head will look too small in proportion with the body. The best style: short to mid-length with enough fullness to balance but not overpower.*

Milwaukee stylist Jeff Setterlund says, "It's really more about balance than anything else. You try to balance the hair to the body. A too-short style may not provide this balance, but it also depends on body shape. Some women may be able to carry it off." The profile is often neglected, he says. "You want to strive to create an oval shape to the profile, rather than a round or square look."

"What is the biggest mistake large women make with their hair?" I asked him. "Trying to make it too big," he replied. "In striving for balance, they overcompensate and the result ends up actually being top-heavy."

Michael Maron, author of *Instant Makeover Magic*, agrees that the key is balance. For full cheeks, he recommends a longer hairstyle with an angular cut. Hair that falls forward, he adds, tends to diminish a full face, while a "bowl" cut can accentuate its roundness.

One way of finding out which hairstyles flatter and which do not is to visit a wig shop and try on wigs in different styles. Another alternative, something I did recently, is to see if you can locate one of the establishments where, via the magic of computers, you can have a photo taken of yourself, pick out different hairdos, and actually have these hairdos generated on computer images of yourself.

Health as part of your image

Designer fashions and top-of-the-line cosmetics won't mean a thing if you're not eating properly, exercising, and getting enough sleep. I recently saw a friend who now lives in Florida. She looked great: tanned, toned, glowing. "People who haven't seen me in awhile think I've lost weight," she said, "but actually I've gained ten pounds." She went on to explain that she's been working out with a personal trainer and that the weight gain represents muscle, not fat. In fact she has probably lost some fat, but muscle weighs more than fat.

We deal extensively with the aspects of good health elsewhere in this book, but I wanted to emphasize that good health is as just as important in creating a positive image as the clothes, the lipstick and the hair spray.

Image is not just for public display

One of our members, a peppy and vivacious woman, always counsels new members to start each day looking good, even if it's not a work day and their schedule calls for relaxing. "Get up," she says "take a shower, splash on a fragrance, fix your hair. Put on some pretty casual clothes. You'll feel so much better than if you spend the day in a ratty bathrobe."

I have to agree. I begin each morning with a shower, shampoo, and skin care. I feel refreshed, alert, ready to do things. If I skip the routine, I'm apt to feel sluggish and unmotivated the entire day. You can pare down the rest of the routine. I often apply some gel to my hair and let it dry naturally. I may give my face a break from makeup—except for lipstick. My around-the-house clothes are soft, loose and casual, but still attractive. When I catch myself in a mirror, the image is fresh-scrubbed and glowing, not dull and bedraggled, and it's a mental boost, too.

I also feel that when husbands complain that their wives have "let themselves go," it may have more to do with simple matters of grooming and hygiene than with size. After years of marriage, you think it doesn't matter how you look around the house, but it *does* matter. You wanted your image to be pleasing in the beginning and the importance of that shouldn't diminish.

Conversation with an image consultant

Roz Thurner is a plus-size image consultant who lives in Milwaukee. Several years ago she created BASICS, which stands for "Bringing All Sizes Into Consideration with Style." She started her business because "I just couldn't find the clothes I wanted. The styles might be okay but the fabrics were terrible. Today I may use the same basic styles over and over, but I use fabulous fabrics."

Roz frequently presents workshops in the Milwaukee area. Here are her basic guidelines:

- Build your wardrobe around solid colors and accessories. It's the most economical way to assemble a wardrobe that will last, will never go out of style, is interchangeable, and always can look different with new accessories. If you know how to accessorize, you could wear the same black dress for a month and no one would realize it. They may realize you like black, but they won't know it's the same dress. Accessorizing is kind of like a Mr. Potato Head. You get the little plain potato and keep adding things to change the look!

- Always buy the best you can afford. If you buy quality pieces, they'll last for years. Just change your accessories. People will think you've got a new outfit.

- Always buy clothes that fit. I know there's a temptation to buy things in the "post-diet" size, but that's being cruel to yourself. You're telling yourself you're not worth it now, and you are!

- Make every purchase a commitment. Ask yourself: "Do I have four pieces to go with it?" If not, ask: "Am I going to get those four pieces?" If you don't think you will, pass it up.

- Take a chance on something different. If you've always worn tent dresses, put on a belt. Or try on a suit.

- Be sure to finish the look. I might see a woman in a black turtleneck and pants, and she looks okay, but there's nothing interesting about her look. It's kind of like cake without frosting. If she had added a big silver pin or a bright red scarf, she would have pizzazz and creativity.

- Pay attention to grooming. You can have on a great-looking outfit, but if your nails are ragged or your hair is greasy, you've spoiled the look.

- Pick a focal point and accentuate that area. If you would rather not call attention to a big bosom, don't plop a pin there. Position it up around your shoulder.

For more information, contact BASICS at 5540 N. 103rd St., Milwaukee, WI 53225; 414-464-1918.

The Largely Positive Image

Now you should be ready to create a personal style that is unique, confident, and striking. You deserve it and you're worth it. When you know you look your best, you'll want to get out and be a full participant in life. Let's sum up the elements of personal style:

- *Clothes* that flatter and fit, that reflect your personality, that make you feel special.
- *Makeup* that enhances and adds glow.
- A *hairstyle* that looks smart and suits your image.
- *Signature accessories* that become your trademark.
- A *confident stride* that lets people know you know who you are and where you're going!
- A *voice* that's pleasant but self-assured, and never utters apologies for your weight.
- A *smile* that says, "I'm happy with who I am right now and I'm happy to be living in the present."
- *Healthy habits* that arise from positive self-regard rather than body dissatisfaction.
- A *positive attitude* that shines through and lets people know that how you feel about yourself is how you expect to be treated in return.

The bottom line is this: Style is not about size. It's about knowing who you are, liking who you are, and reflecting that attitude in the way you look, walk, talk, and behave. The large woman today can make just about any fashion statement she likes. She can be elegant, glamorous, mysterious, corporate, alluring, captivating, playful, whimsical. She is woman. Roar!

♥ ♥ ♥ From The Heart ♥ ♥ ♥

The Largely Positive Christmas Wish Book

I look forward this time of year to arriving home each evening to find the mail slot loaded with holiday catalogs, sometimes referred to as "wish books." As I page through them, I do a lot of "wishing" myself—and sometimes the wishes come true.

In thinking about how to send my own holiday greetings, it occurred to me that I have many wishes for not only the Largely Positive membership, but for all the readers of this book. So I decided to compile a Largely Positive Wish Book. I hope you'll order and enjoy many of the items listed below! The best part is that they are all free if you believe in yourself and your unlimited potential.

The Self-Esteem Coat

Don this coat and you will be enveloped by a luxurious sense of self-esteem, knowing that you are a worthwhile person just as you are. This coat is guaranteed to ward off the chilling winds of prejudice, discrimination, and ignorance. Size is unimportant when ordering this coat, as self-esteem knows no size. Wear it with dignity this holiday season.

Confidence-Building Gloves

Slip these gloves on and you will no longer view your size as a drawback in any situation. You will not allow your weight to keep you from attending holiday events. Your weight will become insignificant as you allow yourself to enjoy the people, the festivities, the laughter, and the message of hope and renewal that the holiday season brings. You will radiate confidence, and people will be attracted by your vitality, vigor, and vibrancy!

Nonjudgmental Glasses

Look through these glasses and everyone becomes beautiful, regardless of size, color, age, or physical status. The most attractive people are kind, compassionate, generous, and self-assured. You are one of these people and you let others know it in your actions, words, and deeds. The "ideal body" is the one you were born with. Dress it up in bright holiday colors and proudly display it at holiday parties.

The Live-for-Today Watch

This watch will not allow you to put your life on hold. It will continually remind you that living your life to the fullest is the greatest gift you can give to yourself, your loved ones, and your community. If it catches you avoiding going places because of your weight, its alarm will sound until you get on out there!

The Stand-on-Your-Own-Two-Feet Shoes

With these shoes on, you will have no trouble standing up to those who, out of ignorance and insensitivity, would choose to comment about your weight. You are knowledgeable about issues related to size and weight and know that what the research really says and what most people believe are two entirely different things. You will not be a target for insensitive remarks. You will help to educate the critics and inform them that they need not be concerned with your weight. Your body is your business and no one else's.

The Self-Contentment Necklace

This necklace, in the shape of a heart, will allow you to be at peace with yourself, just as you are. You know that although you may not be able to change the opinions of everyone you meet, it doesn't matter. You know the kind of person you

are. You know that the essence of who you are does not fluctuate with numbers on a scale. People who also know that are the people you call your friends. They are the people you want to be around. Throw a party for them.

The Healthy Hat

This hat will free you from unproductive dieting and help you to focus on what you can do to improve your health and well-being. Health isn't a number on a scale. It results from all the things you do to nourish yourself, energize yourself, activate yourself, soothe yourself, educate yourself, assert yourself, and enjoy yourself!

Vest Of Compassion

This vest is worn mostly around the holidays, but should be worn the year round. It will remind you that issues of size and weight pale in comparison to issues of poverty, homelessness, hunger, and loneliness. Make a yearlong commitment to one cause and do one thing each month to fulfill that commitment. Your spiritual health will be nourished.

Well-Stocked Handbag

This handbag holds all the tools you will need for a quick repair to your self-esteem. Its contents include an assortment of affirmations you can pop out when you're feeling low, specially-treated tissues for blowing away negative self-talk, an eraser for obliterating self-doubts, and a special mirror that reflects all of your positive attributes back to you.

9

I'm only telling you this for your own good

Since my attitude has changed, and I no longer bring up the subject of my weight, I find that people seem less free to make negative comments about it. But if and when someone does, I will tell them that my weight is not open for discussion.

—KARI

Elizabeth, a gorgeous woman with peaches-and-cream skin, blue eyes and silky blonde hair, told a friend of hers she no longer intended to diet. "I told her I had decided to accept the body God obviously gave me, and that I wanted to nurture and appreciate myself rather than continue to wallow in self-blame and punishment. I said that instead of being an attractive, thin woman, I would be an attractive, large woman." Elizabeth's friend looked at her and chided: "If you really think you look attractive the way you are now, you're sadly mistaken." This is not a friend.

"I'm only telling you this for your own good," they'll say. But being put down is never for anyone's good. Most people who are "looking out for your own good" are really looking out for their own fragile egos.

Finding something about you to put down makes them feel superior and in control.

Part of the process of self-acceptance is letting other people know that you will no longer tolerate criticism about your weight. This may feel intimidating at first, but you must learn to do it.

In the final analysis, size acceptance is really not about weight. It's about being loved and respected exactly as you are with no conditions attached. Love says, "I treasure your existence. You are special to me. Physical changes may occur, but my love and respect for you remain constant."

Reduce your need for approval

Your battle will be half won if you stop worrying about what other people think. If you spend too much time seeking the approval of others, you will have no time left to seek your own. You will never win approval from everyone.

A very wise member of our group once said, "I can't spend my life worrying about what others think of me. I know what I think of me, I know what my wife thinks of me, and I know what my true friends think of me. This is what matters. If someone can't accept me, I no longer regard it as my problem. This has lifted more weight off me than any number of pounds I might ever lose."

How you choose to live your life does not depend on approval from others. I do not need someone else's approval to buy a new dress, take dance lessons, sign up for a cruise, go to the beach and watch the sun come up, or participate in a charity walk. Their opinion of my weight is simply irrelevant.

Large women often get caught up in the notion that they have to please everyone. They want everyone to like them. They have so much self-doubt that they continually look to others for assurance that they're likable people. If you like and accept yourself, this will no longer be necessary. Your own validation is all you'll need.

Remember that most other people really don't know you. They don't know what you eat or don't eat. They don't know your daily schedule. They don't know that you ride your bike several times a week or that you have vegetarian meals every other day. They make assumptions—assumptions that are often wrong. I've decided I can't help what people may think they know about me—how much they think I eat, how much exercise they think I'm getting. I know what I'm doing and that's all that counts. Ricky Nelson said it well in his song, "Garden Party": "You can't please everyone, so you just got to please yourself."

Does sisterhood go down the drain when it comes to weight?

My friend Wendy, who does market research, said she was registering women the other day for a fragrance test. It just so happened that a program about large women and men who admire them was airing on a TV off to the side of the room. At one point, a couple of the women came out on the TV show modeling sexy lingerie. "As the women came up to the registration table and caught a glimpse of the TV, they'd say, 'Isn't that awful?' 'See how disgusting she looks?' 'I can't imagine looking like that!' Some asked for my opinion. I said that while I wasn't sure lingerie was appropriate attire for a daytime TV program—on women of any size—I thought they were all lovely women and obviously the men there thought so too."

Sometimes I think women are hardest on other women when it comes to size and weight, and I don't understand it. We can unite when it comes to issues of job equality, sexual harassment, or the need for child care, but when it comes to cellulite, sisterhood falls apart. Large women even do it to one another. How many times have you said to yourself when a woman who's bigger than you walks by: "Thank heavens I'm not that big!"

A *Family Circle* magazine survey turned up some interesting statistics. Sixty-five percent of the women surveyed thought women judge female appearance more harshly than men do; fewer than nine percent thought men were more critical.

Recently, I was getting dressed after my water aerobics class behind the curtain of one of the dressing rooms. I could overhear two women talking right outside. "Have you seen Cathy lately?" one asked the other. "She just looks awful. And I told her so! She should have more pride in herself. She's an embarrassment to her family!" The other woman agreed. My heart went out to poor Cathy, although I had no idea who she was. With friends like those, who needs enemies? I hurried to finish dressing so I could let them see that a large woman had heard them. I was amused by the sheepish looks on their faces, but angry that they were being so cruel in their assessment of a woman who was supposedly their friend.

My size won't have any effect on my ability to be a friend to you. I'll still be able to pick up a prescription for you when you're sick, take you out to lunch on your birthday, commiserate with you when your kids are having problems, cry with you when your cherished pet dies, pick you up at the car repair shop, have you over for dinner when your stove is on the fritz. If you're my friend, all I care about is that I can trust you and count on you. Your waist measurement is utterly insignificant.

Women rally around one another to fight many forms of discrimination. Isn't it time we unite to protest the damaging impact size and weight discrimination has on all of us?

Responding to criticism

What's the best way to respond when someone is critical of your weight? There are a number of things you can do, starting with:

Education

Attitudes change through enlightenment. You must begin to educate your family, friends, and colleagues about issues of size and weight. We can hope that a "ripple effect" will ensue as they pass on the information to others.

How to do this? You'll need to be armed with some facts. Chapter 2, which summarizes the research, is a good start. Ask the critics and skeptics to read it. Keep an eye out for results of other weight-related studies, clip them, and start a file. This is what I do. I may then make copies and say, "If you don't believe me, here are the findings of some recent research."

Your money will be well spent on some publications such as *Healthy Weight Journal,* that will keep you abreast of recent studies. (See page 362 for information.) Read some of the other books I've recommended.

When an opportunity for education presents itself, do it without hostility or blame. Most people have spent a lifetime hearing only that being fat is unhealthy and unsightly. They will need some time to absorb and process the new information that you are presenting, because it seems to contradict everything they've heard all their lives. Go slowly.

You don't have to get involved in an "I'm-right, you're wrong" standoff. You can agree that there is still debate about many of the issues surrounding size and weight which is true. Researchers will tell you there's still a lot they don't know. But you can say that you've decided to keep your mind open and you hope they can do the same. And remind them that, no matter what the ultimate conclusions are, your weight still has nothing to do with your self-worth.

Know when to walk away

Like Kenny Rogers says in his song "The Gambler": You have to "know when to fold 'em." Some people just don't want to be educated. Jan says, "Sometimes I say nothing when I know it will lead to a pointless lecture on all the stereotypes and misinformation we have been told for years." I have encountered people who refuse to consider that what they've believed for years might be wrong, even when I have the studies in my hand to show them. Save your breath and your energy. What's important is that you understand. If this is a person who is close to you, you may have to agree not to talk about issues of weight at all. If this is not possible, you may have to distance yourself from the person.

When a shouting match about your weight is in full swing, this may not be the best time to try to educate or have a conversation about your feelings, needs, and expectations. At a time like that, it may be best to say: "I need for us to come to an understanding about my weight, but now is not the best time. When can we set aside some time to talk?"

Confront stereotypical remarks

Hard as it may be to defend yourself if you're not used to doing that, you cannot allow others to put you down and make inaccurate assumptions about you. One of our members had the courage to confront someone she met on vacation. While having breakfast with an older couple she had just met at a bed and breakfast, she mentioned that she had slept late the previous day and had missed breakfast. In her words:

After breakfast, my traveling companion went upstairs to our room, and I decided to read in the living room. I was about to sit down on the sofa when I heard the man mockingly remark to his wife: 'Why, with her big size, she could afford to miss a few more breakfasts.' I was horrified as they laughed openly and loudly over his piercing words; my stomach was in my throat (or so it felt), and painful tears streamed down my cheeks. I stood there in a daze, asking myself all kinds of questions: Why did I have to overhear their conversation? What did I do to them to be treated so unkindly? Couldn't I just run away and forget this ever happened? How could they say these unkind words about me and laugh at me? Why does this hurt so much? I realized it was because this was just another example of being unfairly labeled, and I could no longer accept this form of abuse. It was time to make a difference for me.

I stood up, still feeling as if my stomach were in my throat. With my hands shaking and my face stained from tears, I walked proudly back into that dining room. Looking directly into the man's eyes, I said firmly: 'Excuse me, sir. I heard your very unkind words about me from the living room, and I would like to know why you think you can talk about me that way? Why, you don't even know my name or who or what I represent!' His horrified facial expression said it all; he knew he had done wrong. He stuttered something, and then his wife stepped in and began apologizing profusely for her husband's 'inexcusable behavior.' I thanked her for her gesture of kindness, but told her I was very hurt by her husband's remarks about my body, and I wasn't leaving the dining room until I got an apology from him.

Finally, with his face cast down toward the floor, he softly said, 'I'm sorry.' I thanked him and left the room feeling like I had just won the Boston Marathon!

The next morning I awoke to find a note under my door from the man who had made fun of me, professing his deepest apologies for hurting me. In his note he thanked me for confronting him and teaching him a lesson in his later years. He also said how much respect and admiration he had for me. It felt so wonderful to finally have taken care of my needs and to have made the choice to no longer be someone's victim.

This woman says she feels that we all have "that special inner strength and a choice." Confronting someone who has made an unnecessary or negative remark about your weight is very appropriate and very healthy.

Neutralize the criticism

Some experts advise disarming the person who is criticizing you by finding some truth in the criticism. This, they say, will usually defuse the escalating argument. For instance:

"You don't really need to eat that, do you?"

Response: "You're right. I probably don't. But I've found that if I deprive myself, I only end up eating more later, so I'm practicing some new techniques that I feel will serve me better in the long run."

Or:

"Don't you think it's time you did something about your weight?"

Response: "I appreciate your concern and I have decided to do something about my health. Since most weight loss diets fail, I've decided I will be better off focusing on improving my health."

Or:

"Aren't you concerned about your health?"

Response: "Yes I am, and because of that I've been doing a lot of reading about the connection between health and weight. What I've found is that a lot of the popular beliefs about size and weight are inaccurate. Many researchers believe that the health risks associated with being fat have been exaggerated and that repeated dieting is worse than maintaining a stable weight. So the answer to your question is yes, I am concerned about my health, and I plan to take care of it by exercising and eating properly."

This tactic lets people know you appreciate their concern but it's not necessary. It tells them that you are in control of your weight, your health, and your life.

Set ground rules

You may have to make it very clear to family members that you no longer intend to participate in conversations about your weight or eating habits—and then stand firm. You can do it without being hostile. Say: "I know you've been concerned about my weight, but you no longer need to be. Having my weight commented on or criticized is not helpful to me and will only lead to anger and bickering. I am in the process of educating myself about the factors that govern weight, and I will be deciding how to use this information in the best interest of my health and well-being. We have so many other more important things to talk about. Let's not talk about the private matter of my weight any more."

Marion, one of our members, says people don't often comment about her weight, but if they do, she just tells them she's "fat and sassy." You might add: "Any more comments about my weight and you'll find out just how sassy!"

Don't worry that you may be hurting someone's feelings. They haven't minded hurting yours. People need to learn that it is not acceptable to comment on someone's weight, just as it is not acceptable to inquire about other matters of a personal nature.

Our member, Sue, says that when someone close to her is critical of her weight, she asks, "What gives you the right to judge me? Being thin does not mean that you have all the answers to life's problems."

It may help to write a letter to your critics. The benefit of writing a letter is that it can be written and read without interruption and without heated words. You might also want to attach educational material. I've written a sample letter, which appears at the end of this chapter. You can use all of it, parts of it, or compose your own.

Quit apologizing

Kate's family used to nag her about her weight every time they all got together. But she admits that she often raised the subject herself. "I'd tell them how depressed I was about my weight. I'd give them a blow-by-blow account of whatever diet I happened to be on at the time. I really set myself up." When she stopped doing that, the conversations about her weight ceased, as well.

Stop calling attention to your weight by apologizing for it or responding to compliments in a self-deprecating manner. I never mention my weight when I'm around others. As a result, it never becomes a topic of conversation.

Exit weight conversations

Unless I'm giving a presentation on weight-related issues or doing some one-on-one educating, I try not to get drawn into conversations about weight and dieting.

Rhonda's colleague was passing around copies of a diet she'd clipped from a magazine. When she got to Rhonda's office, Rhonda took a look at it and replied: "I've learned from the research on size and weight that dieting doesn't work, and I prefer to accept myself the way I am instead of how society thinks I should be." Period. She then turned the conversation to a project they'd both been working on.

Consider forgiving

You can spend your life blaming other people, especially your parents, for the damage they've done to your self-esteem. Or you can let it go. Many experts believe that the act of forgiving will free you emotionally in a way that lugging around past grievances never can. When you harbor bitterness toward someone, you are usually the one who suffers the most. People who have hurt you may not realize they've hurt you, or they may have long forgotten it. But you end up with the festering inner wounds.

Asked to recall people who criticized their weight, many women cite their mothers. Eating disorders therapist Judith Ruskay Rabinor tries to affirm and heal the mother/daughter relationship rather than spend time blaming. Mothers, she says, need to be understood as also being products of the culture. Often they too have been criticized and blamed for having gained weight.[1]

There is a big difference between a mother who encourages her daughter to diet because she loves her and wants to spare her the misery of being fat in a fat-hating culture and the mother who shames and belittles her daughter. I always knew my mother loved me and that she thought I was fine just the way I was. If she tried to help me cut calories, it was because doctors told her to do it or because I asked for her help.

Mothers usually do the best they can with what they know at the time. A lot of the information we have today wasn't available to women of the previous generation. Your mother wanted you to be happy. She didn't want you to be the fat girl everyone laughed at and no one wanted to date. She didn't realize that her concern simply reinforced your belief that you were inferior and unlovable.

It is helpful to understand the roles various people played in shaping your body image, but after that, you have a choice. You can spend the rest of your life engulfed in self-pity, anger, and blame, or you can simply say to yourself (and your critics if you choose to): "I understand that those who criticized were not operating with accurate information, which I now have. I forgive them for not knowing."

Few people really mean to be cruel when they express concern about your weight. Usually they're worried about your health and happiness. They're afraid if you don't lose weight, you'll be doomed to a life of ill health, sorrow, and unfulfilled dreams. Tell them you know they had your best interests at heart, but that was then and this is now. Thank them for their past concern and advice, but tell them you'll no longer need it. Let them know that you have new information, a new attitude, and a new image, and that criticism won't be part of it.

It is, of course, another matter entirely if people ignore your announcement and continue to criticize. At that point, you must decide if you value your relationship with them enough to shrug off and ignore their remarks—after all, you know it's based on misinformation—or if their attacks are disrupting your own healing process. If it's the latter, you may have to distance yourself from these people. If that happens, remember it's their choice, not yours.

Be around people you like

Who are the people you're always eager to see and like being around? Who are the people that support you and think you're great just as you are? Find more people like them! Maybe some people you've known for a long time or who are members of your family drag you down, but you feel an obligation to be around them. Shed that notion. Often, as you grow older, your values, interests, and attitudes change. You may find that your new "largely positive" attitudes leave no room for people who are "largely negative."

You don't have to worry that you'll end up with no friends. I find that people who have the capacity to accept other people for who they are far outnumber those who are judgmental and narrow-minded. People who are judgmental of a person's size are likely to be judgmental about other characteristics. Who needs them? You don't!

Here's what Noreen says: "I have chosen to respect myself for who I am and expect respect from others. If people don't treat me with respect, I don't bother with them any more. There are too many people in the world to waste my time with a few who can't find pleasure in my company."

Once you've identified the people you like, take a sincere interest in them too. There's nothing people enjoy more than being around someone else who is genuinely interested in what they have to say. Care about other people and their lives. Ask questions and listen closely to the answers. There's nothing more attractive than a person who is interested in what you have to say. People will remember you as that delightful woman with whom they had the best conversation!

If you really want to help

The following advice to people who tend to take on the role of "food police" was developed by Karen Chalmers, a dietitian who counsels patients at the Joslin Center in Boston, and published in the *Tufts University Diet and Nutrition Letter* for February 1995. You may want to share it with those who adopt this role around you:

- Instead of accusing someone of "cheating" on his or her diet and thereby engendering resentment, make an effort to learn as much as you can about the relationship between eating and health. The person on the receiving end of the accusations may, in fact, be making perfectly sound food choices, but the accuser may not have a good understanding of how the diet works as a whole.

- Respect your loved one's privacy by not criticizing, or even discussing, his or her medical condition or diet in front of other people unless you know that person is comfortable about it.

- Be flexible in your attitude about food rather than rigid. If you constantly tell a loved one that a food he or she wants is "bad," your negative attitude can create unnecessary stress and guilt. No one responds positively to negative criticism.

- Refrain from teasing another person about his weight or eating habits. Even people who smile and go along with the joking may be more sensitive than they let on.

- Put yourself in the other person's shoes. Family members and health professionals often expect people with medical problems to be perfect when it comes to their eating habits, but if the critics tried following a strict meal plan for a week or two, they'd see how unrealistic it is to expect perfection. Moreover, many people fail to realize that it is possible to fit "treats" into even the strictest of diets with a little planning—a point worth keeping in mind before accusing someone or having no willpower or self-control.

- Don't immediately blame dietary indiscretions for a "bad" checkup that indicates, for instance, a rise in blood cholesterol levels, weight, blood pressure, or blood sugar. Remember that variations in those measurements can be influenced by any number of factors, including a person's exercise habits, presence of another illness, or change in drug regimen. Instead of quickly pointing a finger at diet, remain neutral and try to pinpoint what the root of the problem actually might be.

- Set a good example. Don't preach one thing and practice another, or expect one person in the family to eat one meal while others dine on something completely different. If the whole family makes an effort to eat healthfully, the person who must follow certain meal plans will feel supported and less isolated.

- Let go. In the end, only your loved one can control his or her own eating habits.

If you really loved me, you'd lose weight

Louise is a funny, intelligent woman with beautiful blue eyes and a cascade of chestnut hair. She came to our group as a soon-to-be-divorced woman whose self-esteem had taken a nosedive when her husband told her: "You're too fat and I don't love you any more." She had, she confessed, been thinner when they met. I immediately recalled a cartoon that said: "My husband kept bugging me to lose weight, so I dumped him. I figure that's 185 pounds in no time at all!"

This line is good for a quick chuckle, but its subject is not a laughing matter. The weight-gain-after-marriage scenario is one of the most difficult of all situations to resolve. What often happens is that a woman loses weight to attract a man; they get married; mission accomplished. Then she regains the weight and the spouse says: "You're not the same person I fell in love with." Of course she *is* the same person in all respects but one. Unfortunately, this particular aspect matters a great deal to many men.

People who marry young often place great emphasis on looks. Many times this spells future trouble. Changes will occur as we age. Not only do most of us gain weight, but we develop wrinkles, lose hair, succumb to gravity, develop aches and pains—possibly more serious illnesses. If you married your spouse for inner qualities, you should be fine. If, on the other hand, you married for a tiny little waist or a tight butt, you could be headed for trouble down the road. People who marry for looks eventually discover that the elements of an enduring relationship have less to do with waist measurement and bra size than with trust, respect, friendship, shared values, compatibility, and laughter. An appreciation of these qualities is more likely to come with maturity. At 20, my primary criteria in a boyfriend was "nice looking." At 30, I wanted a "nice human being." (I ended up with both!)

Ruthanne Olds, in her book, *Big & Beautiful*, talks about a woman who had suffered years of weight-related abuse from her husband. "She finally told him that while she might not be a raving beauty, he was far from the ideal of male perfection. She told him, 'When I look at you objectively, I see a short, bald, skinny, bow-legged man with a crooked nose. When I look at you through the eyes of love, I see the most glamorous, sexy, virile, wonderful man I've ever known.'" She then asked which way he wanted her to look at him. "Through the eyes of love," he conceded and the weight abuse stopped.[2]

Dr. Dean Edell thinks there's a mythology about attractiveness: "I see lots of sexy, attractive, heavy women." Some men, he says, prefer larger women, but "talk to these men and you find out they are afraid to go out with fat women because people think there's something wrong with them!"[3]

I am truly blessed. I have a husband who respects me, cherishes me, desires me, supports me, and is proud of my accomplishments and the way I look. "I like for her to be out in front," I once heard him say to someone. I know that many large women do not have husbands like mine. I wish they did. His love and support has freed me to devote my time to issues that I care about instead of spending time fighting about weight.

I do not blame spouses who nag about weight—at least not initially. They've heard the same antifat messages as the rest of us. They may think they're being helpful by snatching that ice cream cone out of your hand or admonishing you for eating dessert. They may think they're concerned for your health when they buy you an exercise bicycle. But most are concerned primarily with appearance. I know this is true because even after they've been exposed to the educational literature about size and weight, many men still want their wives to be thin. Like most people in this country, they've bought into the idea that the words "fat" and "unattractive" are synonymous.

I sometimes do workshops titled "If You Really Loved Me, You'd Lose Weight." At one of these was a husband who was clearly not buying anything we were saying. Finally he said: "I just want her to be fit." "Who says she isn't?" I replied. Again, we have this notion that big bodies cannot possibly be fit bodies. I suggested they start to find some physical activities they could enjoy doing as a couple, being careful not to make it into some sort of contest. "She may not lose a lot of weight," I cautioned, "but she'll probably be more fit—and you did say that was your main concern!"

Some men are ashamed of their larger wives. "My husband doesn't like to take me out. He says I'm too fat," a woman once told me. She couldn't have been more than 20 pounds over her "chart weight." I felt anger welling up inside of me. Here was a lovely, warm, delightful woman whose husband didn't want to be seen with her because she was nicely rounded. I would like to see what he looks like

Often weight becomes a scapegoat for problems that go much deeper, and those problems will remain no matter what happens to your weight. When a man is insecure, he may feel compelled to conform to all the norms of society, including the one that says, "You should have a thin wife." Carole Shaw, former editor of *BBW* magazine, says: "A man who is confident doesn't need a carbon copy woman to assure him acceptance and verification of his masculinity. He's got enough self-esteem to be his own man."[4]

Many larger women are happily married. In fact, a Cornell University study found that larger women were actually happier with their marriages than other women and that women who gained weight were more likely to be happy than those who lost weight. The latter finding may be at least partially explained by studies showing that dieting (e.g. losing weight) can often be accompanied by depression.[5]

What's really important?

Ultimately it all boils down to what's really important in a relationship between a man and a woman. I can't say it any better than my friend's beau, who took me up on my challenge to commit to paper what he loves about Wendy:

What Do I Love About Wendy?

She makes me laugh.

She laughs at me.

She is considerate of my feelings about things.

We trust each other, giving each other the freedom to be alone, with other friends, doing whatever we would like to do or have to do in our individual lives.

She is attentive to her appearance, and wears a perfume that is absolutely wonderful. It has imprinted itself onto my memory, and I want more of her.

She is intelligent.

She is interesting to listen to, and I want to hear about her day, her children, the things that are bothering or pleasing her, and her ideas about nearly everything.

She listens to me and my superb ideas about all things!

We listen to each other, giving attention to the one who needs it the most at the moment, and truly conversing rather than monopolizing our talking opportunities.

We are like all other people—a mixture of strengths and shortcomings. I see in her strengths that I admire, have very positive emotional responses to, and find inspiring to me. Her shortcomings are minor and don't bother me. This is not a "love is blind" evaluation, but is probably the essence of "compatibility." Our particular mixture of positives and negatives seem to be complementary. She can help me when and where I need it, and I can do the same for her.

We respect each other's opinions, philosophies, politics, desires, and general likes and dislikes. We do not ever require the other to change a deeply-held feeling about anything.

She does not complain about herself.

She does not complain about much of anything. Negative things that go on around her may be observed and commented on, but this is not the same as whining and complaining. It also does not preclude her from voicing a dislike for something.

She is affectionate. She likes me and shows it. I see it in her eyes, in a light touch sometimes, in a short friendly message on my answering machine. Getting home after a day in the world is brightened immensely by her friendly voice.

She is sexy and she acts sexy and flirtatious with me. I find her irresistible.

She is kind to me and others.

She is said to be a "large" woman. I guess I didn't notice.

Sexuality and the large woman

Milwaukee body image therapist Shay Harris says:

Sexuality is a very painful issue for large people. It has come to be synonymous with slenderness and youth. Many of my clients tell me that their spouses or partners refuse to be sexually involved until they lose weight—which simply intensifies feelings of self-loathing and self-doubt. So it's back to another diet. The pounds drop but inevitably return, causing them to feel hopeless, undesirable, and like failures. But this is not the failure I'm concerned about. We need to explore why she fails to confront him and claim her right to be loved as is. Part of it is that he can't fully love her until she loves and accepts herself. How can I convince a partner that I am lovable and desirable if I abuse, reject, insult, deprive, and loathe myself?

As I said earlier, women who marry thin and gain weight later often run into problems. If inner qualities were paramount in the beginning, the relationship usually can be repaired. It becomes more difficult when appearance was the main—and sometimes only—attraction.

Kari notes: "I was slender at my wedding. What he didn't know was that there was a fat person inside demanding to be let out! When that person reemerged, I'm sure he was shocked."

Kari's husband, Chris, loves and accepts her as she is today. I asked him if he would be willing to share his current feelings and here's what he wrote:

Love, honor and cherish until death do us part. Nothing about size, shape, or cellulite. Eighteen summers have passed since that promise was made. She creates a bit more shade. She pleases me as before and we laugh. What more is there?

If all else fails, I say to spouses: "What if she died tomorrow? What would you miss most about her?" I know this is a rather morbid exercise, but it makes an important point because their answers will have very little to do with physical characteristics, and a lot to do with things like: "Her sense of humor," "Her hand held in mine," "The enjoyment of just being together," "Our political discussions," "Our walks by the lake," "When I come home, having someone I can talk to about how my day went." Being able to fit into her wedding dress has never appeared on any of their lists!

You *can* cultivate an appreciation of the larger form

Here are some activities you and your partner can participate in together to dispel the myth that only thin bodies are attractive:

Discuss the cultural influences

Be sure you understand where our ideals of beauty come from. We're not born with them. They're culturally induced—which means you have a choice to accept or reject them. An ideal that has women perpetually looking like adolescents is a fairly recent invention. Before that, it was okay for women to look like women, which included padded hips and soft, rounded stomachs. You need to spend some time discussing and really coming to terms with what's innate and what we've absorbed from the culture.

Visit an art museum

Really notice and admire the variety of bodies that have been considered beautiful throughout history. Note that many larger women are painted quite sensuously. Note that their stomachs almost always protrude and that waves of flesh are never "retouched" as in today's photography. Make a conscious effort mentally to link voluptuous images with erotic thoughts. He may resist, but ask him to try.

Take dance lessons

Dancing is a great way to be close to one another and to get your body moving. Exercise specialists have reported that fast ballroom dancing can elevate your heart rate as much as running or cross-country skiing. But I'm more interested in the sensuousness of your bodies touching and moving in harmony. Romantic evenings on the dance floor often lead to continued romance in the boudoir!

Set the mood

If all you wear to bed are flannel nightgowns or loose-fitting night-shirts, it may be just a matter of putting the words sheer, flimsy, gossamer, and sexy back into your nightwear vocabulary. Large-size lingerie isn't that difficult to find any more. Many plus-size stores (and some department stores) carry a plus-size lingerie line, and there are a number of catalogs that specialize in boudoir attire for the fuller figure. See if modeling a few of these items doesn't light a spark! Don't forget other "mood enhancers" such as soft lighting, candles, perfume, and romantic music.

Make a "date"

Think back to when you were dating. How were romantic feelings kindled? Wasn't part of it anticipation? What about parking in a romantic spot and sharing some kisses and cuddling? Sitting on the beach together and watching a sunrise or sunset? What about getting away to a hotel for the night? Romance sometimes gets lost in the mundane activities of daily living. Use a little imagination and rekindle it.

Be receptive to new information

An open mind is an essential ingredient in this process. You must both be receptive to new information about issues of size and weight, and be willing to discard myths and prejudice. The spouse who has been nagging about weight must be willing to acknowledge that his partner may not have a choice about her body size. When Maggie, a member of our group, took some educational articles home for her husband to read, he came to her afterward and said "I'm sorry." He was willing to acknowledge that he had held some mistaken beliefs, and was able to let go of them.

Make a healthy lifestyle a joint venture

Instead of nagging and arguing about your partner's weight, work to-gether on developing a healthier lifestyle. Go for walks. Dance. Bike. Play tennis or golf. Decide how you can make more nutritious meals. But change your goal from being thin to being healthy.

One of the best remarks I've heard on the subject of men and large women was made by researcher Susan Wooley and quoted by Terry Nicoletti Garrison in her book, *Fed Up!:* "If one morning all the women woke up 40 pounds heavier, how long do you think it would take the men to become sexually interested again?"[6]

In the final analysis, the essentials for a good relationship have nothing to do with a svelte body. They are:

- Really liking to be with this person. Being eager to see him/her walk through the door at the end of the day. Wanting to share the events of your life
- Sharing similar values and goals.
- Laughing together.

These ingredients will not spoil over time.

When all else fails

You may not need to lose weight, but you *may* need to lose the relationship. Lydia's husband wouldn't make love with her anymore. She felt there was little hope for the relationship, but was reluctant to end it because of her own sense of insecurity, fear that she'd never find another partner, and concerns about finances. But after coming to our group for awhile, she gained confidence, returned to work, and was soon promoted. Her self-esteem has shot way up and she says, "I'm learning that I am attractive now. When my image and attitude are positive, other people sense it and like it. So they see me as a beautiful, happy, energetic person, not just a fat person." She said she had thought she had to lose weight before someone else would be interested in her romantically, but since donning her new attitude, she is having no problem attracting the opposite sex.

Your first priority must be your own self-respect. If, despite all your efforts, the only thing that will make your partner happy is for you to lose weight, you are going to have to consider whether the relationship is worth the toll it is taking on your self-esteem. Perhaps it would be better to free yourself to find someone who will love your body in its natural state and who will not make losing weight a prerequisite for kisses, caresses, and caring. In the final analysis, you can't control someone else's behavior or what another person thinks. You can only choose what *you* will do and think.

Still single

Sometimes, women who come to our group feel that men who like large women went out with the dinosaurs, but I keep telling them, "You may have to look a little harder, but the man for you is out there somewhere!" I didn't meet my husband until I was 31 years old. But he was well worth the wait!

Ken Mayer, author of *Real Women Don't Diet*, offers hope when he insists:

> *There are some men in our society who don't judge a female by her body shape and size. Remarkable as it sounds, these males place primary importance on other qualities, such as personality, intelligence, kindness, positive attitude, accomplishments, cultural involvement, organizational skills and strength of character.*[7]

I found a few of these men and here's what they had to say:

- "There's nothing sexier to me than a confident large woman. Her sense of pride is not based on superficial looks but on her knowledge that she's got a lot to offer to me and to the rest of the world."

- "I love to explore the body of a large woman, with all its curves, softness, lushness. I find this very erotic."

- "I think attraction is a very individual thing. I'm attracted to women of all sizes—there are large women I find attractive and there are thin women who do nothing to excite me. There are many large women I find sexy by virtue of their personality, attitude, the way they dress and carry themselves."

- "Once I realized that the culture was dictating to me what was beautiful and what was not, I was able to think for myself. I set aside the cultural prejudices about women's bodies and came up with my own standards of attractiveness. I'm happy to say that my own criteria are much more inclusive. I now feel that men who limit themselves to cultural definitions of beauty are missing out on a lot!"

Another man, writing in the NAAFA workbook, made a list of the things he finds appealing in large women:

- *Femininity:* The sexual characteristics that distinguish women from men—breasts, wide and round hips, mons veneris, etc.—are composed almost entirely of fat!

- *Maturity:* Size suggests maturity, with all of its positive connotations.

- *Cuddliness:* A large woman looks and feels comfortable. Bones are sharp and cold.

- *Sensuality:* A large woman has more body and more skin to feel with, hopefully making her a very sensory-oriented person.

- *Power:* Size is power to most male minds, and to many men, a powerful woman is very attractive.[8]

Self-deprecation is unattractive

Resist the temptation to put yourself down. It's very unsexy and unattractive. A male friend once told me: "I have seen many large women I consider attractive and have asked some out, but all they seem to want to do is belittle themselves, talk about how fat and ugly they think they are and how they need to lose weight. They then proceed to give me a blow-by-blow account of their latest diet. After awhile, I'm bored and start to lose interest. It's not that I don't find them attractive; it's their self-condemnation that eventually becomes unattractive."

Never say things like, "How could you possibly be interested in me?" or "What do you see in me?" or "Only a loser could be interested in me." You might be sowing negative seeds without even realizing it. Of course he's interested in you, and rather than being a loser, he's a real winner—because he's smart enough and secure enough not to be deterred by cultural pressures.

The March 1994 issue of *Mademoiselle* magazine listed things "men wish women would make less of a deal of." They included:

- Food

- Appearance

- The faults they see in themselves

Counselor and media personality Isadora Alman says, "Self-esteem is the ultimate aphrodisiac." While she acknowledges that a large woman may not always be the object of instant attraction on a physical level, "she has to put herself in situations where people see all the other good things about her."[9]

When plus-sized humorist Liz Curtis Higgs interviewed her husband, Bill, for a book she was writing, she asked him if her size made any impression on him initially. He said:

Not in any negative sense. What struck me was that your personality and confidence level did not match what I had come to associate with larger women. You didn't fit the image at all. Some men say they are turned off by larger women, and this may be so for a few. I would venture to say that their negative impression is mainly due to an attitude shown by some larger women rather than size itself. For me, at least, my attitude toward a woman is based mostly on her attitude toward herself.[10]

This sounds like a very secure man.

Letter from an admirer

Awhile back, I received a call from a California gentleman who designs apparel for large women. He wondered if our members would be interested in learning about his designs. I said I was sure they would be. During the course of our conversation, he told me that one of the reasons he started designing for larger women is that he finds them very attractive and appealing. He said he does not feel he is an "isolated case," but that society makes it just as hard on men who like larger women as on the larger women themselves.

He said he enjoyed writing and wondered if he might write something for our newsletter. When I received his letter, I realized that he had done an excellent job of expressing not only his feelings, but I'm sure the feelings of many men. Here's his letter:

Dear Largely Positive Ladies,

The other day while attempting to design apparel for a large-size fashion show, I began to think about what I found sexy and beautiful in large-sized women, and tried to incorporate those aspects into my designs. I found myself exposing backs, exposing arms, lowering necklines, creating slits and shortening hemlines. In other words, I couldn't think of anything not sexy about large-sized women that I felt a need to hide or disguise.

This led me to think about a large woman I dated several years ago. She wore at least a 32-dress size, loved clothes and always looked sharp, projected an image of feeling sexy and full of life. Her friends referred to her as the 'male magnet' since men were always asking her out. I soon realized that how men perceived her was directly related to how she felt about herself. Her unwillingness to apologize for her size discounted size as an issue. Her self-esteem was based on how she perceived herself—a sensual and sexy woman—not what others thought. And her comfort with this image of herself allowed her to defy conventional images of female beauty in American society.

I do not want to imply that self-esteem is important only for projecting sexual attractiveness. Self-esteem in itself is important. Feeling good about oneself and enjoying life is always attractive. And yet, talking to larger women, this often doesn't seem to be a satisfactory answer to the question of what men find attractive, especially since not all larger women are confident. More pointedly, I have been asked what men find physically attractive in large women, since the image of a large woman has often been used comically rather than sensually.

The only way I have of answering that is to say that to some men, what is nice and sensual and sexually attractive in a smaller woman is that much nicer and more sensual and more sexually attractive in a larger woman. Some men simply like the female form in a larger package. They find it more attractive and exciting.

Other men do not find large women attractive. This is a fact of life like so many others, which shouldn't affect how a woman feels about herself. Who are you living for, after all—yourself or some man's perception of you?

So dress yourself up in some self-esteem and you never know what might happen!

Sincerely,
One of your many admirers

Looking for Mr. Right

So now you're convinced now that there are men who are attracted to large women, but where do you find them? Almost anywhere—except a bar. I think bars are an especially poor place for large women to meet men because the men there are often looking for "chicks" with single digit dress sizes. I'm sure there are exceptions, but generally speaking, bars are a dead end for large women.

Looking for men as the sole purpose of an outing is usually doomed to fail, anyway. You'll have better luck if you keep an eye out for an interesting prospect while you're going about your daily activities or pursuing hobbies and other interests. You're better off getting to know someone in the context of an activity you both find interesting and worthwhile. Develop a hobby—one time I took a woodworking class and ended up being the only woman there. Look for classes where there are likely to be a preponderance of men. Be sure, of course, it's something that really interests you—at least a little! That way you'll already have something in common with the men you meet there.

Other ideas: some of my friends swear by the Inernet or the produce section of the grocery store. (Men never know how to pick out melons, says one of my friends.) Another woman met her beau at a museum fund-raiser as they strolled together admiring the paintings. Still another met her boyfriend at a bookstore where refreshments and entertainment are provided on weekends.

Personal ads have worked for some of my friends, but it's important, they say, to state up front that you're a large woman. Many ads express preferences for large women. You may want to find a clever way of revealing what size of "large" you are. I say this because one woman, who ran an ad acknowledging she was large, was devastated when she went to meet a man and he said: "You said you were big, but I didn't know you meant *that* big."

Relationship consultant Susan Page advises women to "go for volume." Page told a Milwaukee audience she has a friend who met 78 people. "She married the 78th!" Another woman offered a class called "Cooking for the Single Male" which allowed her to do something she enjoyed, make some money, and meet a bunch of single men!

Get together with friends and make a list of possible places to meet men: personals, singles organizations, dating services, community theater, adult education classes, especially courses on investing and real estate!

In some ways, you, the larger woman, may actually be more fortunate in the "meeting men" department. When you meet a man who does fall in love with you, you will know it's for all the right reasons. He finds you attractive, yes, but he also appreciates and values the whole person—mind, body, and soul. He is not likely to leave you at the first sign of change in the outer package. These relationships are usually deep and lasting.

Rude remarks

"Sticks and stones can break my bones, but names will never hurt me," goes the old saying. I beg to differ. Unkind words can catch you by surprise and cut far deeper than a superficial flesh wound. A flesh wound will heal in a matter of weeks, but the wounds inflicted with words can take far longer and can be reopened easily.

Why do people make cruel remarks to other people? One of the best explanations I've encountered came out of a TV program about skinheads who had committed crimes against Jews and African Americans. The interviewer asked a jailed skinhead, who now claims to regret his past behavior, why he felt the way he did about people from different racial and ethnic backgrounds. He replied: "By looking down at someone else, it made me feel more important." Keep that in mind. People who make unkind remarks are very insecure and make themselves feel more secure by putting others down. If you weren't so busy being angry at them, you could feel sorry for them (but go ahead and be angry too—it's healthy!).

NAAFA president Sally Smith tells of the time she overheard a table of men joking about her size as she moved through a buffet line. Her strategy? When she had exited the line, she went over and sat with the men! Familiarity often defuses ridicule. If she had been a colleague, they would have been much less likely to make fun of her as she selected her meal. By sitting with them and talking with them, she gave them the opportunity to know her as a person and see beyond the flesh. She was no longer an "object," but an individual—and a delightful one at that!

It's true that the nastiest comments are often made by strangers. What do you do? Do you respond? Ignore it? And if you do respond, do you do it coolly, angrily, wittily? Sometimes there's no chance to respond, as in the case of a drive-by insult. You have to let these go. Say to yourself:

- These are obviously very ignorant people.
- These are strangers. I will never see them again. Why should I care what they say?
- I know who I am. They don't.
- I have many friends and relatives who care about me. These are the people that count in my life. Rude strangers aren't worth a second thought.

There is no one right way to deal with cruel remarks. You have to decide what feels best for you. You can choose to simply ignore them—and chalk them up to the insecurity and ignorance of the perpetrator. Or, you can choose to shoot back a zinger of your own. You can even choose to use the incident as an opportunity to educate—although that's not always possible.

Personally, I don't think it's helpful to become hostile or use profanity in responding to ignorant remarks. This reduces you to the level of those doing the name-calling and makes it more difficult for you to take control of the situation. That doesn't mean you can't express your anger at their callousness. When I asked our members to make "largely positive" New Year's resolutions last year, one woman said: "I resolve to get angry enough to confront others who are always trying to get me to change myself. I'm me!"

If an insult really gets you down and you can't shake it, discuss it with someone you trust. Once, while I was out for a walk, a carload of young boys hollered at me: "You'd have to walk around the world to walk that off!" Here I am, trying to walk for my health and I can't even do that without being insulted! When I arrived back home in tears, my husband comforted me by pointing out: "They're stupid and immature. They're probably hooting things at every woman they see. They're strangers you'll never see again, so why spend another moment letting them get to you?" I realized that as long as the people I love care about me—and they do—why should I care about the antics of a few young boys trying to impress and outdo one another in the verbal assault department.

Columnist Abigail Van Buren has a standard reply for people who ask intrusive personal questions: "I'll forgive you for asking, if you'll forgive me for not answering."

Sometimes put-downs come not in the form of words but in the form of stares and whispers. One of our members walks right up to people who are staring and says, "Pardon me, but do I know you? I noticed you were looking at me. Please refresh my memory as to where we met." She enjoys watching them squirm to come up with an answer.

Do you sometimes find yourself drawn into conversations about other people's weight: "Peggy has lost so much weight and she looks so good now." The implication, of course, is that Peggy looked like hell before and would again should she regain the weight. I am wondering where, as a large woman myself, their remarks leave *me*. My reply is always something like this: "I think Peggy looks good now, but she looked good before, too. Women can be attractive at any size."

Or sometimes it's the opposite: "Have you seen how much weight Peggy has gained?" (asked, of course, in a tone of disgust so there can be no mistaking how they feel about Peggy's weight increase). Now I'm *really* wondering where this leaves me because I'm bigger than Peggy! I've been known to say, "What must you think of me, then?" And the reply usually goes something like this: "Oh, but you always look great and you're meant to be a larger person." Well, maybe Peggy is meant to be a larger person, too. We wouldn't say, "Have you seen how much Peggy's blood pressure has increased?" because, of course, we would have no way of knowing. But let Peggy gain ten pounds and all tongues break loose!

What do you say to someone who has noticeably lost weight? She may feel hurt if you ignore it. On the other hand, you don't want to go the you-look-so-much-better route. I don't ignore it, but I don't congratulate them on looking better. I say something like, "I see you've lost weight. I know that was an important goal for you, and I'm glad you achieved it." This way you acknowledge their effort without tying it to attractiveness.

Be sure you're really the target of ridicule

Before you confront people you feel are having a laugh at your expense, be sure they're laughing at you and not just having a good time. Most people *are* not looking at you and planning how they can insult you. They're more concerned with what they're doing and how they look. It's understandable that we've developed some body paranoia, but be careful not to overreact every time you think someone may be laughing at you. Many years ago I was in a bar with some friends when I became convinced that a group of strangers at another table was laughing at me. I confronted them angrily, said I was aware they were making fun of me and wasn't about to let them think I didn't notice. They looked at me as though I were several slices short of a loaf and one of them said: "We didn't even notice you. Mike here just told a great joke!" They were sure to notice me now!

You're in the driver's seat

You can decide to take charge of your encounters with others and to guard your own dignity. You can decide what you will discuss and what you won't discuss. You can choose whom you want to be around. And you can choose to be loved today, not after you've dropped two dress sizes.

♥ ♥ ♥ From The Heart ♥ ♥ ♥

A Letter to My Weight Critics

Dear _____ ,

I know that you love me and that you've been concerned about my weight. And I appreciate that concern, but I want you to know it's no longer necessary.

I have been learning a lot about issues of size and weight such as:

- *Large people aren't necessarily eating more than thin people, and they're not lazy. Research has proved these stereotypes to be untrue.*
- *I am not to "blame" for my weight. A person's weight is determined by a variety of biological and physiological factors that may have very little to do with food intake.*
- *Studies have found that large people are in just as good emotional health as thinner people.*

I am also learning that dieting is a very poor way of managing one's weight and usually creates more problems than it solves. It wreaks havoc with metabolism, and upon returning to normal eating, 95 percent of dieters regain their lost weight—and often more. I won't be doing that anymore. *What I will be doing is focusing on my health and developing a healthy lifestyle. I may lose weight or I may not, but I will be making the decisions I feel are best for me and my body.*

What I will need from you is to accept me as I am and stop commenting about my weight. Having people nag about my weight has never helped me in the past anyway. In fact, it has only made me feel worse.

I am the same person no matter what I weigh. The essence of who I am does not change with my weight. Society has this misguided notion that you have to be thin to feel good about yourself, but I know this isn't true. I am no longer letting "society" run my life. I am in charge.

I know you may find all this hard to understand, but if you give me a chance, I'll be happy to share what I'm learning with you.

I can no longer wait to be thin to live my life. I want to be a full participant in everything life has to offer, and if I wait to be thin, I may never do this. Because you love me, I hope you wish these things for me too.

Instead of discussing my weight—or anyone else's—let's talk about things we're doing that are fun, interesting and meaningful. You mean a great deal to me and I know you care about me. I don't want to have to distance myself from you, but if the weight squabbles continue, I may have to do that. I'm sure that's not what either of us wants, so even if we have to agree to disagree, let's do that and get on with the things that are important, including our friendship (relationship, kinship).

Thank you for your love and concern.

* Reprinted with permission. For subscription information write *Tufts University Diet and Nutrition Letter,* 53 Park Place, New York, NY 10007.

10

lose weight and call me in the morning

I dismissed a physician for fat discrimination. I then interviewed a new physician for sensitivity to weight and explained I did not want to be weighed. He agreed to a first-time weigh only, and the relationship has been great.

—ELAINE

Betsy recalled her first—and probably last—visit to a doctor who walked in, and without examining her, exclaimed: "I can see what your problem is—you're fat." Although there are many fine doctors who wouldn't think of making such a remark, there are still far too many who do.

The following appeared in an editorial in the *New England Journal of Medicine,* on September 30, 1993:

> *Overt discrimination against overweight people is only part of the problem, however, and we in the medical profession are among the chief offenders. Who among us hasn't heard the horror stories told by obese persons about their treatment at the hands of insensitive and prejudiced physicians? Studies documenting our role in the stigmatization of obesity have been available for years. Our education has done*

nothing to relieve the problem. Not only hospital staff but also medical students are clearly prejudiced against obese persons."

The authors are Albert Stunkard, M.D., and Thorkild Sorensen, M.D. Dr. Stunkard has been a leading and highly respected researcher in the field of obesity since the 1950s. He tells horror stories similar to those we have heard from our members. Among them:

- A doctor calling his large woman patient a "fat pig."
- A doctor who says to his patient upon entering the exam room: "You certainly have gotten humongous!"
- A doctor who, after hearing from his patient about Largely Positive, shoots back: "That's all you need—a bunch of fat people sitting around feeling good about themselves."
- A doctor obviously disgusted with a patient as he catches a glimpse of her in an examination room during a follow-up visit and sees she has not lost any weight. When the nurse asks if he wants to talk to her, he brusquely says "No" and walks away.
- A doctor who told a fat emergency room patient: "I wouldn't have bothered to resuscitate you had you been in cardiac arrest. Your neck is so big I probably couldn't have found a pulse."

A woman wrote to me and said: "I just recently had a doctor's appointment where my doctor read me the riot act about being overweight. Needless to say, I left his office feeling somewhat humiliated and my self-esteem has taken a nosedive."

Kathy Sandow, an Australian social worker and founder of the Australian size acceptance organization Women at Large, tells about going to a doctor with flu-like symptoms: "Somehow my original complaint seemed to escape this woman. She commenced to tell me I must be eating at least twice as much food as my body needs and that I would probably die young. I did not have the energy to argue, so I left thinking that the flu wasn't so bad after all."

Due to similar experiences, many large people avoid going to doctors until problems become emergencies. They routinely put off getting regular checkups, Pap tests, mammograms. I am convinced that fat people are perceived as unhealthy partly because they avoid even preventive health care until they are acutely ill.

Jacklyn Packer of the Medical and Health Research Association of New York City surveyed 118 large women about their health care experiences. The women complained that their doctors often berated them for their weight, acted disrespectfully while examining them, misattributed health problems to weight, and failed to follow standard medical procedures. Nearly all had put off doctor visits, primarily because their doctors made them feel ashamed of their size. Some women who asked for birth control said their doctors seemed amazed they would need it. One woman was asked straight out, "What would you need it for?" Another woman's doctor sarcastically snarled: "Who are you going to get? Captain Ahab?"[1]

A more recent study also found overweight women were less likely to be screened for cervical and breast cancer, and the authors concluded that obesity might be an "unrecognized barrier" to preventive care.[2]

One Largely Positive member admits that she has not been to a doctor in ten years because she's afraid to be weighed. And she is of an age where she should be having regular Pap tests, mammograms, and the like. I am alarmed by this and similar revelations which mean that large women may be suffering unnecessary illnesses, not because of their weight but because they are avoiding insensitive health care providers.

I recently had to have an X-ray at a local hospital. When I arrived at the X-ray department, an aide gave me a pair of cotton pants and a wrap-around robe. The pants were too tight. When I asked for another pair, I was told curtly, "This is the biggest we have." Certainly there are many people larger than I am. I put my own slacks back on and told the X-ray technician the pants I was given didn't fit.

The unspoken message in these situations is: "If you weren't so fat, the garments would fit." And, once again, the belief is that it's our own fault, and we deserve whatever humiliation we encounter.

I have had other, similar experiences and am no longer surprised. The last time I went for a mammogram, the robe was too small. The technician said apologetically, "I don't know why they don't get some bigger ones. They're too small for a lot of people." I don't know why either, except that it's one more way to punish us for being fat.

My gynecologist used to hand out paper sheets that stopped three quarters of the way around me. So I started bringing my own sheet. It always amused him to see me sitting on the exam table in my purple-and-blue-floral sheet. Finally, he got bigger paper sheets and I no longer have to wrap myself in my own bedding.

Not immune from cultural prejudice

Why would doctors be prejudiced against their fat patients? Studies confirm that physicians harbor the same prejudices found in the general population. In one survey, 77 physicians described their large patients as "weak-willed, ugly and awkward."[3] In a more recent study of family physicians, 63 percent of physicians attributed obesity to a lack of willpower, and more than a third described their obese patients as "lazy."[4]

In another study, very large patients were asked to respond to the statement: "I have been treated disrespectfully by the medical profession because of weight." Only 6 percent responded "never," while 79 percent responded either "usually" or "always." Participants in that study also reported that they had been the targets of rude and degrading remarks by professionals such as: "How can I tell if you're pregnant? With this mountain of fat I can't feel anything"; "How many chairs did you break in my waiting room?"; and "All your problems are due to your gross fat."[5]

In a survey of health professionals who were attending a continuing education conference on obesity, a number of stereotypes emerged. The researchers concluded that these biased views were due to the stigma society attaches to obesity rather than any knowledge and skills acquired through professional education.[6]

What do doctors know about obesity?

While some doctors are familiar with the research on obesity, many are not. I'm not sure why this is, but it's disturbing. Like most people, I was in the habit of elevating doctors to superhuman status, assuming their knowledge was always superior to mine. But since I started studying the obesity research, I've noticed that my knowledge often exceeds theirs.

In a survey of Kaiser Permanente physicians in California, it was found that only 17 percent had training in obesity and only 31 percent said they felt qualified to treat it. Kaiser now recommends to its physicians that they:

- Focus on health, not weight.
- Emphasize positive behavior changes patients can make, such as eating more fruits and vegetables, decreasing fat, increasing physical activity, and practicing self-acceptance.

- Focus on managing medical conditions with the same advice they would give thin people.
- Become familiar with the research, which shows the risks of weight cycling and that there are great benefits in a small loss of weight.
- Abandon suggesting dieting as a weight loss strategy.

Educating doctors is a tricky business. If there are no egos in the way, patients can sometimes assume the role of teacher. I have been known to share educational articles on weight-related issues with some of my doctors. For the most part they were receptive.

Part of the dilemma is that doctors like to have answers for their patients, which is understandable. A friend of mine tells about going to a doctor who told her to lose weight. She asked him why, and he finally admitted, "Because I don't know what else to tell you." Contrast that with the experience of my friend Liz Curtis Higgs, who wrote the book *One Size Fits All—And Other Fables*. After she had a complete battery of tests, all falling within normal ranges, her internist looked at her and said: "I should probably tell you to lose weight, but I can't give you a medical reason to do so."

Anthropologist Margaret MacKenzie, speaking at an AHELP (Association for the Health Enrichment of Large People) conference, had this insight: "We don't educate professionals to tolerate uncertainty." Doctors don't like not having answers, and we, as patients, don't like it either. Ultimately, it's easier to blame patients for their failure to lose weight than to admit that medicine does not yet have a permanent cure for obesity. MacKenzie said that if doctors could regard medicine as a permanent internship—always in flux—they would be more receptive to new ways of thinking.

There are, of course, doctors who have a more enlightened attitude. Dr. Fran Watson, a Minneapolis internist, is one of them. Interviewed for the Winter 1990 issue of *Radiance* magazine, she said weight prejudice was instilled in medical school. "But as a practicing physician I couldn't ignore what I saw." What she saw were large women who came into her office only for routine yearly exams. "My large patients were healthy," she said. Within a year of beginning her private medical practice, Watson began to believe, and to advise her patients, that there was no need for them to lose weight as long as they were active, healthy, and eating well.

She continued: "I've heard some real horror stories from patients about doctors who told them they were going to die, their knee hurt, or they had back pain because they were fat. Usually, when those women come to me, it has been five or ten years since they've seen a doctor."

One renowned physician who advocates size acceptance in the medical profession is Dr. Dean Edell. He advises large patients not to put up with any kind of discrimination and to be armed with the facts. He suggests saying something like the following to a weight-prejudiced doctor: "Doctor, haven't you seen the studies that say there are a lot of people like me who don't eat excessively, who are fat and can be healthy? I find your comments discriminatory." People, Dr. Edell says, have to educate the medical profession.

I like the story I read in the Spring 1994 issue of *Radiance* about a woman who was seeing a new doctor:

> *He walked into the room where I was waiting, looked at me, and said, 'You're fat.' I looked at him and said, 'You're black.' He took my history, and afterwards put down his pen and said, 'Is my being black going to be a problem for you?' I looked at him and responded, 'Is my being fat going to be a problem for you?' He looked at me, and I could see a light bulb go off in his head. 'Touché!' he said. He became educated right there. He turned out to be the most wonderful person in the world.*

Some Milwaukee doctors have become allies of Largely Positive. One had been my husband's doctor. One morning as my husband headed out the door for an appointment with him, I grabbed some educational articles and Largely Positive literature and said: "Here. If he hassles you about your weight, just show him these." A few hours later, my husband called me at work and said: "Dr. Palin wants to meet you." Uh oh, I thought. He probably wants to lambaste me for presuming there was something he might not know. My husband quickly set me straight: "No, he likes your stuff and he agrees with it. He'd just like to meet you in person."

So I called and set up a meeting. I was a still a little perplexed by his interest in Largely Positive because I knew that one of his duties was supervising a local diet program. But by the time he met me, he admitted he was growing skeptical of it since most of his patients seemed to be regaining their weight. "I'd see them in the mall," he said, "and they'd try to duck out of my way so I wouldn't see that they'd regained their weight. I felt bad that they thought they had to avoid me."

He said he was eager to read the information I had brought him. A few months later he called to ask if I'd join him in giving a talk on obesity to a group of doctors at the hospital where he practiced. I had done a fair amount of public speaking by then, but never to an audience of doctors. I agreed, but when the time came, I was terrified. I couldn't have been more surprised when he told his fellow physicians that a lot of what he'd learned about obesity, he'd learned from me! I told them what an ordeal it is for many large people to visit doctors when a stern lecture about their weight is about the best they can expect, and outright insults the worst. Also to my surprise, I was warmly received—many doctors came up afterward to say that my message was thought-provoking and much needed.

It's *not* all on account of your weight

I have lived on this earth now for five-plus decades and have never had a serious illness. After my last gynecological checkup, my doctor's exact words to me were: "Carol, you're terrific." I am not an exception. Many of my large women friends are also healthy. I had two large grandmothers who lived to be 87 and 91, respectively.

I will not deny that certain health conditions, most notably hypertension and diabetes, seem to be more prevalent among large people. But some scientists now question, especially in the case of diabetes, whether obesity is the cause or the effect—and whether some as-yet undiscovered factor is responsible for both.

I know many thin people who have high blood pressure and knee and foot problems. Two of my colleagues have severe back problems, and both are thin. Another very slender friend of mine has been frequently hospitalized with heart problems. No health issues are confined exclusively to large people.

I will not belabor the debate surrounding the connection between fat and health. We covered all that earlier. The point is that large people deserve good health care. They deserve the same treatment a thin person would receive. They should not be told flippantly that their problems are all due to their weight.

"Lose weight and then we'll talk" is not an acceptable conclusion to a doctor visit, especially if there is a problem left untreated. My mother's side of the family has a tendency toward hypertension and so do I. When I was told that my blood pressure might go down if I lost weight, my response was, "Yes, but what do I do in the meantime?" I told the doctor that since I have been a big person all my life and have had little success with dieting, I would, in all likelihood, remain this way. Although I am certainly willing to make healthy changes, those changes may or may not result in weight loss. "I don't," I told him, "want to leave your office with untreated hypertension. What would you do if I were a thin person?" He said he'd probably prescribe medication. Please, I said, do me the same courtesy. My blood pressure is now within normal ranges.

Noted researcher Paul Ernsberger, Ph.D., said in the Fall 1988 issue of *Radiance* that "any time thin and fat patients with the same medical problems receive different treatments, discrimination has taken place." He advises overweight patients to ask their doctors whether thin people ever get the same condition. The answer, he notes, will always be yes. Then ask how the thin person would be treated and demand the same treatment. It's your health, after all, that's being put at risk, not the doctor's.

What's the answer?

Is there a way for us to get more respect and understanding from the medical profession? Better education has been shown to help. A University of Kentucky study found that first-year medical students held mainly negative stereotypes about fat people before they took a communications course featuring a video, role playing, and written materials on size acceptance. One year later this group was more positive and less likely to blame the fat person for his or her condition than a comparison group of medical students who didn't get the training.[7]

Medical students should get more instruction like the kind provided by psychiatrist Karen Johnson, M.D., who has taught courses about feminist issues in psychiatry and has written a book, *Trusting Ourselves: The Complete Guide to Emotional Well-Being for Women*. Says Johnson: "In part of the course we question the conventional wisdom that fat is bad." She asks the students to question the effectiveness of dieting as a treatment plan: "If the assumed treatment plan is a diet with a 98 percent failure rate, then that prescription is a debatable medical practice." In Johnson's course "we discuss the research that strongly suggests that genetics programs us to be a certain size and shape, that our bodies have a setpoint, and that only through tremendous physical effort or fundamental deprivation can we change this."[8]

William Bennett, M.D. and Joel Gurin co-authored *The Dieter's Dilemma*. When interviewed for the Summer 1991 issue of *Radiance* and asked what they'd like to see from their medical colleagues, they responded: "We need to be respectful of our own ignorance and realize that there's a lot more to this story still to be told, to not guilt-trip people for factors that are clearly not under their control, to not assume that fat people and thin people are alike except that fat people eat more. It's a much more complicated story."

As the patient . . .

To make sure that your doctor encounters don't end up being one long weight lecture, try the following:

Shop around

Interview prospective doctors about their views on obesity and how they approach it. While managed care has limited the element of choice for some people, usually more than one option is available. Call and say you'd like to speak with the doctor briefly, before making an appointment. Ask the doctor:

- If he/she is comfortable treating large patients—even if they do not lose weight.
- If he/she is willing to focus on measures of health rather than measures of size and weight.
- If the choice to weigh-in can be left up to you (unless, of course, there is a medical reason for it, such as preparation for anesthesia).
- If you will receive the same treatment for your medical problems that a thin person would receive.

Write a letter

Perhaps instead of phoning, you'd be more comfortable introducing yourself and asking the necessary questions in a letter. I have composed a sample letter, which appears at the end of this chapter—or you could compose your own. The important thing is to find out up front if this is a doctor you can feel comfortable with and if the doctor can feel comfortable with you. If not, you'll have saved yourself some time and aggravation, and you can look for someone else.

Ask others

Ask other people if they can recommend a doctor who will be "size-friendly." We have a list of such doctors at Largely Positive and we keep adding to it.

Don't be afraid to be assertive

If gowns are too small, complain. If you are treated disrespectfully, complain. Point out that one-third of the population is "overweight" and that surely you can't be the only one the gowns don't fit. If you have a large arm, *be sure your blood pressure is taken with a large cuff.* A too-tight cuff can produce a false-high reading.

Assume responsibility for your health

Be open and receptive to discussions about your health and be willing to take the steps necessary to improve it. Understand that *you* have a responsibility as well. You must be willing to examine your lifestyle and make improvements where needed.

As the doctor . . .

In the absence of weight loss, there are still a lot of things patients can do to improve their health. Doctors always assume that weight loss is a necessary prerequisite, which is unfortunate because it causes many large people to ignore what other steps they could take. Why bother, they reason, with healthy habits until I have a thin body to house them in?

It's time for some reality. Americans aren't getting any thinner, despite the proliferation of weight-loss programs. We can accept this and try to help them be as healthy as possible, or we can continue to deny reality and keep insisting that weight loss is the only option.

I understand that physicians feel they have an obligation to inform their patients of conditions, such as diabetes and hypertension, that sometimes accompany higher weights. And I certainly have no quarrel with this, but keep in mind:

- Studies show that even a modest weight loss can often alleviate these conditions significantly.

- Patients who engage in regular exercise programs often improve their health even if they do not lose a great deal of weight.

- There is no reason to believe that weight loss will be any easier for people with health problems than for other large individuals. Some researchers believe that weight loss becomes even more difficult for Type II diabetics because excess insulin promotes fat storage. (Most Type II diabetics develop a condition known as insulin resistance, where the body actually produces excess insulin, but the cells become resistant to it.)

- Rather than helping, repeated episodes of weight loss, followed by weight gain, may cause harm. In some studies the healthiest people were those who maintained a stable weight, even if it was higher than what the charts recommend. Researchers continue to debate whether weight cycling contributes to the development of heart disease.

- Dieting may be more risky for diabetic and hypertensive pa-tients. If they regain lost weight, and we know that many will, often they will be even heavier, and the regained weight will accumulate in the most dangerous spot of all—the abdomen.

So talk to your patients about their health. Talk to them about starting an exercise program. Talk to them about watching their sodium. Talk to them about eating less fat and more fruits and vegetables. Talk to them about medications that may help. Talk to them about reducing stress. They may not end up thin, but I'll bet they end up healthier.

To mental health professionals . . .

"Are you bothered by your weight?" a therapist testifying in a legal case asked my friend Laura, an attorney who in bygone days would likely have been referred to as a "big, handsome woman." "Emotional problems can manifest themselves in weight," the therapist told her. Now it was Laura's turn! "I was angry at her," she said, "for trying to play that game with me and insinuating that my size was evidence of an emotional prob-lem. I told her that, on the contrary, my size is an asset to me in my legal work. It confers a certain sense of power. I am a presence, a force to be reckoned with—especially when I'm dealing with abusive spouses. I told her that my weight has never caused me any problems with my self-esteem and that I simply regard it as one of my physical characteristics."

Laura is one of the most well-adjusted women I know. She would not allow anyone to intimidate her. "I think you need to address this issue in your book," she said to me one day. "Why is it that just because you're a larger person, they think you have emotional problems?"

She's right. I see it all the time in larger women. They've convinced themselves that their weight is emotionally driven. Why? Because it's what they've been told for so long. I spent years combing my psyche for an emotional explanation for my weight before I realized I was searching for something that didn't exist. I don't deny that disordered eating usually has an emotional component, but the majority of large people are not disordered eaters. Weight *can* be emotionally based, but more often it is biologically and physiologically based. Like me, many people have been big since they were babies and toddlers. Was I eating at that point to blot out emotions? Hardly. My body had simply decided to be a big body!

There is no evidence that large people suffer to any greater degree from emotional problems than thinner people, and since the majority aren't eating compulsively either, it's a mistake to view largeness as indicative of deep-seated psychological problems. But some professionals still assume this to be true.

In one experiment, a group of therapists was given copies of identical case histories with a photo of the client attached. The only difference was that some of these professionals were given a photo of a large person and some were given a photo of an average-weight person. The therapists who received a photo of a large person attached a much more negative psychological profile to that person than the other therapists did to the average-weight person.[9]

In a more recent, but similar experiment reported in the January 1999 issue of *Allure* magazine, psychologist Kristen David-Coelho sent a photograph of the same woman to members of the American Psychological Association. In some photos, the woman was made to look heavy, while in others she appeared to be of average weight. The case history provided was identical in both cases. The 200 psychologists who responded diagnosed the "overweight" woman with more severe problems and said it would take much longer to treat her than the average-weight woman. David-Coelho encouraged large women to interview prospective psychologists about their attitudes toward fat and choose one who considers body acceptance, rather than weight loss, a desirable goal.

When a large woman seeks therapy, her wounded self-esteem is often the result of the effects of cultural prejudice and stigma, not a psychological abnormality. What she needs is not to search for the emotional underpinnings of her fat, but to disconnect her self-esteem from her weight, learn how to confront those who put her down, and expose the fallacies of the cultural messages. In the long run, this approach will be much more helpful. Weight loss may be temporary, but a strong sense of self will be permanent. You don't ever have to worry you won't be able to zip it up!

I believe it is the responsibility of therapists to:

- Provide their clients with accurate information about issues of size and weight, including the fact that most weight-loss diets do not work in the long run.

- Help them understand that there are alternatives to dieting that can result in significant improvements to health and well-being even if weight loss does not occur.

- Help them to disassociate self-esteem from weight and recognize that size has nothing to do with one's value as a person.

- Help them to quit postponing their lives by asking, "Is there any reason you can't do this right now?" and then helping them to take the steps, one by one, they need to take to do the things they want to do.

- Help them to start thinking for themselves, challenge the anti-fat messages society sends women, and realize that they are not "flawed," but that society has made them feel that way.

- Help them develop strategies for dealing with people around them who are critical of their weight.

- Help them to become more *resilient* to psychological distress caused by the stigma of overweight. Research has shown that people who are most resilient have not internalized negative stereotypes about overweight people; do not base their self-regard on others' evaluations and opinions; realize that not all things (including weight) are under personal control; and have the resources to cope with rejection so as to not experience any long-lasting psychological distress.[10]

♥ ♥ ♥ From The Heart ♥ ♥ ♥

The Large Patient's Bill of Rights

1. Assume that an overweight patient knows she is overweight.

If she hasn't heard it from a health care professional, she has likely been told by friends, family, or even strangers.

2. Treat larger patients as individuals.

The circumstances that determine an individual's weight differ from person to person. Take time to discuss these factors with the patient. Was she a big child? Has she been a chronic dieter? Has her weight fluctuated considerably or has it been relatively stable?

3. Listen carefully to the patient's presenting problem independent of weight.

Very few patients consider weight to be their primary problem. As Stunkard[11] points out, it is important to remember that patients define the presenting problem. If weight is a precipitating factor, focus on the factors that affect the presenting problem *and* weight. For example, it is not likely to be useful to tell a patient with hyperlipidemia to "lose weight." However, encouraging the same patient to decrease the intake of saturated fat and make small changes in activity will likely influence both weight and lipids. Such advice will be better received by patients who are often told to lose weight as a treatment for many medical problems.

4. Don't assume a large patient is eating excessively.

Studies show that many are not. On the other hand, people with bulimia or binge eating disorder should be referred to the appropriate eating disorder specialists.

5. Consider giving the same advice to larger patients as you do to average-weight patients.

What advice would you give to average-weight patients who present with diabetes, hypertension or hyperlipidemia? Such advice would likely include some combination of diet, activity, and medication and no mention of weight loss itself.

6. Let the patient decide if he/she wants to be weighed unless there is a medical reason that makes it necessary.

It may sound basic, but buy a scale that can weigh all of your patients. You wouldn't think of using a sphygmomanometer that couldn't easily assess high systolic and diastolic pressures. Similarly, scales should not be only for people who weigh less than 300 or 350 pounds. Getting weighed is among the most unpleasant experiences for a large patient in your office; it becomes tortuous and humiliating if a patient weighs more than your scale can accommodate.

7. Have gowns available that fit larger patients.

Many patients report the experience of waiting for a physician examination in a gown that barely covers them. Your patients deserve better.

8. Use larger blood pressure cuffs when appropriate.

Train your staff about the criteria for when larger cuffs are necessary (e.g., arm circumference exceeds a critical value). Such criteria are available from the manufacturer. Inappropriate cuff sizes will lead to inaccurate measurements and treatment recommendations.

9. Provide some armless chairs in your waiting room.

Patients come in different sizes. Larger patients should not be made to feel uncomfortable in chairs made for lean persons.

10. Be hesitant to set a goal weight for the next visit.

Weight loss is extremely variable across patients, even assuming equivalent adherence to diet and exercise. Not reaching a specific number will only lead to frustration. Focus instead on specific lifestyle changes (decreasing the amount of high-fat snack foods, walking at the mall two times a week for 15 minutes).

11. Stay up to date on the latest research about obesity treatment.

You and your patients should know, for instance, that there are limits to how much weight can be lost, and that a ten percent reduction in body weight has positive effects on health. Don't be offended if a large patient brings an educational item to you. Some spend a lot of time keeping up with the research, and just want to share what they've learned with you.

12. Focus on non-weight outcomes.

Discuss how weight and behavior changes can lead to decreases in medication, and improvement in blood pressure, glycemic control or lipid values. Obesity should be treated because of its relationship to health, not to some specific number on a scale.

13. Don't blame patients for a less than desired outcome.

Acknowledge and accept that despite their very best efforts, many patients will not become thin. Obesity remains a complicated issue with few simple, long-term solutions.

14. Emphasize to your patients that their weight has nothing to do with their self-worth.

It is especially important for them to hear this from you because doctors are often regarded as some of the harshest critics of overweight people.

15. Finally, please don't make us afraid to come to you.

Once that happens, we end up avoiding doctors and neglecting essential preventive care.

Letter to a prospective doctor

Dear Dr. _____ ,

I am very interested in my health. I am also a large person. I know the medical profession often feels that fat and health are incompatible, but I seem to have little choice in the "fat" part. I have tried many times to lose weight, but it doesn't seem to be in the cards for me. It's not that I don't care about my health. It's just that dieting hasn't done anything to improve it. I've read that weight cycling may even be harmful in the long run.

I am interested in finding a doctor who will work with me toward better health despite my size. I am also looking for a doctor who understands that:

• Large people are not necessarily overeating, nor are they lazy and inactive.

• *Many of the factors that contribute to a person's size and weight are biological and physiological.*

If I have a medical problem, I hope you won't automatically blame my weight and that you will recommend the same treatment you would prescribe for a thin person with a similar problem.

I understand that you may feel an obligation to point out the risk factors associated with obesity, and I don't object to that. But I also hope that you are familiar with the studies that question whether the consequences of obesity are as dire as we've been led to believe. I am hoping that by focusing on development of a healthy lifestyle, I may alleviate some of these risk factors even if I don't get thin. Perhaps I will also slowly lose some weight. But even if I don't, I will still want to take care of my health.

What I am asking for is unprejudiced care and that my weight be treated as one, but not the only, aspect of my health profile. Will you work with me? I hope the answer is yes. If not, I'll seek medical care elsewhere. Thank you for your consideration.

>*Most sincerely,*
>
>*A Proactive Patient*

11

movers and shakers

I have decided to be a participant in life instead of a spectator. This includes trying things I always thought would be fun and interesting if I lost weight. I am striving to 'un-isolate' myself, get involved in the world around me, become more spontaneous, and join in without trying to figure out how I look or what someone might say.

—RUTHIE

Fat people are lazy—or so the assumption goes. Yet most Americans do not participate in a regular exercise program. According to the results of three national surveys, only 28 percent of adults meet the recommended levels of either moderate or vigorous physical activity, and nearly one-third report no regular physical activity outside of their work.[1] "If you think of yourself as a couch potato, look around—there are spuds of all sizes lounging right there with you," note Pat Lyons and Debby Burgard in *Great Shape: The First Exercise Guide for Large Women*.[2]

Physical activity actually accounts for a very small proportion of our total daily energy expenditure. Involuntary energy expenditure, which is the energy it takes simply to keep our bodies running, uses up about 80 percent of the energy in our daily account.

What is fitness anyway? An American College of Sports Medicine publication says it's the ability to carry out daily tasks without becoming overly tired, and involves participation in both planned and unplanned exercise. By their standards, I am fit. I have a fast-paced day that usually begins at 6:30 a.m. and ends about 11 p.m. I go to a "planned" exercise program twice a week and I use a treadmill at home another couple of days a week. I also get plenty of "unplanned" activity.

We now have so many labor-saving devices that we can literally shop, order food, turn on the TV or CD player, and answer the phone from our couch. While this is all very convenient, it has significantly reduced the time our bodies spend moving—and many experts feel it's the real reason people are getting heavier even though they don't seem to be consuming more calories. In fact, the average daily caloric intake in the U.S. was higher in 1900 than it is now, but Americans are heavier today than they were then.[3]

We're not having fun any more

For many people, the problem with exercise is they have grown to view it as painful and grueling work, certainly not fun. It is something to be "endured," something we have to make time for even though we'd rather be doing almost anything else.

It shouldn't be like that. Exercise should be a way of retreating from the stresses of everyday life, a way of reconnecting with nature, a way of rejuvenating our bodies, minds, and spirits. Lyons and Burgard agree and see it as even more than that: "Movement is a fundamental way of helping women heal damaged self-esteem tied to body image. Living confidently in your body comes from the inside. Feeling at home in your body and getting back in touch with what it needs involves rediscovering the connections between body and mind."

Unless we are exercising for 30 minutes at our "target heart rate" at least three times a week, we feel we have not really done what we're supposed to do, but that just isn't so. We never thought about things like checking our pulse when we were kids, and yet most of us moved significantly more then than we do today. Dallas-based researcher Steven Blair, Ph.D., says: "The greatest benefit comes from changing from being virtually sedentary, which most Americans are, to being moderately active."[4]

You don't have to huff and puff for 30 minutes straight to be more fit. In a Stanford University study, some men walked briskly or jogged for 30 minutes five times a week. The rest exercised at moderate intensity for only ten minutes at three different times during the day. After eight weeks, both groups had achieved virtually the same level of fitness.

The key is finding an activity you truly enjoy, something you like doing *while* you're doing it, not just for the health benefits you assume it provides. "If you don't enjoy it," says Pat Lyons, "you won't keep it up. It becomes just another type of diet. You must find things that bring you pleasure, that energize you, that peel away stress, that make you sleep better at night."

Fitness expert Gail Johnston says that when people struggle with exercise, it's not because they're fitness failures. Most often the activity doesn't match their personality. She recommends distinguishing between play, exercise, and sport, then finding out which one suits you. Most adults, she says, focus on exercise and tend to forget about play and sports.[5] Play, explains Johnston, is meaningless activity. "It is free flowing, incites creativity, stimulates your imagination, and challenges the joyful child inside you." Play can be things like going to an amusement park, dancing, boating, flying a kite, roller blading, ice skating, walking around a zoo. Exercise is what most adults think they have to do to be fit. Exercise is mechanical and very routine. It suits some people, however, who like the structure and predictability of knowing precisely when they will exercise and what they will do. Sports are usually played according to rules, often involve an element of competition, and appeal to people who enjoy a challenge. Again, you need to make sure your personality and the type of exercise you choose are in harmony.

Why exercise?

"Do you know how many calories I'll burn during this workout?" a pretty young newcomer to our water aerobics class asked the other evening. "That's not what's important," I told her. "What's important is that you're improving your health and your fitness level. Since I've been coming here, my blood pressure has gone down, I'm stronger, and I have more endurance. I just feel better." Being very young, she's probably coming for the sole purpose of losing weight, and if that doesn't happen, or doesn't happen fast enough, she may not continue to come.

Although studies clearly show that regular physical activity is essential to achieving and maintaining a healthy weight, there are lots of other reasons to move your body. These include:

- Lowering blood pressure
- Improving glucose tolerance and lowering insulin resistance
- Raising "good" cholesterol, lowering "bad" cholesterol
- Speeding up metabolism
- Preserving muscle
- Perhaps lowering set point weight
- Increasing strength and flexibility
- Improving endurance
- Enhancing self-image
- Increasing energy and mental alertness
- Improving sleep quality
- Relieving stress
- Having fun

Evidence continues to mount that regular exercise is a *bona fide* enhancer of psychological well-being and self-esteem.[6-8] Going further, there is even evidence that exercise is effective in the treatment of clinical depression.[9]

If you are dieting, you should know that dieting without exercise might cause you to lose as much lean muscle tissue as fat. Men and women who combined exercise with dieting lost more weight as fat and preserved more of their muscle and lean tissue.[10, 11] More recent studies are finding that the type of exercise makes even more of a difference. Resistance training appears to preserve more muscle than any other form of exercise.[12]

Memories of gym class

The stereotype is that large people are lazy, and while this may be true for some, it also is true for many thin people. Laziness usually plays very little part in large people's exercise avoidance. So what are the real reasons?

If you're like me, you don't have many good memories of gym class—the uniforms didn't fit, you often felt awkward and uncoordinated, the big kids were often picked last when choosing teams, and the boys may have been laughing at you from the other side of the gym. Pretty soon you developed a mental association between the words "physical activity" and "unpleasant."

Many large people cannot recall any "successful" exercise experiences. They weren't good at it, they received no praise for it, they may have been laughed at. So, as time passed, they learned to avoid it.

Fear of ridicule

"I like women, not horses," a man she didn't know said to a friend of mine who was out walking for exercise. Let's face it. It's no fun to be striding along briskly and suddenly hear a group of fellows making "oinking" noises in your direction, or to be working out at a health club while other patrons are obviously whispering, pointing, and laughing at you.

How many times has an insensitive aerobics instructor bellowed: "Come on ladies—sweat off that ugly fat!" Pardon me, but I think you've just told me that I'm ugly, and this is not very inspiring.

People who make jokes at the expense of large people seem to come out of the woodwork when one decides to engage in some form of physical activity. "It is ironic that while the world screams at fat women to exercise, when we do go out we have to prepare ourselves to deal with insults from all directions," say Lyons and Burgard.[13] I mean, here we are, doing what people say we should do, which is exercise, and our reward is ridicule. We can't win!

If you do become the target of ridicule, "What's most important is not to swallow it," said Lyons when I interviewed her. "Call a friend and get it off your chest. Write it down. Get it outside of you. You can't control other people's comments. But you can control your own reaction. Strengthen your courage muscles while you're strengthening your body muscles!"

Fear of "the spirit's willing, but the body isn't"

"Elbows together!" the water aerobics instructor shouted to us. "Mine won't touch," I replied. "Oh, yes they will!" she shot back at me. "Oh, not they won't," I countered angrily. "I have these two things in the way!" This is a perfect example of the insensitivity of slim instructors to the realities of what larger bodies can and can't do. And I'm not indicting them all. Prior to her, we had an instructor—also very slender—who used to challenge us to touch "opposite elbow to opposite knee." When I pointed out to her that my stomach prevented this, she immediately revised her instruction: "opposite elbow toward your opposite knee is just fine," she said.

I don't think instructors are being intentionally cruel or rigid. They just don't understand that certain movements will be difficult for larger bodies to accomplish. It is for this reason that the Milwaukee YMCA asked me to do a training session with their fitness instructors. It went extremely well and resulted in the initiation of plus-size exercise classes at many of their branches.

When large people can't do what the instructor demands, and if this happens repeatedly, many will feel defeated and simply give up. If, on the other hand, the instructor is sensitive and insightful, she may say something like this: "I know that I'm not a large person, and because of this I may not know how you and your body are feeling about the various movements I'm asking you to do. That's why I will appreciate it if you let me know how specific activities are working out for you and help me create a routine that will be comfortable and satisfying for everyone."

Belief that dieting is more important than exercise

Many people don't bother to exercise if they are cutting calories because they think dieting should be enough. Once they're thin, they rationalize, then they'll exercise. This is another example of the things people put on hold waiting to be slender. For years, people who wanted to lose weight were told to "go on a diet." Rarely did the advice include exercise. We now know that exercise is more important than dieting and that people rarely maintain lost weight without it.

Lack of privacy

Because many have had unpleasant experiences with onlookers, large people often prefer to exercise in a space that is private and removed from "gawkers." Some don't want to watch themselves in a mirror.

The YMCA generally has tried to find private rooms for their plus-size exercise classes rather than hold them in an open area where people can stop to look. They say it has worked well.

Fear of injury

Some large people have physical problems and worry they will hurt themselves if they exercise. Some of our members have knee problems, some have arthritis. For many of the reasons listed earlier, some have not been active for a long time and need to begin very slowly. If this is true for you, consult an exercise physiologist, or consider a form of activity called chair dancing, which I encountered for the first time several years ago at a conference. The program was developed by dance expert Jodi Stolove who, because of a fractured ankle, had to teach dance classes for a time while seated in a chair. For more information try 1-800-551-4386, 619-793-1177, www.chairdancing.com, or write to Chair Dancing International, Inc., 2658 Del Mar Heights Rd., Del Mar, CA 92014.

Some people think they're just too fat to exercise. But consider the saga of Lynne Cox, a woman with an impressive history of long-distance swimming achievements. Cox has broken the men's and women's world record for swimming the 21-mile English Channel, and she was the first swimmer to cross the notorious stretches of water between Denmark and Sweden, Norway and Sweden, and the Strait of Magellan between mainland Chile and Tierra del Fuego. In 1986 she swam 12 bodies of water in a route that took her around the world in 80 days! At the time she was five-feet six-inches tall and weighed 209 pounds.[14]

Not having appropriate attire

It's interesting to note that in one survey, women said they avoid exercise classes because they don't know what to wear or don't feel they'll be able to find appropriate exercise clothing. Once again, the women in fitness club ads are usually attired in fancy, skin-hugging leotards. Many wouldn't want to wear this kind of outfit, and even if they did, wouldn't know where to find one.

This situation is rather easily remedied. First, it matters little what you wear to move about in. Almost anything in a loose knit or fleece will do fine. And some manufacturers are catching on and making exercise wear in larger sizes, which can be found in many catalogs. I have listed mail-order sources for plus-size exercise wear in the Resource Section, but want to single out one of them for special mention as they do such a great job in this area. If you want to be a "fitness fashion plate," call or go online for a Junonia catalog (www.junonia.com or call 800-671-0175).

Removing barriers

Pat Lyons and Debby Burgard suggest taking a sheet of paper and dividing it into two columns. In the first column list all your fears and anxieties about getting involved in physical activity. In the second column write: "What I can do about them." There's almost always a solution. If you're concerned that your knees can't take the jarring of hard surfaces, consider water activity. If you're afraid of being heckled, opt for a more private location, such as an exercise video in your home, or decide that there's strength in numbers and walk with friends.

Probably the biggest obstacle for people of any size is time. I've found it's true that "you just have to make time." I have what amounts to two jobs at this point, in addition to taking care of a home, doing errands, and finding time for my husband and friends. It would be all too easy for me to say, "I have no time" when it comes to exercise. But I've decided that exercise is a top priority in my life, even if it means saying no to other things.

Planning is key

You don't necessarily have to exercise in one burst. Experts now say that exercise spaced throughout the day is just as effective as one 30-minute session. So if you can find ten minutes several times a day, you're all set. How about ten minutes with an exercise video in the morning, a ten-minute walk at lunch and ten minutes of activity after dinner?

Be sure you're exercising at your peak times. Some people can jump out of bed and put in their daily exercise right then and there, while some are best right after work. You know your internal time clock best. Be sure you're paying attention to it.

Pat Lyons advises: "Instead of viewing exercise as a separate part of your life, look at what you already do and add to that. Do you go grocery shopping? Park farther away. Do you do housework? Put on music and stretch and boogie while you're dusting. Walk up the stairs a little more. Walk to stores that are near you." In fact, a study done at the Cooper Institute for Aerobic Research in Dallas found in a two-year trial that while structured exercise led to bigger temporary gains in fitness, changing habits was a more lasting way to improve health. After 18 months of follow-up, the gains made by the exercise group declined, while those who had changed their daily lifestyle into a more active one made steady and lasting improvements.

If all else fails, you may need to schedule exercise as an appointment on your calendar.

Go to a class or go it alone?

You've made the decision to get more activity, but should you go to a class or do something at home? In one study, women were divided into two groups. Group exercise participants attended three supervised exercise classes per week, while the second group was told to complete all exercise in their home environments. After 12 months, the home-based people were doing much better in terms of performance and adherence. They had also lost more weight.[15] In another study, people who exercised at home with a treadmill maintained the highest level of exercise, and the researchers felt that easy access to equipment was a big factor in their ongoing progress.[16] (As an aside, it was found at the Sports Performance and Technology Laboratory at the Medical College of Wisconsin that people burned more calories and improved cardiovascular fitness more effectively on a treadmill than on five other common pieces of exercise equipment, including stationary bikes.)

In the final analysis, only you can decide what works best for you—going to a class, going it alone, or perhaps a combination of both.

Fit and fat

One common assumption is that fat people can't possibly be fit. Some experts disagree. A female walker with an ample rear is probably more fit than a slim sedentary woman. West Georgia College professor Krissa Baylor has found that women who were pleased with their weight and appearance regarded themselves as fit even if they did not exercise. This is simply another offshoot of the misguided notion that we have to be thin before we can be healthy. Let's stop regarding "fitness" and "fatness" as either/or conditions. Try putting an "and" there for a change and see what happens!

Low fitness was associated with greater mortality in men of all weights. In a ten-year study of more than 25,000 men, larger men with low fitness were more than twice as likely to die compared with larger men who were fit.[17] Lead researcher Steven Blair says large people can improve their health solely by exercising, even if they don't become thin—and exercise, he says, is an attainable goal. "Thirty years ago, I was short, fat, and bald," he said. "Today I am short, fat, and bald. But I have run 100,000 kilometers (62,500 miles) in the last 30 years."

What did you like to do as a child?

This is one of the first questions that a friend of mine, an exercise physiologist, asks people who come to him for help in designing an exercise program.

We moved a lot more when we were young. I was at the beach every day during the summer—and not to lie on a blanket and get a tan. I was there to do some serious swimming, and eventually I got my lifesaving badge. I went horseback riding, roller skating, dancing. And many evenings I'd call my girlfriend and say, "Want to go for a walk?" Usually past the house of some boy one of us liked! We got plenty of activity and we weren't making a conscious decision to "exercise." Moving our bodies was just a natural part of our lives. And we didn't call it "exercise." It was "play," "fun," "recreation." Look closely at the last word—recreation. Recreate. We were "recreating" ourselves, doing things that left us mentally and physically refreshed and renewed. Think back to how you felt after an afternoon of dancing or roller skating. You felt good, reinvigorated, and you slept well.

If we could rekindle the spontaneous playfulness of our youth, we would not have to view exercise as a burden to be squeezed into a busy schedule; it would come automatically. It would be integrated into the part of our lives earmarked for fun and recreation.

So if you were to ask yourself the question, "What did I like to do as a child?" what would your answers be?

- Swimming
- Bike riding
- Roller skating
- Ice skating
- Jumping rope
- Playing tennis, badminton, volleyball
- Sled riding
- Making a snowman
- Dancing
- Flying a kite

You can still do these things! One friend of mine just bought some roller blades and is having a ball. She sometimes takes them to the lakefront, where she can glide along enjoying the view and the breeze.

Glenna Dunaway, president of Big in Sports, based in Lansing, Michigan, suggested in an interview with *BBW* magazine that large women consider the benefits of skating. She feels skating is an ideal sport for large women: "It's great for strengthening and developing the body without jarring. It's a non-impact sport."

Did you like to dance? Dancing is one of the most enjoyable, yet one of the most neglected, forms of cardiovascular conditioning. You don't even have to leave your home. As a collector of old 45 records, this works well for me. I still have a 45-record turntable. A couple times a week I stack 'em up and stage my own personal sock hop! A tape or CD player can work just as well, given all the dance music collections that are now available—disco mixes work great.

My dad and I used to go to the beach and fly kites. I don't think there's any age limit on this activity! And it's one of those things that can be a family affair.

Rediscover the outdoors

I don't think we spend enough time outdoors. Once again, we did when we were young, but then we got older, acquired more responsibilities, and came inside. Gradually we forgot the refreshing, invigorating feeling of being outdoors, soaking up the fresh air, the warm and cool breezes, the aromas of nature.

Playing was often done outdoors. "I'm going outside to play," I'd tell my mother. We'd do things outdoors as a family. Every summer my father put up a badminton net in the back yard. Or we'd toss balls back and forth. Even a game of croquet, while not terribly strenuous, got us out from in front of the TV and into the fresh air.

While you may not be ready to strap on a backpack and go camping in the Sierra Nevada mountains like exercise enthusiast and size acceptance-advocate Pat Lyons, you may be interested in some of her other suggestions: hiking, rowing, canoeing, cross-country skiing. Or if those seem too strenuous, how about archery, golf, sailing, Frisbee?

Staying indoors may also relate back to the fear of ridicule. Stepping outside instantly renders you vulnerable to the scrutiny of strangers, and sometimes this scrutiny leads to cruel remarks. But the outdoors belongs to you every bit as much as it does to "them," and I've decided that the benefits of being outdoors far outweigh the momentary sting of an infrequent insult.

Other options for outdoor activity:

• Planting and tending a garden
• Bird watching, star gazing
• Taking a nature walk and identifying different flowers and plants
• Walking your dog
• Picking your own apples, cherries or strawberries
• Washing your car

And if you simply prefer indoor activity, that's fine. Going to a class does take more time, and some people just aren't "groupies." There are plenty of options for indoor activity, including home exercise equipment, exercise videos, and dancing. Several exercise videos featuring large women are available (see Resource Section).

Walking

Walking is the form of exercise most often recommended to large people. It's assumed to be something everyone can do, and it requires no special equipment except a good pair of walking shoes. While this is generally true, it may or may not be your "thing." Frankly, I would much rather swim than walk, although I do try to take a walk a couple of times a week.

What's more, if you haven't been getting much physical activity, brisk walking can be taxing. As far as I'm concerned, the guidelines for walking are too ambitious for people just starting out. They often advise: Start with a mile and work up to three miles in a few weeks. Some people—and not just large people—would have trouble starting with a mile. For them, a block might be a good starting point and a mile the long-term goal. Many people will never ever walk three, four, or five miles. And if they think that nothing less will do, they often don't do anything at all.

I also think we would be better off to forget going at a gallop to "get our heart rates up" and to concentrate on walking for the enjoyment of being outdoors and flexing our bodies. So why not:

- Take a "stroll." If you never walk more than a few blocks, it's better than doing nothing at all. Find a pace that's enjoyable. Count trees, flowers, or stars—not heartbeats. One study showed that regular strolling can dramatically reduce the risk of heart disease. People who covered a mile in 15 to 20 minutes reaped the same six percent hike in HDL or "good" cholesterol as people who walked a 12-minute mile.[18]

- Vary your route. Find new places to walk, such as along a river or lake, through gardens, a park, historic district, college campus, trendy shopping area, or neighborhood with interesting homes; across a college campus. Drive there and park if you have to. Why not sit down each week and decide where you'll walk? Do it as a family and take turns picking spots.

- Walk with friends. Kill two birds with one stone. Move your body and catch up on your friends' lives. We often say we're too busy to exercise and too busy to see our friends. Make a walking date and you've accomplished both.

- Visit museums. Museums and galleries usually require a good deal of walking, plus you'll be seeing some interesting things.

People who have avoided exercise for a long time and may not have the stamina initially to go around the block, should consider "house walking." I have a friend who goes to her basement and walks around as if she were walking on a track.

Make it a family affair

Kids are getting larger—but they're not really eating any more. What's going on? Many experts feel it's got little to do with food, but a lot to do with activity levels. We were having dinner with friends the other night and got to talking about what kids do nowadays for fun. "They just sit," my friend said, "with their electronic games and play for hours on end." We never had electronic games. As I said before, our "play" was usually physical.

Parents have to take the lead in making physical activity a family priority, perhaps by earmarking several hours each week for "family physicals." Some suggestions are:

- Have a family dance: Play tapes from now and from when you were young. Demonstrate the dances you did as a teenager and have your kids show you today's steps.
- Go out walking as a family and alternate having each family member pick the spot where you'll hike.
- Set up some backyard games, such as volleyball or badminton.
- Go biking.

A message to the fitness industry

Generally speaking, the fitness industry has not put out the welcome mat for large people. I often hear, "The only people who go to fitness clubs are people who are already thin and fit."

When I do seminars for fitness professionals, I ask them, "Why should you bother with large people?" My answer is because:

- We're one-third of the population.
- It makes economic sense: We have money and we're willing to spend it if you provide services that meet our needs.
- The market for plus-size fitness is wide open. Very little has been developed for this population.
- Research clearly shows that weight management without exercise will not be effective.
- We deserve to reap the same health and fitness benefits as thinner people.

Ads for fitness clubs portraying reed-thin celebrities do not convey the message that we're welcome. Most of us will never look like them no matter how much we bounce up and down. Just once I'd like to see a picture of some "real" people in these ads.

It's ironic that the fitness industry tends to ignore the very people who are being told that exercise is what they need most. A veritable bonanza awaits those who discover we exist and extend us an invitation to the ball.

I often tell large people that they may need to take the lead in advocating for development of plus-size fitness programs. There's no reason why you can't approach your local YMCA, YWCA, or other fitness facility about starting a class, or why you can't help to educate them using the material presented here (along with anything else you may choose to add). Here's what I advise when I do seminars for fitness club personnel:

- Do treat large patrons with respect and understanding. Have an educational session for your entire staff. Dispel myths about large people and provide accurate information.

- Do pay extra attention to the large people who are new to your facility. Chances are it took courage for those people to walk through your door. Make an extra effort to be sure they're comfortable, that they have what they need, and that they know they're welcome.

- Do be a keen observer of what's working and what isn't. Large bodies may not be able to perform the same moves that thin bodies can. Be ready to suggest an alternate movement or a different piece of equipment. Demonstrate at a pace that's sustainable for most.

- Do invite and be very receptive to feedback from participants. Tell them you're counting on them to help you develop the program and you would welcome their advice and suggestions.

- Do let your large customers know where they can buy plus-size exercise clothing.

- Do try to find a private setting for a plus-size exercise class. Do you have a private room where you could hold a class? It doesn't have to be fancy, but free of mirrors might be best.

- Do focus on what your large members can do rather than what they can't, and praise them for it. Many big people have never been praised for anything physical.

- Do not make weight loss the only goal. Tell your large-size clients it's more important that they improve their health.

- Do not bellow things like "Let's get rid of that ugly fat!" Remarks such as this just drive another nail in the coffin of a negative self-image.

- Do not permit staff or other patrons to ridicule large-size patrons. After a seminar I gave at a fitness club, an especially sensitive young man said: "It's not only our staff that we may have to educate, but our other patrons. We have to make it clear that we will not tolerate rude remarks about fat people from anyone on our premises."

I have noticed that in some facilities the exercise equipment is so crowded together, a larger body might have trouble fitting between the machines. Seats on exercise bicycles may be small and uncomfortable. This does not mean redesigning the whole facility, but how about just a couple of bicycles with larger seats?

I understand that an exercise facility without scales would be like Beavis without Butthead. But that doesn't mean weighing and measuring have to be mandatory. When I spoke recently at a local health club, I advised the staff that a lot of large people prefer not to be weighed and measured. One of the club owners was genuinely surprised. "I thought everybody wanted to be weighed," he said. He had no problem with the idea that they didn't. He just wasn't aware of it.

But will I lose weight?

If weight loss is your only goal, you're bound to be disappointed. Studies show that losses resulting from exercise are small. But researchers continue to point out that the health benefits that accrue from exercise are much more important.[19]

If you have been inactive and you start exercising regularly, chances are you will lose some weight (I'm assuming your food intake remains about the same). But unless you start to value equally the multitude of other health benefits of exercise, you may not be able to keep yourself motivated. If losing weight is your only reason for exercising and the weight loss ceases or isn't all you expected, you're apt to throw in the towel.

Every time I take my blood pressure and see that the numbers are lower than they were before I started exercising regularly, I know I will keep it up. Every time I slip into the pool after a busy day at work and feel the stress melting away, I know I want to keep coming back. Every time I run from my basement to the second floor of my house and realize I'm not out of breath, the benefits of my exercise are evident. Every time I come home from the pool with more energy than I had before I went, I know this is a lifelong habit!

 From The Heart

Moving Experiences

I want to be a cheerleader, and so I try out.
But they reject me, saying: You're just too stout."

I'd like to be a majorette and twirl a baton—
I'm hurt when they say, "The uniform won't fit you," but I don't let on.

I yearn to be a modern dancer and interpret the songs,
But to be seen in a leotard, they say my body's all wrong.

I decide to play basketball, and I'm not half bad,
But no team wants me—I feel kind of sad.

I love rock 'n roll, and I go to the dance.
The thin girls have partners, but I don't stand a chance.

I go to the beach—at swimming I excel.
But back on the sand, "It's Orca!" they yell.

Ice skating's fun, but people aren't very nice.
When they see me glide by, they yell, "She'll just break the ice!"

After awhile, the message is clear:
You should get some exercise, but just not right here.

But if I don't move it, my body bridles,
It needs to move; it's not happy being idle.

So I'll risk the taunts and ignore the jeers.
I can't allow my body to be governed by fears.

I'll continue to swim and twist and shout;
My health, after all, is what it's all about!

12

so you still want to lose weight?

For a long time, I sat in the house not wanting to go out and be with people. I hated what I looked like. I felt people judged me according to my size. One day my doctor suggested I see a dietitian. With tears in my eyes, I sat down with her and poured my heart out. She suggested that I needed moral support and a change in my self-esteem more than I needed to be put on a diet. She then gave me some literature about a group called Largely Positive. I started coming to the meetings. I now have a different viewpoint about food, and I'm beginning to like myself.

—BRENDA

People who come to our group for the first time are sometimes surprised—and disappointed—to find out that we don't have a diet to give them. When I explain that our goals are health and self-acceptance, some ask: "But isn't that just giving up? Aren't you just fooling yourselves?" My answer is: "I'd be fooling you if I said I knew of a sure way to lose weight and keep it off."

That doesn't stop people from continuing to try. In a year 2000 survey of almost 4,000 adults and 500 adolescents, more than half (53 percent) said they were currently engaged in "weight-control behaviors." Regrettably, about one-fourth of all those surveyed and one-third of adolescent girls were using methods deemed "unhealthy."[1] The bottom line is that no one really knows how to help the majority of larger people lose weight and keep it off permanently.

When I created Largely Positive, I promised that I would always try to tell people the truth. I have found, however, that when it comes to issues of size and weight, the truth is not always what people want to hear. Researcher Janet Polivy agrees: "What I have to say—that there is no magical solution to losing weight—the public doesn't want to hear." She adds: "It's time we started treating body weight more like height, as a biologically-determined trait. You don't see short people hanging from door frames trying to stretch themselves out or tall people carrying around weights in hopes of shrinking a few inches."[2]

The problem with most commercial weight-loss programs is that their advice often bears little resemblance to that of experts who conduct studies on obesity. Rapid weight loss is a prime example of something the diet industry advocates and the research community repudiates because quick weight loss carries with it an almost 100 percent guarantee that the weight will be regained.

Mixed messages

Lately, there seem to be a lot of mixed messages in the news about issues of size and weight.

"Yo-yo dieting okay after all!" the headlines proclaim. But since no one has found a way to keep weight off permanently, does that mean we should just continue to yo-yo? And how is it that *all* the studies that have found yo-yo dieting to be harmful are suddenly discredited?

"Search is on for fat genes," another headline announces. One researcher involved tells me he hopes their investigation will someday make it possible to intervene genetically to prevent the development of obesity. Until then, he feels "diets are no more successful than they've ever been." A few days later we're advised of a national campaign to help Americans lose weight. Thankfully, those issuing this challenge acknowledge that the billions of dollars spent on traditional dieting haven't helped much. But what do we do instead? They advise lifestyle changes, such as increased exercise and healthy eating. Largely Positive advocates the same. But there's still no guarantee every large person who makes these changes will become thin—although moderate weight loss may occur for some.

Often, when the difficulties of permanent weight loss *are* acknowledged, people with health problems, such as diabetes, are advised that they should still try to lose weight. While I don't disagree that moderate weight loss has been shown to improve blood sugar control in diabetics, how are these individuals expected to be any more successful losing weight than other large people? What's more, some experts believe that weight loss for Type II, insulin-resistant diabetics may be even more difficult, due to the presence in their bodies of excess insulin (and an overload of insulin is believed to cause weight gain).

Why all the mixed messages? Because the popular desire for weight loss often operates independent of science. How then does one sort it all out? Here's my thinking:

1. Science does not yet have the answers.

2. That fact won't stop people from trying to lose weight.

3. Some people may be able to lose some weight by making lifestyle changes and losing the weight slowly.

4. Even so, many large people will still not become thin, but they may become healthier.

How many Americans are "overweight?"

The government now says that about 97 million American adults, or 55 percent of people over 20 years old, are overweight or obese.

What's the difference between being "overweight" and being "obese?" It depends on your body mass index, or BMI, the measurement that is now in vogue. The National Institutes of Health (NIH) says that anyone with a body mass index (a ratio between your height and weight) of 25 or more—someone, for example, who is five foot four inches and 145 pounds—is "overweight." People with a body mass index of 30 or above—such as someone who is five foot six inches and weighs 186 pounds—are considered "obese." NIH estimates that more than half of U.S. adults are "overweight" and about one-quarter of these are "obese."

The number of people considered "obese" has risen much faster since 1960 than those considered "overweight." Between 1960 and 1994, the prevalence of obesity almost doubled (from 13 to 22 percent)—with most of this increase occurring in the decade of the 90s.[3]

Why the increase? One observer offered this explanation: "As a nation, we do not seem to be hearing the message about the long-term risks of being overweight, or we do not care, or we are woefully unsuccessful in being able to control our weight." I take issue with statements like this. First of all, "not getting the message" implies I'm stupid or I've been living on another planet. How could a person in this society "not get the message?" It's just that getting the message and having an answer for it are two different things.

"Do not care?" Now we're back to the "lazy and slothful" stereotype. Once again, I beg to differ! I'm exercising. I'm eating well. I'm looking after my health. Does this sound like a person who "doesn't care?" How about "woefully unsuccessful at being able to control our weight?" It's true that most weight loss attempts fail, but the use of the words "woefully" and "control" signal that the writer believes it's the fault of the dieters. Sorry, but the research indicates otherwise.

There continues to be a widely-held belief that large people are ignoring the advice of health experts and that they just don't care or have given up. I don't see that in my work. I see people who are genuinely concerned about their health and are trying very hard to do things that will improve it. Obesity experts seem to agree:

> *Obesity is not increasing because people are consciously trying to gain weight. In fact, tens of millions of people in this country are dieting at any one time . . . Obesity is a multifactorial disease of appetite regulation involving genetics, physiology, biochemistry, and the neurosciences, as well as environmental, psychosocial, and cultural factors. Unfortunately, the lay public and health-care providers, as well as insurance companies, often view it simply as a problem of willful misconduct— eating too much and exercising too little. Obesity is a remarkable disease in terms of the effort required by an individual for its management and the extent of discrimination its victims suffer.[4]*

Are we just eating more? Studies suggest that Americans are *eating out* more, relying more heavily on convenience foods, and eating larger portions ("supersizing"). And the U.S. Department of Agriculture (USDA) claims that, despite the low-fat frenzy, Americans' daily fat consumption slightly increased between 1989 and 1995, as did calorie intake.

Many experts point to increasingly sedentary lifestyles as the primary cause for the rise in obesity, especially childhood obesity. Television, they say, is one of the biggest culprits. Seems obvious, right? As we have already seen with many other weight-related issues, the findings are conflicting. Examples:

- Among adolescent girls, television-viewing time appears to have only weak, if any, meaningful association with fatness. *(Pediatrics, February 1993)*

- Television viewing behavior was not associated with body composition in children. *(Pediatrics, October 1994)*

- Children who watched TV for more than five hours a day were more likely to be overweight than those watching two hours or less. *(Archives of Pediatric and Adolescent Medicine, April 1996)*

- Fast food and TV viewing hours were linked with fatness in women, but not men. *(American Journal of Public Health, February 1998)*

- The more hours spent watching television, the more likely Australian adults were to be overweight; however "physical activity was not directly associated with being overweight." *(International Journal of Obesity, May 2000)*

Most experts believe that environmental factors have to be the cause of recent increases in the number of people considered overweight. Genetic factors, they say, take much longer to manifest themselves. But maybe genetic factors *are* involved, even in the short term. At least one intriguing study asks us to consider the possibility of "assortative mating." This means that larger women tend to tie the knot with larger men—and that the children resulting from these unions have a much greater chance of also being "overweight."[5]

Are we pathologizing the normal?

"Should obesity be treated at all?" is the question posed by Susan C. Wooley and her husband Orland W. Wooley in a chapter from *Eating and Its Disorders.*[6] The Wooleys, who are affiliated with the University of Cincinnati, point out that:

- In many cases, obese patients have little or no abnormality of behavior to be corrected.
- Most people regain lost weight.
- A number of studies have called into question the belief that to become thinner is to become healthier.

Given the ineffectiveness of current treatments, mounting evidence that obesity is rooted in biology, and the debate over health risks, the Wooleys conclude: "It is very hard to construct a rational case for treating any but massive, life-endangering obesity." They are quick to add, however, that the largest patients are often among the most difficult to treat by conservative methods, and that risky procedures, such as surgery, may produce more complications than the condition they are meant to correct.

More recently, Dr. Susan Wooley was joined by eating disorders expert David Garner, Ph.D., in taking a comprehensive look at traditional dieting as a cure for obesity. After an exhaustive review, they concluded: "Most approaches lead to weight loss during active treatment, and many individuals continue to lose in the interval directly following treatment; however, most participants ultimately regain to levels that approximate their pretreatment weight."[7]

Are we pathologizing normal behavior? Do we label eating behavior that is normal in non-overweight people as abnormal in larger people? In many cases, I think we do. My friend Debbie, who is thin, says she and some friends were having a conversation about food one evening. "We were talking about how we can sometimes go through a whole bag of potato chips or a box of Girl Scout cookies or a quart of ice cream. Another friend, a large woman, wasn't saying much. But after awhile, she looked at us and said, 'You mean you do that too?' She was so surprised that we all had experiences like that."

There are times, my friend confessed to me, while driving home from work that she thinks about the ice cream she knows is waiting for her in her refrigerator and how good it's going to taste. When large people do this, it's called pathology and they have to record it in their food diaries.

I spoke with another colleague, also slender, about eating habits. I told her I no longer deprive myself of foods I enjoy. "If I want candy," I said, "I eat a few pieces–I don't eat the whole bag though." She replied, "I sometimes do!"

Anthropologist Margaret Mackenzie sees a curiosity of the human species: "We blame ourselves, not the method. It's a human trait in all parts of the world—to keep trying the same solution, even when it's not working. You think it's you, not the solution, that's not good enough."[8] *You* have not failed—the process of dieting has failed you!

Why dieting isn't a good idea

Personally, I will never "diet" again, if by dieting we are referring to food taboos, restriction, and deprivation. Why do I say this? Plain and simple, it doesn't work. The long-term results haven't changed:

- In follow-up studies of dieters between 1977 and 1986, the average weight loss was 8.5 percent (of total body weight)—no different, the authors noted, from the average weight loss of 8.9 percent in similar studies between 1966 and 1976.[9] And they concluded: "Weight regain was the usual outcome."

- In a 1995 study, it was the "same-old": Those who completed weight-loss programs lost approximately 10 percent of their body weight, only to gain two-thirds of it back within one year and almost all of it back within five years.[10]

As we have already seen in Chapter 2, repeated dieting has been linked in some studies to decreased metabolic rates, the development of hypertension, long-term weight gain, loss of muscle and redistribution as fat.

Other dieting woes can include:

- Fatigue, dry skin and hair, intolerance to cold temperatures, constipation and depression.[11]

- Intensified cravings for fatty foods as well as sweets. People who are not restrictive dieters, it has been found, are naturally satisfied after eating a relatively small quantity of sweets. Dieters, however, find that their desire for sweets greatly intensifies.

- Gallstone formation. University of Alabama researchers have found that very low calorie levels and rapid weight loss are associated with increased gallstone risk.[12]

- Bone loss. Large women in one study lost two to three percent of their bone mass while dieting even though they were getting more than the recommended 800 milligrams of calcium each day.[13]
- Possible drinking problems. Eating disorder specialist Dean Krahn, professor of psychiatry at the University of Wisconsin at Madison, has found a "pretty direct relationship between the severity of dieting and drinking." The reason for the relationship is not fully understood, said Krahn, although he speculates that "perhaps a woman who deprives herself of good-tasting food is making herself vulnerable to the rewarding aspects of alcohol."
- Depression. Being chronically hungry causes all sorts of unpleasant physiological and psychological effects. Albert Stunkard concluded in his book *The Pain of Obesity* that "most forms of dieting carry with them a high likelihood of emotional disturbances," most notably depression.[14]

Dieting's unpleasant effects were dramatically demonstrated in a 1950 study of human starvation involving 36 normal, healthy men who agreed to three months of normal eating, six months of semistarvation, and three months to resume normal eating. The semistarvation calorie level? 1,570 calories a day! In the semistarvation phase, the men became obsessive about their daily food intake, their metabolic rates dropped, and they experienced a host of other unpleasant side effects including weakness, fatigue, edema, and skin problems. They withdrew socially, spent more time alone, and became quite self-centered. Sound familiar? Kind of like a dieting person? When the men resumed normal eating, they ate compulsively, even after they were no longer hungry, until they returned to their pre-starvation weight.

The normal daily intake for adults is around 2,400 to 3,000 calories. Yet most commercial weight-loss programs range from 945 to 1,200 calories a day. The World Health Organization defines starvation (the point at which the body is dying) as 900 calories or less a day.

Noted obesity researcher Dr. Jules Hirsch of Rockefeller University, interviewed for this book, says that while he feels science is closer to some answers about obesity, "diets are no more successful than they've ever been." Yes, he said, people can lose weight—"it's just that we don't know how to help them keep it off permanently." But he agrees that "absolutely, we need to absolve large people of the guilt so many of them feel because of their weight."

What is binge eating?

You are *not* a binge eater if you:

- Have dessert.
- Have a candy bar or an ice cream cone a few times a week.
- Go out for a steak dinner and eat every morsel.
- Eat to soothe yourself after a hard day.

Everyone does these things now and then. If I ask at a workshop: "How many of you consider yourselves to be binge eaters?" almost every hand will go up. And yet, when we do a careful assessment using criteria developed by researchers, few actually fit the profile. This is because many people have come to regard restrictive dieting as "normal eating" and feel they must be out of control if they give in to the desire for an ice cream cone. What they don't realize is that "normal eating" *includes* occasional sweets and most of the foods dieters regard as "forbidden."

Binge eating has two main features:

- A sense of loss of control over eating, and
- Eating a significantly larger amount of food in a given period of time than most people would eat in this same time.

Other symptoms of binge eating are:

- Eating more rapidly than usual
- Eating till uncomfortably full
- Eating large amounts of food though not hungry
- Eating large amounts of food throughout the day with no planned mealtimes
- Eating alone because of embarrassment over the amount of food one is eating
- Feelings of distress and disgust after overeating[15]

When women at a Largely Positive workshop took a quiz designed to identify binge-eating patterns, only three of the 18 attendees fit the binge-eating profile. Most were surprised they didn't meet the criteria. So I asked: "What made you think you were a binge eater?" They replied:

- "Sometimes I eat six or seven cookies at a time."
- "Sometimes I eat dessert when I know I shouldn't."
- "Sometimes I eat when I'm not hungry."
- "I eat candy every day."
- "I eat food that I know is 'bad.'"

What most end up describing is normal eating. What is normal eating? The best definition I've encountered comes from dietitian Ellyn Satter's book, *How to Get Your Kid to Eat, But Not too Much*. It goes like this:

> *Normal eating is being able to eat when you are hungry and continue eating until you are satisfied. It is being able to choose food you like and eat it and truly get enough of it—not just stop eating because you think you should. Normal eating is being able to use some moderate constraint in your food selection to get the right food, but not being so restrictive that you miss out on pleasurable foods. Normal eating is giving yourself permission to eat sometimes because you are happy, sad or bored, or just because it feels good. Normal eating is three meals a day most of the time, but it can also be choosing to munch along. It is leaving some cookies on the plate because you know you can have some again tomorrow, or it is eating more now because they taste so wonderful when they are fresh. Normal eating is overeating at times; feeling stuffed and uncomfortable. It is also under-eating at times and wishing you had more. Normal eating is trusting your body to make up for your mistakes in eating. Normal eating takes up some of your time and attention, but keeps its place as only one important area of your life. In short, normal eating is flexible. It varies in response to your emotions, your schedule, your hunger and your proximity to food.*[16]

The amount of food eaten in a true binge can range from 15,000 to 20,000 calories in one sitting. People who *think* they binge often eat far less than that—the "binges" of people in one study contained fewer than 600 calories.[17]

How common is binge eating?

Binge eating appears to be more common among people *who seek treatment* for weight loss than among those who don't. It was found in one study that 30 percent of the participants in weight-control programs met the criteria for binge-eating disorder (which still leaves two-thirds who were *not* binge eaters, even among this population). What about larger people in general? In a random sample of people regarded as "overweight," only three percent reported problems with binge eating.[18]

Binge eaters may not be big. "There appear to be a substantial number of normal weight individuals who engage in binge eating . . . Binge eating is not confined to the overweight population, nor does it invariably produce overweight," say the husband/wife research team of Janet Polivy and C. Peter Herman.[19]

What causes binge eating?

Although researchers have found similarities among people with binge-eating disorder, this doesn't mean they know what causes the problem or how to effectively treat it. Rena Wing, Ph.D., says: "At the present time, we know very little about the causes of binge eating among overweight people."

Other researchers, most notably Janet Polivy, believe they do have some answers. Polivy's research has led her to the conclusion that dieting is the precursor to binge eating. "Bingers, in short, tend to be dieters," she says. Some experts agree. Some don't. One study links binge eating to "dietary restraint";[20] another says that dieting is a "risk factor," but not necessarily a precursor to the development of binge eating;[21] and a more recent study says "concerns that dieting induces eating disorders . . . are generally not supported by empirical studies."[22] But guess what? This same study concluded that "nondieting approaches seem to lead to improvements in mood and self-esteem," although weight loss is minimal. Sound familiar? Sound pretty close to what I'm advocating in this book?

Newer studies are looking into biological explanations for binge eating. Evidence is accumulating that the tendency toward binge eating may actually be inherited,[23] that metabolic abnormalities may be involved,[24] and that a lack of serotonin may play a part.[25] (Serotonin is a biochemical in the body that plays a part in controlling moods.)

Treating binge eating

There is still a lot to be learned about treating binge eating. Cognitive-behavioral therapy seems promising.[26] This is a process that helps people to stop dieting, abandon distorted thoughts and "rules" concerning food, and identify and alter triggers for binge eating. Increasingly, drug therapy is being used, including the antidepressants fluvoxamine[27] and sertraline.[28] More recently, topiramate, a drug used in treating epilepsy, is being tested as a treatment for binge-eating disorder (after it was noticed that the patients being treated with this drug for epilepsy had a reduced appetite and had lost weight).[29]

Other approaches for treating compulsive eating have been set forth by people who have experienced the problem firsthand and have found their own way to conquer it. Once again, I think it is important to remember that a particular approach may work for one person but not another. Your best bet may be to have a professional help you sort out the alternatives. Among these approaches are:

- *Overcoming Overeating.* Developed by Jane Hirschmann and Carol Munter, the core concept of this approach is "demand feeding." Their treatment involves an end to dieting, "legalizing" all food, learning to distinguish between stomach hunger and mouth hunger, and reconnecting with stomach hunger through "demand feeding." I heard Munter and Hirschmann say at a conference that the only way to confront compulsive eating is to accept yourself and begin living as if you will never lose another ounce. This, they say, will free you to deal with issues of self-awareness rather than dieting.

- *Breaking Free.* Geneen Roth, creator of this concept, believes the basis of compulsive eating is emotional and that people need to learn to eat when hungry and deal with the emotional conflicts they bury with food. She delivers her message in her "Breaking Free" workshops. Roth has written a number of books.

Dr. Janet Polivy firmly believes that the only way to stop people from overeating is to stop them from restraining their eating. "If people are allowed to eat everything, they are less inclined to overeat. People overeat when they think it's their one opportunity to eat a food they like."[30]

Women worry that if they stop restraining themselves, they'll go on a feeding frenzy. But this is not the experience of many people who've tried it. Here's what one of our members had to say:

When I decided to go into business at home, my biggest fear was that I would eat all day long, being near the refrigerator. But since I have given myself permission to eat what I want, when I want, I don't fear the proximity of food. I know that since I won't be dieting tomorrow, I can choose not to eat something today and it will still be in the refrigerator when I'm ready. Giving myself this type of permission to eat and promising myself that 'I won't starve myself tomorrow no matter how much I pig out today' finally stopped the bingeing. It really did! No need to stuff myself simply because it was the 'last day before the diet.' I thought I would just eat and eat and eat if I 'let myself go,' but I didn't. It was the self-imposed starvation and dieting that made me so ferociously hungry that I couldn't stop.

Another member found much the same thing to be true:

I am now doing almost everything with the confidence and poise that comes with true self-esteem. I have also been more consistent in my pursuit of a healthy lifestyle. I'm now on the right course to my 'healthy best' even if that is not fashion model thinness. Since I've done this, any episodes of overeating disappeared on their own without any effort on my part—a completely unexpected bonus of finding peace with myself.

Beware the "nondiet" diet

One result of all the negative publicity surrounding dieting is that many programs now insist that theirs is a "nondieting" approach. And yet I find most of these are diets in disguise. In one article called "Stop Dieting and Lose Weight," the advice included:

- Keeping foods that trigger overeating out of the house.
- Grabbing a handful of veggies whenever cravings hit.
- Avoiding buffets—and eating at home as often as you can so as not to be tempted by fatty, sugary items in restaurants.

- Being sure to ask, "What's in the sauce?" and asking to have your chicken broiled, not fried. Stuffed, sautéed, or fried are *no-nos!*

If this isn't restrictive thinking, I don't know what is! My feeling is this: if you're asked to follow a set plan, if you're asked to eat less than 2,000 calories a day, if you're asked to avoid certain foods, or if you end up hungry—it's still a diet.

Keeping the weight off

It is often said that losing weight is the easy part—keeping it off is what's difficult. In a three-year follow-up of people who went to a commercial weight loss program, 57 percent had kept off at least five percent of the weight they lost, but 40 percent gained back more than they lost during the diet.[31] Many experts advise waiting five years to follow-up. In one study where follow-up occurred at six years and again at 15 years, only six percent of the study participants maintained at least a five percent weight loss.[32] "Long-term weight loss maintenance is rare," the authors of the study concluded.

There has been some feeling that the "success rate" may be higher in the general population among people who just go it alone, don't go to any kind of weight-loss program, and don't come to the attention of researchers. But this possibility was put to the test in 1999 and proof was lacking. Said the study authors: "The current data are inadequate to draw any definite conclusions regarding the cure rate of obesity."[33]

Still, there must be some people who are keeping their weight off. Yes, but at what cost? A woman featured in a TV documentary on obesity admitted she could maintain her weight loss only by running five miles every day and limiting her daily calories to 1,000. Is this how you would want to spend the rest of your life? Another man who lost a significant amount of weight and regularly appears on talk shows says he walks between 30 and 70 miles a week to keep his weight off. This is an average of four to ten miles a day. How many people would realistically be able to adhere to such a routine for a lifetime?

The National Weight Control Registry was created to document weight loss success stories. Initial enrollees had maintained their weight loss for five years. Women in the registry reported continued consumption of a low-energy, low-fat diet and were eating an average of 1,306 calories a day. Men were eating 1,685 calories a day.[34] Long-term maintenance of weight loss in another survey was associated with "highly restrained eating, regular physical activity, and perhaps with increased anxiety."[35] Does this sound like fun? And what kind of person could live on this spartan of a regimen for a lifetime?

Researchers Susan and Wayne Wooley, who are also therapists, have seen this firsthand: "Many treatment successes are in fact condemned to a life of weight obsession, semistarvation and all the symptoms produced by chronic hunger. Some consume as few as 800 calories per day, struggle constantly to ward off or compensate for loss of control, and seem precariously close to developing an eating disorder."[36] When they do encounter people who successfully lose weight, the Wooleys point out that these are often "simple overeaters who gain weight during transitory periods of stress or indulgence and who are able to return to a lower natural weight without undue difficulty." I found the same to be true while examining one diet program's roster of people who had reached their "goal weight." Most had lost only ten to twenty pounds to achieve that (and are probably not among those whose weight has genetic and physiological roots).

What about behavior therapy?

Behavior modification has been a component of many weight-loss programs for some time. Has it lived up to its promise? Long-term results have been mixed, says G. Terence Wilson, Ph.D., in the book *Obesity*.[37] Behavior modification is based on the premise that all large people are eating excessively and have a different style of eating from thin people. But, says Wilson, it's been shown in people of all shapes and sizes that "some are responsive to external food stimuli and some are not." And many large people are not eating compulsively. In other words, people are being provided with techniques to correct problems they may not have in the first place. Still, Wilson believes that behavioral strategies may help some people to develop better eating habits.

Do behavior clients do better at keeping weight off? Unfortunately, the answer seems to be no. University of Rochester researchers found after five years that "nearly everyone had regained to initial weight or higher." Stanford University researchers were similarly disappointed and concluded that theirs was "just another episode in a long series of weight loss efforts."[38] Louisiana investigators found after two and a half years that most women had regained all their weight and more. Their average weight was 214 before the program and 217 at the follow-up.[39]

What about exercise?

It's often said that people who exercise regularly do better at keeping weight off, but studies have found that exercise helps primarily to minimize weight regain. In one study, dieters were assigned to one of four groups: 1. aerobic exercise; 2. strength training; 3. aerobic exercise plus strength training; or 4. no exercise at all. "Participants in all four conditions regained approximately 35 to 55 percent of their weight loss in the year after treatment," although those who continued to exercise regained less.[40]

In another project, some people dieted but did not exercise, some exercised but did not diet, and some dieted *and* exercised. After one year, "no significant differences were noted among the three groups," and all were regaining their weight, although the exercisers were regaining less.[41] When investigators reviewed 15 studies of exercise's impact on weight reduction, they concluded that exercise produces "modest" benefits for weight loss.[42] Does this mean we should abandon exercise? Absolutely not! It simply means that exercise should be viewed as an important tool in maintaining fitness and good health and not just as a means for losing weight.

"Secrets of slim women"

I am always intrigued by magazine articles with titles like "The Secrets of Slim Women" and testimonials of newly-reduced individuals who proclaim, "If I did it, anyone can!" Some people do manage to lose weight and a few even manage to keep it off over time (and we saw earlier what that entails for many of them). These are often people who end up dispensing weight-loss advice on the talk show circuit or in how-I-lost-weight magazine articles. Of course, many haven't had their weight off for *that* long and will need to be revisited in five years.

In one of these articles, the "secrets" we were let in on included: calories count; low-fat is best; exercise is key; downsize portions; eat out wisely. These lists always invoke the "duh" response in me and insult my intelligence. They assume that because I am large, I don't know any of these things when I've been hearing them—and doing most of them—all my life.

Then there are what I like to call the "gurus of girth," the celebrities with diet books or those who have become well-known through infomercials and the like. Most of these diet evangelists are not people with any particular expertise in obesity or the research surrounding it. The people you *should* be listening to are not usually famous. Obesity expert Dr. Wayne Callaway points out: "During the past 20 years, my colleagues and I have been involved in serious research and clinical studies designed to gain insight into the causes and cures of human obesity . . . You don't usually see our names and faces plastered all over the media, or hear us expounding on miracle treatments on national talk shows." He's right. For whatever reasons, the people who know what they're talking about don't get booked. And that means the truth never really gets told.

Magic bullets?

There have been a number of prescription drugs and over-the-counter weight loss formulas hyped in the last five years. Do any of them work? Let's start with what's known about the prescription drugs.

"Fen-Phen"

When I was writing the first edition of this book, the buzz had just started about a new diet drug called "fen-phen," short for the combination of fenfluramine (brand name Pondimin) and phentermine (brand name Redux). Touted as safe and free from the hazardous side effects of amphetamines, people scrambled for it. In 1996, the total number of prescriptions in the United States for fen-phen exceeded 18 million.

The euphoria was short-lived. In July, 1997, doctors at the Mayo Clinic discovered heart valve problems linked to fen-phen use in 24 of their patients. This prompted the Food and Drug Administration (FDA) to examine the records of 291 people from five medical centers who had been taking either fen-phen or Redux alone; 30 percent were found to have abnormal echocardiograms.

In September, 1997, the manufacturers of the drugs pulled them from the market. On October 8, 1999, it was announced that $3.75 billion would be paid to individuals with fen-phen-related health problems. About 4,100 lawsuits, involving 8,000 people, were filed, making it one of the largest product-liability cases ever.

Meridia (sibutramine)

It wasn't long before a new drug called Meridia (sibutramine) came along to fill the vacancy left by fen-phen. Approved in 1997, sibutramine works by affecting appetite-regulating chemicals in the brain. It was originally intended to be sold as an antidepressant, but didn't work well enough. Researchers noticed that sibutramine users shed pounds, and so shifted their attention to turning it into a weight loss drug. It is not known to cause heart valve damage, but can greatly elevate blood pressure and cause rapid heartbeat.

In clinical trials, patients lost modest amounts of weight, but not unless they also ate fewer calories and exercised more. When they stopped taking the medication, they regained weight. And up to 15 percent of the people studied didn't respond to the medication at all.[43]

Xenical (orlistat)

The drug orlistat, sold under the brand name Xenical, was approved on April 26, 1999, by the FDA. Orlistat blocks the absorption of dietary fat by about one-third and is the first diet drug that works not by suppressing appetite, but by blocking the digestion of fat.

In a two-year study, patients taking orlistat did lose a bit more weight than those in a placebo-treated group (9.7 percent of their body weight as opposed to 6.6 percent for the placebo group). But the best that could be said for the drug in the second year of treatment was: "During the second year, orlistat therapy produced *less weight regain* than placebo."[44] The side effects of orlistat can be very unpleasant, including, according to the FDA, "oily spotting, gas with discharge, fecal urgency, fatty/oily stools and frequent bowel movements." So all that can really be said for orlistat is that you may lose a modest amount of weight in the beginning and won't gain as much back. And you had better be near a bathroom at all times!

Not everyone on the FDA advisory panel wanted to approve orlistat. Dr. Jules Hirsch, an obesity expert at the Rockefeller University in New York, was one of them. He cited both the drug's limited effectiveness and the dangers of previous drugs.

Meridia and Xenical are called "supporting drugs" for weight loss, meaning that those taking the medications will also have to eat a reduced calorie diet and exercise regularly—which begs the question, "Why take drugs at all if dieting and exercise are required for them to be effective?"

Non-prescription diet aids

What about the over-the-counter concoctions? Some of the most common ingredients in these formulas are as follows:

PPA

For years, phenylpropanolamine (PPA) has been an ingredient in over-the-counter diet pills, as well as in cold remedies. In September, 2000, the FDA became concerned about products containing PPA because of a Yale University study that "provides compelling evidence of increased risk of hemorrhagic stroke in young people who use PPA-containing appetite suppressants."[45] On November 6, 2000, the FDA issued a public health advisory concerning the risk of hemorrhagic stroke, or bleeding into the brain, associated with PPA, and asked that all drug companies discontinue marketing products containing it.

Ephedrine (Ephedra, Ma-huang)

Ephedrine is known to increase heart rate and blood pressure. The FDA has also been concerned about ephedrine amid reports that it can lead to heart attack, stroke, seizures, psychosis and even death. In June, 1997, the FDA proposed limiting the amount of ephedrine products could contain, as well as the length of time ephedrine-containing products could be used. Ephedrine would also have been prohibited in supplements already containing known stimulants.

But the Government Accounting Office (GAO) said that additional evidence was needed to support these proposed restrictions, so in April, 2000, the FDA announced it would suspend its recommendations until further information could be gathered. The FDA then requested an independent review of health problems thought to be related to the use of ephedrine. The reviewers, from the University of California and the California Poison Control System, found that 31 percent of the problems reported to the FDA were "definitely or probably related" to ephedrine use and 31 percent "possibly related." That is a very high percentage. Among the health-related problems linked to ephedrine: hypertension, palpitations, tachycardia, stroke, and seizures.[46]

Other reports in the scientific literature have linked ephedrine to:

- Myocarditis (inflammation of the heart muscle)[47]
- Kidney stones[48]
- Acute hepatitis[49]

Given this new information, it seems likely that the FDA will reinstate its warnings and perhaps issue a ban. While we wait, I would be quite reluctant to use any ephedrine-containing products, especially if you have any history of hypertension. "Consult with your physician" is probably the best advice. Also, beware of "herbal phen-fen," a prescription sound-alike which contains neither phentermine or fenfluramine, but *does* contain ephedrine.

Chromium Picolinate

There are those who claim that chromium picolinate increases muscle mass and decreases body fat, but there is no scientific proof of this. Here is what *Tufts University Diet & Nutrition Letter* had to say: "As for chromium picolinate as a fat burner or weight loss aid, the idea doesn't have any basis whatsoever. Only if you consume too *little* chromium might you lose weight; a chromium deficiency can lead to weight loss since it means sugar from the food you eat can't get into the muscle cells and other body tissues."[50]

In November of 1996, the Federal Trade Commission (FTC) ordered three companies to stop making unsubstantiated weight loss and health claims for chromium picolinate. More recently, chemists from the University of Alabama told attendees at the 1999 national meeting of the American Chemical Society that chromium picolinate can cause DNA breakage—which may lead to genetic mutations and cancer in humans.[51]

Garcinia Cambogia (hydroxycitric acid)

There has been some suggestion that garcinia cambogia, or hydroxycitric acid, may have the ability to aid dieters in losing weight by preventing carbohydrates from being turned into unwanted body fat. But in a 12-week study where some people received either an herbal compound containing garcinia cambogia and some got a placebo, "garcinia cambogia failed to produce significant weight loss and fat mass loss beyond that observed with placebo."[52]

Chitosan (chitin)

Billed as a "fat trapper," chitin is found in the skeletons of shrimp, crabs, and other shellfish. It supposedly attaches to fat in the stomach and prevents its digestion. To test this theory, study volunteers received either four capsules of chitosan or indistinguishable placebos twice daily for a month. At the end of the trial, investigators concluded that "chitosan in the administered dosage, without dietary alterations, does not reduce body weight in overweight subjects.[53]

Bottom line: No magic bullets yet! The FDA and FTC caution:

- Any claims that you can lose weight effortlessly are false.
- Fad diets rarely have any permanent effect.
- Be wary of claims that sound too good to be true. Be particularly skeptical of claims containing words and phrases like: easy, effortless, guaranteed, miraculous, magical, breakthrough, new discovery, mysterious, exotic, secret, exclusive, ancient.

Hucksters will continue to prey on the desperation of people who are willing to spend any amount of money for a jar or bottle of anything that might finally contain the miracle they are seeking. Their money would be better spent on a pair of walking shoes, a pool membership, or a plus-size exercise class.

High-protein/low carb? High carb/low-fat? Who's right?

They're b-a-a-a-a-ck! Since the first edition of this book, there has been a resurgence of the high-protein diets that first became popular in the late 60s and early 70s. Why? Partly because of the adage that "everything old is new again" and certainly because people continue to search for diets promising quick and easy weight loss. High protein diets can do that, at least in the beginning, by putting devotees into a state of "ketosis," leading to water loss, which in turn produces rapid weight loss. Because of strict food limitations, most people are also eating fewer calories. With rehydration, these initial rapid losses tend to disappear.

For a long time—certainly during the years I was growing up—carbohydrates or, as we called them, "starches," were the bad guys.

When dining out, I was always encouraged to order a steak rather than spaghetti. Then the tables turned completely and spaghetti was in, steak was out. The USDA now advises that "most of the calories in your diet should come from grain products, vegetables, and fruits," including grain products high in complex carbohydrates such as breads, cereals, pasta, rice, and potatoes. All major professional health organizations, including the American Heart Association, National Cholesterol Education Program, and the American Cancer Society now endorse a diet composed of 10 to 15 percent protein, 55 to 60 percent carbohydrates, and 25 to 30 percent fat. This was fine with me. I like pasta better than meat anyway.

But dietary guidelines are always a work in progress, and some are calling carbs into question again. They point out that the switch to high-carb diets has not resulted in the population becoming thinner, but quite the opposite. And even the USDA has changed its tune slightly where fats are concerned. Between 1980 and 2000 the advice went from "avoid too much fat" to "choose a diet low in fat" to "choose a diet low in saturated fat and cholesterol and moderate in total fat."[54]

The high-protein aficionados believe that carbohydrates wreak havoc with the body's insulin-producing mechanism. Their theory is that eating carbohydrates triggers the secretion of insulin, causing carbohydrates to be taken to the cells and stored as fat instead of being used for energy. But other, more neutral experts point out that all calories are converted into glucose to be stored for energy, and that glucose is stored as fat only when you have consumed excess calories.[55] "I disagree strongly with the notion that having high blood insulin, by itself, makes you gain more weight," says Gerald Reaven, an endocrinologist at Stanford University. "There are many studies showing that if you decrease calories, people lose weight, and it doesn't matter if you do it by cutting fat, protein, or carbohydrate."[56]

Another misconception is that eating too many carbohydrates causes insulin resistance. What is insulin resistance? The popular newsletter, *Environmental Nutrition,* provides a good explanation: "Blood sugar (glucose) levels normally rise after eating—relatively quickly when you eat carbohydrate-rich foods. The hormone insulin, acting like the hall monitor of the bloodstream, instructs glucose in the blood to enter cells, where it is stored or used for energy. Insulin resistance occurs when cells resist insulin's commands."[57] Many people who develop insulin resistance become diabetic, so this is a real concern. But insulin resistance probably has a genetic component, and blaming it on eating too many carbohydrates is far too simplistic.

High-protein critics are extremely worried that the lack of fiber and overload of fat associated with these diets can have a variety of adverse health effects. High fiber foods are thought to protect against heart disease and cancer, and many fear that a rise in fat consumption will lead to increased cardiovascular disease.

The one notable exception to current dietary recommendations involves people with diabetes and/or "Syndrome X." The term "Syndrome X" was coined to refer to people with multiple risk factors including central obesity (the "apple" shape), glucose intolerance, high triglycerides, low HDL cholesterol (the "good" cholesterol), and high blood pressure. Current American Diabetes Association guidelines for such individuals call for a moderate increase in monounsaturated fats and a reduced intake of carbohydrates.[58] There are reasons for this. Research has shown that high-carbohydrate diets, as compared with high-monounsaturated-fat diets, cause blood sugar control to deteriorate in non-insulin-dependent diabetic patients.[59] Studies have also shown that patients such as these benefit from a high intake of dietary fiber.[60,61]

If you have any of these conditions, your best bet is to consult with a registered dietitian who is knowledgeable about current dietary recommendations for diabetics and people with Syndrome X.

What's a body to do?

"What is needed is a new approach to weight loss that doesn't blame the victim for past failures, doesn't exploit the desperation of dieters with hit-and-run approaches, and does offer a treatment based on current well-researched and documented knowledge," says Dr. Callaway.[62] Perhaps we should take our lead from Canada's "Vitality" program. Designed by Health and Welfare Canada, "Vitality" takes a non-diet approach and recommends feeling good about oneself, eating well, and being active. It de-emphasizes body weight and advocates being proud of how your body looks and believing in your own self-worth.

The prescription: health at any size

Let's try something really radical! Let's replace the frustrating and unrealistic goal of getting thin with the satisfying and positive goal of becoming healthy. We have already heard from researchers who believe that it is entirely possible to be big and healthy at the same time.

Let's hear from yet another. Jane Moore, Ph.D., who has been working in the field of nutrition for 25 years, has no doubt that women can be both fit and fat. Moore worked with 15 women who were from 40 to 100 percent above their ideal chart weight. The women learned to improve fitness and decrease health risk factors by eating less fat and exercising regularly. Weight loss was not a goal. At the end of nine months, 11 of the 15 registered significantly lower blood cholesterol levels, significantly lower blood pressure, and increased aerobic capacity. Only six lost any weight. Moore said she felt all the women in her study were unique and special: "And they didn't have to lose a pound for me to feel that way!"[63]

More proof that fat and fit can co-exist comes from anthropologist Margaret MacKenzie. The Samoan women MacKenzie studied averaged five foot four inches tall and 200 pounds. Fitness tests, however, showed them to be twice as flexible as their American counterparts. Overall, they had good blood pressure readings and strong hearts.[64] But these were very active women. In the United States, large women are not encouraged to be active, and they encounter barriers if they try. Many have convinced themselves they need to lose weight *before* they can be active, or *before* they can be healthy. It has not occurred to us to try to be healthy at any size.

It stands to reason that if large people ignore their health, they'll have more health problems. But many ignore their health because they believe big bodies can't be healthy. What would happen if we turned the tables and said, "First, develop a healthy lifestyle, then worry about weight?" Would we see fewer of the health problems traditionally associated with obesity? I don't think we have nearly enough research on this question, and I challenge the researchers to address it. Some of the health perils attributed to obesity may be more the result of fat-laden diets or lack of exercise.

Instead of using weight to measure health, let's rely more on what former *BBW* editor Carole Shaw calls the "inner stats"—things like blood pressure, cholesterol and blood glucose levels. These are the numbers that really measure health, not the numbers on the scale.

Strive for a "healthy weight"

"Maintain a 'healthy' weight" seems to be the latest advice. Others use the term "reasonable weight." Janet Polivy, cited earlier for her studies of binge eating, recommends that people learn to be comfortable with their "natural weight"—the weight that results from healthy eating and regular exercise. Similarly, Kelly Brownell, a Yale University researcher, defines reasonable weight as "the weight that individuals making reasonable changes in their diet and exercise patterns can seek and maintain over a period of time."

I asked Francie Berg, editor of the *Healthy Weight Journal*, how she defines "healthy weight." She feels that the concept is still evolving, but has some definite thoughts about it. "It is dangerous and unrealistic," she said, "to define healthy weight within a narrow range, as has often been done in the past using height and weight tables. It is becoming clear that a person's healthy weight begins not with height or a number on a chart, but with the person's current weight." She continues:

> *We know that there are risks associated with losing weight, especially losing and gaining repeatedly. So regardless of how high a person's weight is, it may well be the healthiest for that individual at that point in his or her life. There is much evidence in favor of keeping a stable weight. Instead of constantly trying to lose weight, we need to focus on being healthy at the weight we are right now.*

Even the American Dietetic Association (ADA) acknowledges that there is a lot of individual variation in healthy weights: "Your healthy weight is likely to be quite different from anyone else's. A variety of factors are at work, including your genes, physical activity, age, dieting history, and the foods you eat."

Most organizations have abandoned the "chart on the doctor's wall" as an indicator of healthy weight. The National Institutes of Health (NIH), U.S. Department of Agriculture (USDA), and the ADA all recommend taking into account these three guidelines to help you determine your own healthy weight:

1. Body mass index (BMI), a measure of weight relative to height. How to calculate yours? Do a web search for "body mass index" where there are many sites that will calculate it for you.

2. Waist circumference. You know—are you an "apple" or a "pear?" According to NIH, health risks increase with a waist measurement of over 40 in men and over 35 in women.

3. Any other risk factors you may have, such as high blood pressure, high cholesterol, high triglycerides, high blood glucose (sugar), physical inactivity, cigarette smoking, and a family history of premature heart disease.

"From a medical point of view, achieving an ideal weight is not always necessary to achieving a healthy weight," say John Foreyt and G. Ken Goodrick. "For example, a reduction from 180 to 170 pounds may bring blood pressure under better control for some people.[65] Some authorities now advocate the "ten percent solution," meaning that losing just 10 percent of your body weight is enough to reap health benefits. George Blackburn is one of these people. According to Blackburn, "weight loss as low as five percent has been shown to reduce or eliminate disorders associated with obesity."[66] Modest weight loss, he found, improved glycemic control, reduced blood pressure, and reduced cholesterol levels.

In the end, healthy weight is an individual thing. For some it may mean stabilizing weight and not continuing to gain. For others it might mean losing a modest amount of weight—enough to bring a medical problem under better control. Your healthy weight may be higher than your friend's, even though you're both the same height. A generous helping of fat cells may run in your family, but not in hers.

For now, you may have to make your own decision about a healthy weight. At what weight are you relatively free of health problems? At what weight do you feel strong and energetic? What is a weight you can realistically maintain over time? A healthy lifestyle can help your body to find that weight.

Weight management the "largely positive" way

Although some of my size-acceptance colleagues may criticize me for including this section, I think we run a risk if we ignore it altogether. Some of our members used to keep mum if they were in a weight-reduction program because they thought I'd be "mad" at them. Of course I wouldn't have been, but I realized we needed to give them permission to talk about it. I also realized I would much rather have them base their weight-loss efforts on facts, not fads. Although science has not provided us with methods that work for the permanent loss of large amounts of weight, currently-available research may hold some clues for at least moderate weight loss.

Nothing new under the sun—except how you mix it up

There really isn't anything new under the diet sun—or is there? What may be new is how *you* choose to combine these strategies—in other words, your own recipe for weight management. More than one study has demonstrated that weight management works best if you take the available advice and package it to suit your individual preferences and lifestyle. I can share *my* recipe with you, but ultimately you have to decide which ingredients *you* will use—and in what amounts.

Self-esteem as the fuel

"It's not that I'm stupid," one member said. "I know the things I should be doing to look after my health. What I need is motivation. Where do I get that?" We spent some time discussing that, and ended up agreeing that self-esteem fuels motivation.

It's very hard to want to do good things for someone you loathe—and that includes yourself. If you don't believe you're worthy of being treated with love and respect, you won't expect others to treat you well and you won't treat yourself well. You *must* get to a point where you understand that you're a person of value even if you never lose another pound. In fact, you may need to spend time repairing your self-esteem first before you try to make lifestyle changes. You don't want the foundation to be shaky, which it will be if you use bricks labeled "self-loathing." Pay a little more and get bricks labeled "self-esteem."

Put the pleasure back into food

We think we're supposed to eat primarily to meet nutritional requirements and that we shouldn't enjoy what we're eating too much. We're taught that eating for emotional reasons is always bad and that we need to substitute other activities instead. Sometimes a good swim may be what I really need to shed piled up stress, but other times eating a hot fudge sundae may do a better job for me. It would be a problem if the latter were my only reaction to stress and other emotions, but it isn't. Noted chef Julia Child says she is saddened by the "fear of food" that is making Americans feel guilty about the foods we enjoy. To try to alleviate this fear, she has been joined by chefs, dietitians, food and health writers, educators, physicians, product developers and researchers in a project called "Resetting the American Table: Creating a New Alliance of Taste & Health." The project's goal is to help Americans rediscover the joys of eating while moving toward a healthier diet. Their brochure advises:

- Balance over several days. There is no need to deprive ourselves or feel guilty about enjoying a favorite rich food—as long as we plan for it.
- Don't think of foods as "good" or "bad." Moderation is the key. With moderation, it really is okay to eat beef, to enjoy butter, to have a slice of wonderful chocolate cake, to accept all the foods we like as life-giving and pleasant.

No one starts from zero

Constantly keep in mind that no one starts from zero. You're already making a lot of good, healthy choices. As a nation, we like to point out all the things people are doing wrong. We're getting fatter. We don't exercise enough. We don't eat right. Are we doing *anything* right?

I think we'd be a lot better off if we commended people for what they're doing right, for where they are now—and then identified ways to build on that. You make good health decisions every day, from the orange juice you pour at breakfast to walking Fido around the block after dinner. Could you do more? Probably. Everyone could. But instead of lamenting the things you don't do, say: "This is where I'm at right now, and it's a good place to be. Here's where I'd like to be a year from now." Then map out your route. This way it becomes a matter of "bonuses" rather than "deficits."

Personalize your eating plan

"Not all overweight people are alike," states Dr. Callaway, "and no single program is suited to every need."[67] Studies show that you will be better off if you create your own eating plan, rather than adopt one that is handed to you. But if "personalizing" is the way to go, are there any guidelines? How do you go about creating a personalized weight-management plan for yourself? Anne Sprenger, a registered dietitian who has worked with Largely Positive members, has these tips for developing a personalized plan:

1. Consider asking a registered dietitian to help you customize a food plan, but be sure it's not someone who is simply going to put you on a low-calorie diet.

2. While it's not necessary to become a slave to food diaries, it's useful to keep one for a couple of weeks so you can be clearly aware of your eating habits. This will make it easier to zero in on where you might want to make some changes.

3. In advance, plan each day for three meals and a couple of snacks. Decide if you will bring food with you to work, eat out, or cook at home.

4. The U.S. Department of Agriculture's food-guide pyramid is a very simple and useful tool for meal planning. Get a copy of it from a dietitian or go to their website at www.usda.gov.

5. A healthy diet consists of 50 to 60 percent carbohydrates, 20 percent protein and 20 to 30 percent fat. Keeping your fat intake within 50 to 60 grams per day will guarantee that it is less than 25 percent of your total intake.

6. Eat enough to supply energy. For women, I recommend at least 2,000 calories per day; for men, at least 2,800.

7. Experiment with low-fat foods and cooking techniques. Don't buy more than one or two low-fat cookbooks. Too many is overwhelming. Try just one or two new ideas each month.

8. Fluids are important; you need about eight cups of fluid each day to stay well hydrated. Thirst can sometimes be confused with hunger. On the other hand, don't use fluid consumption to try to cover up hunger.

"Developing a healthy eating pattern takes time," Sprenger cautions. "A person really needs a year to go through the seasons, integrate new ideas, and set short-term goals. Give yourself the luxury of time and permission to develop your new eating plan."

The Basics

I think there are some "basics" that belong in all weight management plans. Specifically:

Go slow

"Quick start. Rapid weight loss. Pounds melt away quickly." We are a nation preoccupied with instant gratification, from fast food to ten-minute oil changes. It may work for your car, but it *won't* work for your weight. It has been estimated that a medium-built woman in her 30s or 40s needs about 2,500 calories a day to maintain weight. A daily intake of 2,000 - 2,200 calories should result in a gradual loss.

Plateaus are your friend

Dieters get very nervous when they reach a plateau, but plateaus are a good thing. Many researchers believe people would be better off losing weight in a series of starts and stops.

Planning is the real key

Planning is an important element for everyone. Plan ahead each week what you will eat, and prepare food in advance as much as you can. Cook it, chop it, mix it, whatever it takes. The less you have to do when it's actually time to eat, the better. That old stand-by, the Crock-Pot, is a great planning ally.

The two-minute salad

Nowadays you can buy mixed greens already washed and ready to toss, cut up broccoli and cauliflower, shredded cabbage and carrots, little cherry or grape tomatoes. It then takes seconds to fling them all together! If you prefer to cut up your own vegetables, do it ahead of time and have them ready to go.

Cut the fat, but not too much

One of the best ways to eat healthier is to cut back on fat. But be careful. Low-fat can be taken to the extreme. So how much fat can we eat and still be healthy? You need 20 to 25 grams a day to keep the body in top working order. Thirty grams are considered ideal, but a dietitian friend of mine warns that creating unrealistic eating plans is just as futile as perpetuating unrealistic body ideals. She feels that most people would be fine if they tried to stay under 60 fat grams a day. Be careful of low-fat substitutes, say the experts. People think they can eat as much as they want of anything labeled "low-fat." They forget that these items may have just as many calories as the original versions.

Do not deprive

Swear off M&M's completely, and it's a pretty sure bet you'll be dreaming about an "attack of the giant M&M people." Get rid of the notion that foods are "bad" or "forbidden," although there may be some foods you choose to eat less often than others.

Don't eat around a craving. Here is a typical scenario: You're craving a piece of chocolate, so you eat some carrot sticks. That doesn't satisfy you, so you eat some popcorn. That still doesn't do it, so you have some yogurt. By now, you'd walk across hot coals (or at least drive across town) for some chocolate. A perfectly manageable "one-alarm" craving has now escalated to a "five-alarm" and is out of control. Don't let the fire burn. Put it out early.

Eat chocolate—for the sake of your health!

While we're on the subject of "cravings," here's a real surprise: chocolate may be good for you! It turns out that chocolate contains phenols, the same antioxidant compounds found in red wine and believed to help lower the risk of heart disease. And the fat in cocoa butter is in the form of stearic acid, which, for reasons not yet understood, does not appear to raise cholesterol levels, as most saturated fats do. In fact, a diet high in stearic acid was found to reduce the size and activity of "platelets," the cells that help to produce blood clots.[68]

Don't let hunger persist

It's been said that large people don't know when they're truly hungry. That's not so for me. The signals are very clear. But if you need some guidance, you might be interested in what Dr. Art Ulene had to say in the February 1992 issue of *Good Housekeeping:*

- You're probably not hungry if you've eaten in the last few hours (provided, of course, you ate enough).
- Hunger is usually accompanied by physical sensations like a rumbling, gnawing feeling in the abdomen
- Hunger usually comes on gradually.

Set priorities

Steak, baked potato with sour cream, salad with Roquefort dressing—

a pretty high-fat meal. Decide what you want most and where you'd be willing to compromise. If you really want the steak, eat your salad with low-fat dressing and sprinkle some chives on your potato. French fries don't automatically have to accompany a burger—substitute a salad. Sometimes you can balance diet and non-diet strategies in a way that feels right for you.

There's always tomorrow

Remind yourself that since you're not starting a diet tomorrow, you don't have to stockpile favorite foods. If you crave Hershey's Kisses, have some, but because you can have some more tomorrow, it won't be necessary to eat the whole bag.

What's the worst thing that could happen?

This has been particularly effective for me. If I know I'm no longer hungry, but the food tastes good and I want to keep eating, I ask myself, "What's the worst thing that could happen if I stop eating right now?" I usually realize I won't be in any physical or emotional pain and that nothing bad is really going to happen. (I'm not suggesting you do this if you still really feel hungry.)

Have something good at each meal

It's important for me to have something I really like at each meal. If I don't, I'm just not satisfied at the end of the meal, and soon I'm looking for something that "tastes good."

Forget what's "traditional"

I once heard a dietitian recommend a ham sandwich or a slice of pizza for breakfast. I took her advice, and I'm no longer famished by midmorning. And three meals a day isn't sacred (although it's the minimum you should eat). I sometimes save part of my lunch until midafternoon. My "most hungry" time is around 4 p.m. (Research shows most people fall off their diets at 4:30 p.m.!) It made a lot of sense.

Slow down

It supposedly takes 20 minutes for your stomach and brain to agree that you're no longer hungry. I found this to be true when I had dinner with a friend to plan a presentation. We had a lot to discuss and were spending considerable time in conversation between bites. After 45 minutes, I realized that although I'd only eaten half my meal, I was full. Strive to make meals last at least half an hour and you may not want seconds. You'll also have time to really savor your food.

Try new things

I'm always looking for different vegetables to try in salads—recently I found I like the crunch of jicama and kohlrabi. I also enjoy sampling fruits that are a little off the beaten path, like mangoes and papayas.

Be discerning

Recently I ordered a piece of key lime pie in a restaurant. When it came, it wasn't very good—it wasn't genuine key lime pie (like the kind I usually get in Florida). There was a time when I would have finished it anyway, but I decided that since I wasn't really enjoying it, I wouldn't eat any more of it.

Snack creatively

Snacks don't have to be high in fat, and they don't have to be carrot or celery sticks either. There are lots of things you may not have considered as snacks that I think will please you:

- A baked white or sweet potato
- An ear of corn—nuked
- Popcorn (watch for the fat content), pretzels, breadsticks
- A slice of whole grain bread
- A small bowl of plain pasta with some Parmesan cheese sprinkled on top (try the flavored varieties, such as spinach or tomato)
- A slice of veggie pizza. Buy a ready-made crust and top with tomato sauce, mushrooms, green peppers, onions and any other favorite vegetables.

This doesn't mean I don't sometimes want a snack of ice cream or potato chips, but when I do, I put a portion in a small bowl; I don't eat straight from the bag or container.

Don't get in a rut

Pasta has the green light now, but there's more you can do than pour tomato sauce over it. The same goes for other foods. Buy some cookbooks that will help you expand your "pastabilities" and other types of cooking.

Bite size treats

When I crave chocolate, I often go for a couple "bite-sized" treats and often this satisfies me. This isn't to say that sometimes I don't have a regular-sized candy bar or a hot fudge sundae. It just means that I go more often for the bite-sized goodies. Recent research has shown that craved foods taste best in the first few bites.

Evaluate your intake of artificial sweeteners

One of our members said she started losing weight when she gave up diet soda. Studies are conflicting. Some say artificial sweeteners increase your appetite; others have not found this to be the case. A Leeds University study found that people who drink aspartame-sweetened drinks are hungrier an hour later than people who drink plain water. The researchers speculated that the artificial sweetener fools the body into thinking some high calories are coming—but when serotonin and blood sugar levels don't rise, the hypothalamus is confused and sends more hunger signals.

Other studies show that saccharin promotes weight gain. When the only difference in the diets of lab rats was that some drank water and some drank a saccharin solution, the saccharin drinkers gained weight, while the water drinkers did not.[69]

What about this "emotional eating" thing?

Sometimes theories worm their way into the culture, and eventually become accepted thinking without anyone really knowing where the logic came from in the first place. Such is the case with "emotional eating"— which all larger people are assumed to do. David Allison, Ph.D., of Columbia University has done extensive research in this area and, in trying to pinpoint the origins of this theory, lets us in on some interesting history:

> 'Kummerspeck' is a German word meaning 'fat of sorrow.' This term was used to describe the unexpected weight gain observed among some women during World War I. These women either had uncertain or

unpredictable lives, or had lovers who were killed in war. Thus, their weight gain was attributed to excessive emotional trauma.[70]

The theory has come to be known in the scientific lingo as the psychosomatic model of obesity or "PMO." Allison continues:

The observation that stress-induced eating promotes obesity has existed for many years and has even been traced back to philosopher David Hume in the 18th century. However, it was the psychoanalytic community's acceptance and perpetuation of the PMO that legitimized it as a scientifically credible theory in the 20th century . . . Early psychodynamic proponents of the model argued that emotional eating represents a psychosexual fixation, typically at the oral stage of development.[71]

Many people, health professionals included, appear to accept the tenets of PMO at face value. Why is this? As far as I can tell, it's because it's what they've heard all their lives—one of those things that is just taken for granted and rarely questioned. But when scientists like Allison do stop to question it, they find that "the balance of laboratory studies have not consistently detected greater emotional eating among obese than nonobese individuals."[72]

Allison acknowledges that there do appear to be subgroups that might be more prone to emotional eating, especially restrained eaters and those suffering from binge eating disorder, but as of now, "the relationship between emotional eating and obesity has not been firmly established."[73]

Once again, you must start challenging assumptions like these. I decided some time ago to challenge the emotional eating assumption. When I did, I realized that most of the time I was eating because I was hungry, not emotionally distressed. But there were times, as with *everyone,* that an ice cream cone hit the spot! Emotions may sometimes cause me to eat, but just as often they may cause me *not* to eat, to cry, to laugh, or to get mad. This sounds pretty normal, don't you think?

Will I lose weight?

A better question is: How will my body respond to a healthy lifestyle? My body, for instance, has not responded with a great loss of weight, but it has responded with reduced blood pressure, lower cholesterol levels, greater endurance, more energy, better tone. Again, you can't make weight loss your only measure of success.

Many of the people I work with eventually want to pinpoint their setpoint weight range. Is there a way to do this? And once you've gone through years of dieting and regaining, hasn't your body long since forgotten its original setpoint? Sometimes I joke that your original setpoint may be the weight that appears on your driver's license, but if you want a more scientific way of estimating it, here are some guidelines:

- Try to estimate the lowest weight you maintained for at least a year after age 21.

- Do other close relatives tend to be large? If so, your setpoint weight range may be higher than what the height/weight charts prescribe.

- How heavy were you as a child? What did you weigh in high school? I weighed 175 pounds in the eighth grade. It would be all but impossible for me to weigh any less than that as an adult.

- What is the weight you are able to maintain effortlessly without dieting?

- What is the weight to which your body returns once you have stopped dieting?

The problem with the last point is that post-diets weights are often higher than pre-diet weights, meaning that your setpoint weight range may become higher with each successive diet. So the next question becomes: Can I bring my setpoint back down? Researchers seem to agree that the two main things you can do to try to rediscover your natural setpoint are to start exercising regularly and to lower the amount of fat in your diet. The key seems to be allowing your weight to fall naturally without sending the body into its weight-defending mode.

You can try these strategies, but don't be disappointed if you don't lose all the weight you think you should. I have seen people make these adaptations. Some lose, others don't—which illustrates, once again, the danger of making weight loss your only goal. Start checking your blood pressure, your cholesterol, your ability to walk up a flight of stairs without being out of breath, your overall feeling of alertness and vitality. These are the true measures of health and well-being.

All people do not arrive at the weight-loss starting line with the same potential to lose weight. You are already at a disadvantage if:

- You've been big since childhood. You probably have both more and larger fat cells. People who gain weight as adults have bigger fat cells, but not an above-average number of them.

- You've been yo-yo dieting for years. Your metabolism may have slowed. You may have lost muscle tissue and added more fat in the process of losing and regaining.

- You're very large. The heavier you are, the more difficult it becomes to lose weight. Dennis Remington, M.D., author of *How to Lower Your Fat Thermostat,* notes that only 24 percent of dieters succeed in losing 20 pounds, and of those who feel they need to lose more than 40 pounds, only 5 percent are able to do so.[74]

- You've always found it difficult to stick to a very rigid diet. "The dieter with a high setpoint weight who enters into battle with her weight begins to experience constant hunger, presumably as part of the body's attempt to restore the *status quo,*" says William Bennett, M.D., in *The Dieter's Dilemma.*[75]

- Your family members tend to be large. We've already talked about the genetic studies.

Steps toward regulation

In March of 1990, a congressional subcommittee held an informational hearing investigating the safety and effectiveness of commercial weight loss programs and products. Representative Ron Wyden, who chaired the hearings, said:

> *American consumers are spending over $30 billion on weight loss programs and products. All too often the results are poor, and occasionally even life threatening. And federal regulators are doing very little to assure that products and procedures are safe, and that consumers aren't being ripped off by grossly misleading advertising.*

As a result of these proceedings, the Federal Trade Commission (FTC) alleged in September, 1993 that "five of the nation's largest commercial diet program companies have engaged in deceptive advertising by making unsubstantiated weight loss and weight loss maintenance claims and by using consumer testimonials without substantiation that the testimonials represented the typical experience of dieters on the programs." All eventually agreed to stop "misrepresenting the performance or safety of any weight loss program they offer in the future." Claims that weight loss is maintained over time must now be based on evidence of consumers followed for at least two years. Consumers have the right to ask for details about maintenance and should ask not about people featured in the company's ads, but about the *average* weight loss maintenance for all customers of the program. The maintenance success claims must also be accompanied by prominent disclosures that:

- For many dieters, weight loss is temporary.
- This result is not typical. You may be less successful.

Before signing up with any weight loss program, the FTC advises asking:

- What are the health risks?
- What data can you show me that proves your program actually works?
- Do customers keep the weight off after they leave the program?
- What are the costs for membership, weekly fees, food, supplements, maintenance and counseling? What's the payment schedule? Are any costs covered under health insurance? Do you give refunds if I drop out?
- Do you have a maintenance program? Is it part of the package or does it cost extra?
- What kind of professional supervision is provided? What are the credentials of these professionals?
- What are the program's requirements? Are there special menus or foods, counseling visits, or exercise plans?

In March of 1997 the FTC launched "Operation Waistline" to alert consumers to misleading and deceptive weight loss claims, to steer them to accurate information about healthy weight loss, and to continue to bring law enforcement actions against those who violate the law. As part of this campaign, the FTC is sending letters to publications that run fraudulent weight loss ads, asking them to step up their advertising review efforts to prevent blatantly deceptive ads from reaching consumers.

In a similar vein, the Partnership for Healthy Weight Management has launched "Ad Nauseum," a campaign to identify dubious weight loss claims and the media carrying them. The Partnership is a coalition of scientific, academic, health care, government, commercial, and public interest representatives committed to promoting the responsible marketing of weight loss products and programs. They plan to take their campaign one step further, in that they will encourage mainstream media to demand proof before accepting advertising copy that contains extravagant promises of weight loss success. You can help them by sending examples of "ads that promise the impossible" to Partnership for Healthy Weight Management, Federal Trade Commission, S-4302, 601 Pennsylvania Avenue NW, Washington, DC 20580.

The Food and Drug Administration (FDA) to date has banned 111 ingredients once found in over-the-counter diet products, including products containing alcohol, caffeine, dextrose and guar gum. They also advise consumers to beware of diet patches, fat blockers, starch blockers, "magnet" diet pills, the plant root glucomannan, bulk producers or fillers (designed to absorb liquid and swell in the stomach) and a species of algae called spirulina. Legal action has been brought against marketers of a number of these products.

Among the more bizarre weight loss devices the FDA has branded as fraudulent over the years:

- Electrical muscle stimulators
- Appetite suppressing eyeglasses, which turned out to be common eyeglasses with colored lenses that claim to project an image to the retina which dampens the desire to eat.
- Magic weight loss earrings that purport to stimulate acupuncture points controlling hunger.

You can obtain a great deal of valuable information at the websites of the FDA and FTC. Go to www.fda.gov or www.ftc.gov.

Some states and localities have also taken steps to regulate weight loss programs. All weight loss providers in New York City are required to display the "Weight Loss Consumer Bill of Rights." The bill resulted from a

New York City Department of Consumer Affairs investigation which found numerous "dangers and deceptions" in weight loss centers and programs.

The bill states in part:

- Rapid weight loss may cause serious health problems.
- Only permanent lifestyle changes promote long-term weight loss.

It also gives consumers the right to know the qualifications of the program's staff and to ask questions about the potential health risks of the program. The department's report said customers are led to believe they are receiving a health care service, but in the "commercially driven atmosphere, too often the center's goal becomes sales, not health."

The state of Michigan has also set guidelines for weight loss programs. These guidelines provide for a comprehensive screening "so programs can be individualized and weight goals reasonable, based largely on past weight and family history rather than 'ideal' weight." Clients are also entitled to full written disclosure of all phases of the program, including long term results. Slow, gradual weight loss through permanent lifestyle change is recommended. Even at that, the task force that developed the guidelines acknowledged that no techniques have been proven to result in permanent weight loss.[76]

Connecticut is the latest state to jump on the bandwagon. Its new law prohibits companies from misrepresenting the likelihood that customers will maintain their weight loss for an extended period of time. Weight loss success stories must be based on reliable scientific evidence using a representative sample of all customers.

My friend Kari summed up the Largely Positive philosophy toward eating when she said, "The freedom that comes from not having to worry about everything I put in my mouth is the best freedom I have ever known."

♥ ♥ ♥ From The Heart ♥ ♥ ♥

Unfinished Business

I was never really "finished."

I graduated from high school near the top of my class, wrote an award-winning newspaper column, captured the lead in the sophomore, junior, and senior class plays. But I wasn't "finished." Only after I lost weight would I be "finished."

I graduated from college magna cum laude and went on to get a master's degree. It wasn't enough. I wasn't thin, so I wasn't "finished."

I got a job with the title of "director." I was well regarded professionally. I had other job offers. Lost some weight, but not enough. Not quite "finished."

I married a wonderful man, bought a house, made good friends. Regained the weight. Will I ever be "finished?"

I changed jobs. My reports won praise. Still big. Still "unfinished."

Gradually I became better educated about issues of size and weight and absolved myself of blame and guilt. I stopped putting my life on hold. I uncoupled my self-esteem from my weight. I released the flamboyant woman within.

Suddenly I realized I had been "finished" all along. And it was a "big" finish!

13

the size acceptance movement

When I first heard about the size acceptance movement, I cried. I had no idea I was part of a human rights "movement." I didn't realize I had any "rights" as a larger person. I thought of myself as a misshapen person deserving of society's scorn. No more! I have joined the crusade!

—JULIA

Evolution of the size acceptance movement

NAAFA

The official beginning of the size acceptance movement is best traced to 1969, when NAAFA, the National Association to Advance Fat Acceptance, was founded by William Fabrey. Fabrey, an average-sized man, was distressed at the way his wife, a large woman, was often treated solely because of her size. NAAFA works to eliminate discrimination based on body size and provide larger people with the tools for self-empowerment through public education, advocacy, and member support. NAAFAans do not mind being called "fat." For them, the word has no negative connotations. It is viewed as simply another descriptive term, such as blonde, brown-eyed, short, or tall. Currently there are more than 50 local chapters in the United States (www.naafa.org).

Council on Size and Weight Discrimination

Since 1990, the same William Fabrey who founded NAAFA has devoted a great deal of his time and energy to the Council on Size and Weight

Discrimination, a nonprofit group working to change people's attitudes about body size. The Council acts as consumer advocates for fat people, especially in the areas of medical treatment, job discrimination, and media images. Among their current projects are a media project, medical advocacy project, kids' body image project, attorney referral, and bibliographies in many areas of size acceptance. The Council also coordinates International No Diet Day, which occurs each year on May 6th. Council president is Miriam Berg and Medical Advocacy Director is Lynn McAfee. McAfee frequently speaks at conferences of health professionals and obesity researchers, advocating for the health rights of larger people (www.cswd.org).

Early professional advocates

In 1982, Dr. William Bennett, then editor of the *Harvard Medical School Health Letter,* joined with Joel Gurin, editor of *American Health,* to publish a landmark book called *The Dieter's Dilemma.* This is the book, as I mentioned earlier, that was responsible for my own "rebirth and conversion." Bennett and Gurin stated:

> *The failure [to lose weight] does not lie in your weak will. It lies in the misconceptions about weight and weight control that dominate our belief system . . . [1] Fatness, in most cases, is not the result of deep-seated psychological conflicts or maladaptive eating behaviors; usually it is just a biological fact.[2]*

In 1984, Susan and Wayne Wooley, weight and eating disorders specialists at the University of Cincinnati, wrote a textbook chapter titled "Should Obesity Be Treated at All?"[3] The question they posed was "whether the generally modest benefits of successful obesity treatment clearly outweigh the negative effects of unsuccessful treatment and the general impact on an already weight-obsessed society of our continuing efforts to prevent or eradicate fatness." It was a pretty radical question, but probably one of the first times it had been raised by individuals who were not consumer advocates, but health professionals. In 1991, Dr. Wooley was joined by David Garner, Ph.D., a Toledo-based psychologist and eating disorders expert, in writing a journal article titled "Obesity Treatment: the High Cost of False Hope." In it, they stated:

Although millions seek treatments for obesity, the benefits of treatment have been overstated. For most people, treatment is not effective; the majority of the obese struggle in vain to lose weight and blame themselves for relapses. Repeated experiences of failure add to the psychological burden caused by the social stigma and the presumption of psychopathologic conditions attached to obesity. Many therapists may be contributing to this psychological damage by giving their patients false hope for success."[4]

Meanwhile, back in the lab, a scientist by the name of Paul Ernsberger, Ph.D., was conducting a series of animal experiments from which he concluded that high blood pressure does not develop because of weight gain, but as the result of repeated cycles of losing and regaining weight. In 1987, together with Paul Haskew, he released a special issue of *The Journal of Obesity and Weight Regulation* titled "Rethinking Obesity: An Alternative View of Its Health Implications." According to Ernsberger and Haskew, the prevailing view that obesity is completely detrimental to health "represents an unbalanced view of adiposity and health." They contend that while medical literature has documented elevated risk factors in heavy people, "These risk factors fail to translate into high mortality rates. In fact, many studies show that maximum longevity is associated with above-average weight."[5]

Congress gets into the act

The "nondiet" movement got a boost in 1990 when congressional hearings looked clearly, for the first time, at what was going on in the diet industry and whether consumers were really getting the facts. As a result, the Federal Trade Commission ordered commercial diet programs to inform consumers that weight losses of people in their testimonials are not typical—until such time as the companies can prove otherwise with solid data. (We're still waiting!)

Two years later the National Institutes of Health convened a conference to take a look at how Americans were faring in weight loss programs. Among the findings of those proceedings:

- Weight loss strategies have caused harm.
- Most often the weight lost is regained.
- Dropout rates are high.

- Repeated lose/gain cycles may have adverse effects.
- Trying to achieve body weights and shapes presented in the media is not an appropriate goal for most people.
- Unrealistically thin ideals create problems.
- Many Americans who are not overweight are trying to lose— which may have significant physiological and psychological health consequences.
- Most major studies suggest increased mortality is associated with weight loss.

Interestingly, terminology has evolved along with changes in thinking. In 1980, the government advised people to strive for their "ideal weight." In 1985 that changed to "desirable weight," and by 1990, Americans were told to aim for a "healthy weight."

AHELP

In 1991, some folks got together in a place called Mountain Lake, Virginia, and decided they could no longer in good conscience continue to prescribe dieting to their clients. The man who summoned them was Joe McVoy, Ph.D., then director of the eating disorders program at St. Albans Hospital in Radford, Virginia.

Said McVoy at the time: "There is no flag to gather around. We are a disenfranchised group. There is NAAFA (National Association to Advance Fat Acceptance) for large people, but nothing exists for the professionals who treat large people. Health professionals have the greatest potential for harm, but they also have the greatest potential for change. We want to alter the thinking of those who stigmatize large people into dieting, forcing their patients into unhealthy practices and promoting self-hate."

The organization that grew out of this gathering was called AHELP, Association for the Health Enrichment of Large People. AHELP sponsored a series of conferences throughout the 90s, but then fell dormant due to lack of resources. There was little funding and no paid staff. AHELP's leaders were basically trying to run the organization in addition to holding down full-time jobs. Anyone who has done something like this knows the difficulty of sustaining that sort of schedule for any length of time.

Health at any size

In recent years, the health component of the size acceptance movement has morphed into a concept now widely known as "health at any size." At the forefront is the *Healthy Weight Network*, which evolved from a publication now known as the *Healthy Weight Journal*. Editor Francie Berg has been advocating for "healthy weight" and "health at any size" for 16 years. Berg, a licensed nutritionist and professor at the University of North Dakota, is committed to reporting issues of size and weight in a clear, objective manner. She speaks extensively on this topic and has written several books, including *Women Afraid to Eat* and *Children and Teens Afraid to Eat*.

Soon another professional voice joined the size acceptance choir. He was Glenn Gaesser, Ph.D., professor of exercise physiology at the University of Virginia and author of the book *Big Fat Lies*.[6] Like Ernsberger before him, and after a comprehensive and rigorous review of studies on the relationship between obesity and ill health, he concluded that "you can be overweight and still be fit and healthy." Gaesser employs scientific data to refute the doctrine that obesity is a major health hazard and that dieting is the answer. He advocates larger people focusing on trying to be healthy by eating nutritionally and exercising.

Another leader in the "health at any size" movement is Steven Blair, Ph.D., of the Cooper Institute for Aerobic Research in Dallas, TX. Blair has conducted studies showing that larger men who exercise regularly end up healthier than thinner men who do not. He insists that you do not have to choose between being fat *or* fit—you can be both.

One of the first advocates for fitness among larger women is Pat Lyons, R.N., who, with Debbie Burgard, wrote the book *Great Shape: The First Fitness Guide for Large Women*.[7] Lyons is credited with bringing forth the idea that larger women can—and should—be physically active. She says: "Physically active large women have found that we can be fat *and* fit. We don't have to wait for a size 7 body to have efficient hearts, capable and graceful bodies, and good feelings about our physical selves."

Overcoming Overeating

The size acceptance movement is often referred to as the "non-diet" or "anti-diet" movement. Two women who have been teaching this concept for years are Jane Hirschmann and Carol Munter, authors of the book *Overcoming Overeating.*[8] For years, "overcoming overeating" meant dieting in the form of restricting food intake. But after years of working with clients in a clinical setting, Munter and Hirschmann came to the conclusion that this was backwards. According to their philosophy, "Diets never solve weight problems; they cause compulsive eating." And, "Food is not the compulsive eater's problem; it is the solution." Overcoming Overeating centers are located in Houston, Atlanta, and some New England cities (www.overcomingovereating.com).

Children and young adults

One of the first professional voices warning of the dangers of putting kids on diets was registered dietitian and therapist Ellyn Satter, who has written and spoken extensively on this subject. Her book, *How to Get Your Kid to Eat But Not Too Much,* is highly regarded by both professionals and parents (www.ellynsatter.com).

Size acceptance in the classroom

Another leader in the movement is Cheri Erdman, Ed.D., who designed a college class around the concept of size acceptance. Called "Body Image and the Larger Woman," it is offered at the College of DuPage in Illinois (for more information on this class, call the college's Field and Interdisciplinary Studies at 630-942-2356). Erdman is also author of the books *Nothing to Lose: A Guide to Sane Living in a Larger Body* and *Live Large: Ideas, Affirmations, and Actions for Sane Living in a Larger Body.*

Size acceptance and the research community

More recently, some size acceptance advocates and certain members of the obesity research community have joined forces, recognizing that there are a number of things we do agree on and that, even though we may disagree on the methods for achieving it, our mutual goal is to enhance the health and well-being of larger people.

The olive branch was first extended to me by Gary Foster, Ph.D., Clinical Director of the Weight and Eating Disorders Program at the University of

Pennsylvania School of Medicine. I had noticed that my book was listed in the "Recommended Reading" section at the end of one of his articles. Subsequently we met, and he has been instrumental in bringing the size acceptance perspective into the obesity research community. Dr. Foster contributed the Foreword to this book, and he and I co-authored a journal article titled "Facilitating Health and Self-Esteem Among Obese Patients." Size acceptance advocates and researchers agree that we must unite to prevent and fight weight discrimination. As this book goes to press, an initiative to do just that is commencing.

The struggles

Ask anyone who works in the size acceptance movement and they will tell you it's not easy. The prejudice against larger people is so deeply ingrained in our collective psyche that even people who insist they are not weight-prejudiced often are. A newspaper reporter recently told me in an email debate we were having over an article he wrote that he strongly disagreed with my suggestion that genetics plays a major role in obesity. I offered to send him copies of genetics studies, but I doubt they will change his mind. He may not think he is prejudiced, but he is unwilling to consider that obesity is caused by anything more than "simple overeating and inactivity." Those of us who work in size acceptance face these kinds of situations all the time. A colleague of mine, debating size acceptance with a doctor on a TV program, was told, "We better hope that you don't drop dead right here on the stage." It's easy to burn out when you are continually met with skepticism at best and outright hostility at worst.

Size acceptance organizations have come and gone. Most have had to operate with very little or no funding, minimal staff, and, let's face it, not a widespread demand for their services. Size acceptance events are not always well attended. Many larger women, I have found, feel that size acceptance signifies "giving up." I tell them it's not giving up, it's taking charge, but there are so many pressures and forces working against our message that even those who choose to come and listen may not be able to overcome the tug-of-war in the opposite direction.

Yet we persevere. Those in the vanguard of any human rights movement know how difficult it is to promote acceptance of people who are in any way different—especially if they are believed to be responsible for their own condition. And every time I've thought about throwing in the towel,

I hear from someone who says, "Thank you for all you're doing for us," and I know I must keep going.

Size acceptance worldwide

Lest you think that size acceptance is confined to the United States, there are size acceptance organizations in a number of countries, including Canada, Australia, France, Germany, Italy, New Zealand, Netherlands, Russia, South Afria, Sweden, Switzerland, and United Kingdom. You can connect with these organizations, by going to the website, www.sizewise.com. Click on their search index, click on "activism," and then click on "organizations."

Size aceptance Canada

In many ways, Canada is far ahead of the U.S. in promoting size acceptance, even at the governmental level. HUGS™ International originated in Canada in 1987 with registered dietitian, Linda Omichinski, who was searching for a more effective way to help her clients. Her group counseling format is based on an empowerment model that emphasizes "eating for energy, physical activity for fun, and self acceptance of genetic size and shape variations." She laid down her philosophy in her book, *You Count, Calories Don't*, and, more recently, *Staying Off the Diet Roller Coaster* (which can be purchased at the HUGS website, www.hugs.com). Along with Canada, HUGS groups can be found in the United States, Great Britain, South Africa, and New Zealand.

Then there is Vitality, which can be thought of as the Canadian government's version of Shape-Up America. Vitality doesn't scold people for being overweight. Instead:

> *The Vitality approach represents a major shift in thinking about weight and its relationship to healthy living. It calls for a shift from negative to positive thinking about how to achieve and maintain healthy weights. Rather than focusing on weight loss, Vitality aims to enhance Canadians' physical, psychological, and social well-being by encouraging them to enjoy eating well, being active, and feeling good about themselves. Vitality's 'feeling good about yourself' message draws attention away from society's preoccupation with weight and negative body image. Self-respect and acceptance of others are shown as the way to enhance enjoyment and family life.*

Britain's "Thin Summit"

In June of 2000, Britain's Minister for Women, Tessa Jowell, asked that country's leading figures in fashion, modeling, and the media to join her for a "Thin Summit" to grapple with the issue of young girls who feel under pressure to keep their weight down. "Young women are tired of feeling second rate because they can't match the ideal that they often see in the media," Jowell said. "We will look at any links which may exist between imagery and eating disorders, identify what research we need to carry out, and consider what action the government should take."

Spain's social pact

In an attempt to halt a surprising rise in the incidence and prevalence of eating disorders in Spain, the Spanish Senate commissioned a report on nonmedical factors that contribute to the problem. Reflecting how seriously the problem is taken in Spain, the report recommended that the government encourage a "social pact" against eating disorders. The Senate agreed that the family, the media, and the fashion industry are the main culprits in establishing a series of social values that favor "body cult and extreme thinness" over more important values. Under the terms of this Social Pact, print, radio, and television media were to release public service messages encouraging young people to imitate what Spanish experts consider admirable in intelligence, effort, and culture as a countermeasure to the emphasis on an external "look."[9]

Largely Positive, Inc.

When people ask me if I have children, I say that my child's name is Largely Positive. At times she gives me fits, and other times she is the joy of my life. I created Largely Positive in 1988 as an organization to promote health, self-esteem and well-being among large people. We strive to:

- Provide settings where people can feel safe, accepted, and valued regardless of size or weight.
- Illustrate that weight is never a measure of their self-worth, and that body size need not be a barrier to living a full, happy life.
- Provide accurate information about issues of size and weight to the public and health professionals.

- Promote research-based weight management and the "health at any size" approach.

- Join other size acceptance advocates and the obesity research community to help prevent and fight weight discrimination.

Largely Positive discussion groups

You may want to consider starting a Largely Positive discussion group to talk about issues of size and weight. There are any number of ways to do this, including within the context of a women's health program, a women's studies program, or even with a few friends at your home. A discussion guide is available from Largely Positive.

On a Positive Note newsletter

Largely Positive publishes a quarterly newsletter called *On a Positive Note*. The newsletter features columns by a registered dietitian, a body image therapist, and a plus-size style expert, as well as self-esteem advice and information on the latest size/weight research.

Contacting Largely Positive

For information on purchasing the discussion guide, subscribing to the newsletter, or just to share your thoughts with us, you can write us at P.O. Box 170223, Milwaukee, WI 53217; email us at positive@execpc.com. Also, check out our website at www.largelypositive.com.

♥ ♥ ♥ From The Heart ♥ ♥ ♥

Size Acceptance

What it isn't	*What it is*
Giving up	Taking charge of your own body, deciding what you will put into it, and how you will move about in it.
Fooling yourself	Learning the truth about issues of size and weight.
Abandoning hope	Embracing a new hope—a hope based on living fully in the present, not some future "waiting to be thin" fantasy.
Forgetting about losing weight	Devising a personal weight management plan that is based on what the research really says, not on hype.
Feeling oppressed	Becoming an advocate and standing up for your rights as a larger person. Not feeling as though you "deserve" to be treated poorly due to your size.
Being an outcast	Taking center stage and saying, "Look, world, I'm here and I'm here to stay!"

14

fitting in

I always thought I would hate the day and die from embarrassment if I would have to request a seatbelt extender on a plane. But that day did arrive on a dinky little commuter flight to Chicago and rather than feeling embarrassed—thanks to Largely Positive—I knew it was my right to fly safely and comfortably. I now ask for one on any flight and if I don't need it, fine. But it sure is nice to be able to breathe on an airplane!

—Kari

Sometimes it's tough fitting wide bodies into a narrow world. But don't give up, and don't avoid doing things you enjoy because you're afraid the accommodations won't accommodate you! In most cases there's a solution. Here are some tips to help you.

Airplanes

- Call around to find out which airlines have the widest seats. I am lucky enough to live in Milwaukee, the hub of Midwest Express Airlines, which has wide leather two-across seating throughout the entire plane. It's almost like the whole plane is first class. The coach seats on most airlines, however, are only 16 to 19 inches wide.

- Book far enough in advance so that you can have a good choice of seat assignments. Window or aisle will be best; I prefer a window seat because aisle seating makes you more susceptible to jolts from the beverage cart and passersby.

- Ask to have an empty seat between you and the passenger beside you. (If flying with someone you know, you may not mind the "coziness"). Explain that you are a larger person and that everyone will be more comfortable if your request can be accommodated. If the plane is not full, the airline will usually be happy to oblige.

- Ask the airline which flights are likely to have the fewest passengers. I have been told that the likelihood of a nonfull plane increases on late-night flights and during midweek.

- If you have a choice, you're better off with three-across seating. Airlines generally will fill the aisle and window seats first, leaving the middle seat empty. In planes that are two-five-two, the aisle/window duos will usually fill up first. You may then be better off with an inside aisle.

- If there are empty seats on board but not next to you, ask the flight attendant if you can move so that all concerned can be more comfortable.

- Don't be bashful about asking for a seatbelt extension. You can make the request when you book the flight and it will be given to you discreetly. If you haven't asked for it in advance, ask as soon as you board. You can order your own seatbelt extension from a company called Amplestuff at 914-679-3316 (Fax: 914-679-1206).

- Give yourself a little extra room by putting up the middle armrest. If someone is sitting next to you, suggest in a lighthearted tone that you'll both be more comfortable with this arrangement. Try not to get stuck in a bulkhead seat. There, the armrests are usually stationary and can't be raised.

- Does the tray table hit you in the stomach? If there's an empty seat next to you, use its tray table instead. You might try placing your meal tray on a pillow. Or bring your own bag lunch filled with items that won't be messy to eat, like apples, cheese and crackers, a sandwich, cut-up vegetables, or some cookies.

- If price isn't an issue, consider flying first class—the seats are anywhere from four to six inches wider—or take advantage of the "half-fare" policy. Many airlines will sell you a second seat for comfort at half price, but the offer usually applies only to full fares. You may be better off buying two economy fares. If you do that, be sure to tell the flight attendants when you board so they won't try to fill your extra seat.

According to *Conde Nast Traveler* (September 2000), most major U.S. airlines have placed seat maps and dimensions on their Internet websites. You can find out whether your armrest won't move, your seat won't recline, or if there are any other drawbacks to the seats you've been assigned. Most long-distance jets have 18-inch-wide seats, but the typical 737 seat is only 17 inches across (keep in mind that this measurement is from armrest to armrest; it is not a seat cushion measurement). The magazine also notes that your best bet may be a 767: "Thanks to its 2-3-2 seating arrangement, and the fact that airlines fill middle seats last, a 767 can be 86 percent full before anyone gets a middle seat."

Theaters

- If you can book tickets to a performance in advance, always ask for an aisle seat. This may require going to the box office because phone agents may not be able to pinpoint your seat exactly.

- Box seats may be your best bet. They often have more room—and sometimes they're individual chairs. I know it's more expensive, but my philosophy is this: I don't go that often; I may as well pay a little more for comfort when I do go.

- Eyeball the seats in movie theaters before you sit down. I have been told that some rows have wider seats, and I found this to be true one night when I did a little "seat hopping."

- Most movie theaters have space reserved for wheelchair patrons. You might ask if you could bring your own chair and sit in that area. This may or may not work—there is a court case right now involving a woman who asked to bring her own chair, was told she could, and was then asked to leave when she arrived with it.

Restaurants

• Call ahead and ask about seating arrangements. Find out if they have booths, tables, or both. Ask if all the chairs have arms, or if there is a combination of ones with and without arms.

• If the restaurant has both booths and tables, you can always say, "I prefer a table," even if you have to wait. I have no qualms whatsoever about doing this.

• Send a "scout" to look the situation over in advance—or go yourself. If all you see are very tiny booths, you may want to choose another restaurant.

Educational institutions

• Inspect the classroom before the course begins. I don't usually have a problem with the desks in colleges and universities; classrooms often have tables and chairs, but if the desk comes as a nonadjustable unit, ask for a separate table and chair.

You have a right to fit in. Don't be timid. Accommodations will improve to the extent that large people become assertive about their rights. The next time you encounter a "tight fit" in an establishment, phone or write the manager. Explain that you enjoyed being there but that the seating was not comfortable for a larger person. Suggest that some armless chairs or a few rows with wider seats be added. Explain that if you had this problem, other larger people are experiencing it as well.

Usually there is a solution, even if circumstances are not the best. Be inventive. Above all, don't let a narrowly-designed world keep you from doing the things you enjoy. You have just as much right to a plane ride, a restaurant meal, or a movie as a smaller person. And you needn't be embarrassed.

Automobile seat belts

Currently, 49 states have laws requiring seatbelt use by all front seat passengers. However, federal law requires only that cars be equipped with belts that adjust to fit drivers weighing up to 215 pounds. Most automobile manufacturers recognize that provisions must be made to enable larger passengers to buckle their seat belts, so they offer seat belt extenders. At press time, the only manufacturers who did not offer seat belt extenders were Honda, Hyundai, and Subaru. In most cases, all you need to do to obtain an extender is phone the 800 number of the appropriate manufacturer (these numbers are listed in the resource section).

Big news

There are signs that manufacturers are starting to take the needs of larger people into account. Writer David Jacobson reported in *The Detroit News* (September 8, 1994) that "as America changes shape, merchants are stretching to accommodate our growing proportions." For instance:

- Automakers such as Ford Motor Co. have increased the length of their seat tracks, allowing drivers to push back about 9 inches. A decade ago it was 5.5 inches.

- Steelcase, a leading manufacturer of office furniture, has introduced an office chair that can handle up to 500 pounds. The chair is wider and has adjustable arms.

- The European plane maker Airbus Industrie has sold more than 100 of its A320 jetliners partly by stressing that the plane's cabin is seven inches wider, allowing for wider seats and aisles.

- American Seating Co. reports that theaters and stadiums are ordering seats a few inches wider.

♥ ♥ ♥ From The Heart ♥ ♥ ♥

Things I Don't Deserve

I don't deserve:

- A restaurant booth that saws me in half.
- A hospital gown that exposes me and takes away my dignity.

- An airline seat that I am forced to share with the people on either side of me.

- A seatbelt that constricts rather than protects.

- A chair that accommodates only three-quarters of me.

- A theater seat so narrow I am looking forward to the end of the movie before it even starts.

- A classroom desk that cinches me so tightly I may never be able to extricate myself from it.

I don't deserve any of these things. What I do deserve is recognition by society that people come in all shapes and sizes and accommodations that take this into account. It's not a "small, small world." It's an "all size world!"

epilogue

As I near the end of this book, I am struck by an underlying theme that pops up again and again. That theme is "attitude."

People with a positive attitude are living their lives with little thought to their weight. When asked, "What do you say to people who put you down?" they say they don't have that problem. They like themselves, and other people respond positively to them. "You get back what you give off" is an oft-repeated saying among our members. What surprises me is that this also holds true for the teens I meet. Project a good attitude, they say, and others will like you.

Like yourself and you'll want to take care of your health, spruce up your image, delve into your career, and immerse yourself in interesting activities. Like yourself and you won't accept substandard treatment from anyone and you'll attract other positive people like a magnet.

The more that you learn about issues of size and weight, the easier it will be to like yourself. Strip away the blame. You are not inferior to anyone. Small is not better; it's just different. You can be anything, accomplish anything today, not 40 pounds from now. Try for that 40 pounds if you still feel it's important, just don't stop living. Don't say, "I can't go to that party until I'm thinner" or "I can't go on that trip until I'm thinner." That party will never happen again. That trip may never get taken. These moments will never be repeated in quite the same way. You might miss the opportunity of a lifetime!

Your attitude will get you a lot farther than a few lost pounds. Other people will enjoy being around you, and *you'll* enjoy being around you! Self-esteem doesn't come with a loss of weight. It comes from the inner peace of knowing that you're doing what's right for you. You may not be thin, but you know you are doing your best to take care of yourself, care about other people, and make a contribution to the world around you.

I am not naive. I know that attitude is not guaranteed protection from insults or discrimination; nor will a positive attitude stop them. But you'll be much better equipped to fight. You really have only two choices: punish yourself and your body, or say, "I'm a fine person just as I am," and get on with living a full life.

- A positive attitude is contagious. When you radiate warmth and vitality, others will want to be around you. Your good vibrations will make them feel better about themselves.

- A positive attitude is more fun. You get to laugh. You get to say nice things to other people and have them say nice things about you.

- A positive attitude will get you much farther in your career. People will say, "Let's get *her*. She's always ready for a new challenge."

- A positive attitude will make you more attractive to the opposite sex. Men are attracted to confident, upbeat women, not those who are depressed about some adipose tissue.

- A positive attitude will deflect comments about your weight. It will cease to be an issue.

You *can* develop a "largely positive" attitude. The energy that fuels a gloomy outlook can just as easily fuel a positive frame of mind. Try it—I think you'll like it. The world needs all the positive people it can get. Become one of us!

I would like to end with a piece written by Karina Young, the sixteen-year-old daughter of my friend Kari, following a discussion I had with her about research showing that some kids are ashamed of a fat parent.

> *To me it's outrageous to think that a child would be ashamed of his or her mother because she was overweight. At least that's what I think now. I was never ashamed of my mom because she was overweight. I was more afraid that people would make fun of her behind my back. But I got over that real quick.*
>
> *It's too bad that the only way to gain self-esteem for some people is by losing weight. I remember my mother going on diets on and off,*

losing weight and gaining it back. Finally she went into depression and it was over for her with dieting. Then came a group called Largely Positive.

Largely Positive is a group for overweight people that helps build self-esteem and acceptance. People any age or sex can attend. I have always loved my mother for who she is, but with the help of Largely Positive, now she loves herself for who she is.

notes

Chapter 2 • separating fact from fiction

1 *Pediatrics,* July 1999.

2 A. Catania et. al. "Evidence for Differing Dopaminergic Activity in Childhood or Adult Onset Obesity." *Clinical Endocrinology* 22, January 1985, pp. 75-81.

3 D. Janjic. "Android-Type Obesity and Gynecoid-Type Obesity." *Schweizerische Rundschau fur Medizin Praxis* (Switzerland) 85, December 3, 1996, pp. 1578-83.

4 G.N. Wassef. "Lipoprotein in Android Obesity and NIDDM: A New Member in 'the Metabolic Syndrome." *Biomedicine and Pharmacotherapy* 53, December 1999, pp. 462-5.

5 G. Kolata. "How the Body Knows When to Gain or Lose." *New York Times,* October 17, 2000.

6 J. Hirsch and R. Leibel. "The Genetics of Obesity." *Hospital Practice* 33, March 15, 1998, pp. 55-9, 62-5, 69-70.

7 A. Stunkard et. al. "Body Mass Index of Twins Who Have Been Reared Apart." *New England Journal of Medicine* 322, May 24, 1990, pp. 1483-87.

8 D.B. Allison et. al. "The Heritability of Body Mass Index Among an International Sample of Monozygotic Twins Reared Apart." *International Journal of Obesity and Related Metabolic Disorders* 6, June 20, 1996, pp. 501-6.

9 A. Stunkard et. al. "An Adoption Study of Human Obesity." *New England Journal of Medicine* 314, January 23, 1986, pp. 193-98.

10 M. Griffiths and R. Payne. "Energy Expenditure in Small Children of Obese and Nonobese Parents." *Nature* 26, 1976, pp. 698-700.

11 C. Bouchard et. al. "Linkage Between Markers in the Vicinity of the Uncoupling Protein 2 Gene and Resting Metabolic Rate." *Human Molecular Genetics* 6, October 1997, pp. 1887-9.

12 M.S. Faith et. al. "Evidence for Genetic Influences on Human Energy Intake: Results from a Twin Study Using Measured Observations." *Behavior Genetics* 29, May 1999, pp. 145-54.

13 M.S. Faith et. al. "Putting the Behavior Into Behavior Genetics of Obesity." *Behavior Genetics* 27, July 1997, pp. 423-37.

14 R. Considine et. al. "Serum Immunoreactive-Leptin Concentrations in Normal-

Weight and Obese Humans." *New England Journal of Medicine* 334, February 1, 1996, pp. 292-95.

15 S. Heymsfield et. al. "Recombinant Leptin for Weight Loss in Obese and Lean Adults." *Journal of the American Medical Association* 282, October 27, 1999, pp. 1568-75.

16 "Unhappy Fat Cell Seeks Balance." *Obesity & Health*, March/April 1992, p. 25.

17 O. Bosello et. al. "Behavior of Adipose Tissue Cellularity in Gross Obesity." *Minerva Medica* 69, November 17, 1978, pp. 3831-3.

18 J.L. Knittle et. al. "The Growth of Adipose Tissue in Children and Adolescents." *Journal of Clinical Investigation* 63, February 1979, pp. 239-46.

19 B. Lowell et. al. "Development of Obesity in Transgenic Mice After Genetic Ablation of Brown Adipose Tissue." *Nature* 366, December 30, 1993, pp. 740-42.

20 P.A. Kern et. al. "The Effects of Weight Loss on the Activity and Expression of Adipose-Tissue Lipoprotein Lipase in Very Obese Humans." *New England Journal of Medicine* 322, April 12, 1990, pp. 1053-9.

21 S.F. Leibowitz and T. Kim. "Impact of a Galanin Antagonist on Exogenous Galanin and Natural Patterns of Fat Ingestion." *Brain Research* 599, December 18, 1992, pp. 148-52.

22 S.F. Leibowitz et. al. "Obesity on a High-Fat Diet: Role of Hypothalamic Galanin in Neurons of the Anterior Paraventricular Nucleus Projecting to the Median Eminance." *Journal of Neuroscience* 18, April 1, 1998, pp. 2709-19.

23 J.S. Flier et. al. "Severely Impaired Adipsin Expression in Genetic and Acquired Obesity." *Science* 237, July 24, 1987, pp. 405-8.

24 N.V. Dhurandar et. al. "Increased Adiposity in Animals Due to a Human Virus." *International Journal of Obesity and Related Metabolic Disorders* 24, August 2000, 989-96.

25 T.A. Wadden et. al. "Effects of Weight Cycling on the Resting Energy Expenditure and Body Composition of Obese Women." *International Journal of Eating Disorders* 19, January 1996, pp. 5-12.

26 R.L. Leibel et. al. "Changes In Energy Expenditure Resulting from Altered Body Weight." *New England Journal of Medicine* 332, March 9, 1995, pp. 621-8.

27 A. Astrup et. al. "Meta-Analysis of Resting Metabolic Rate in Formerly Obese Subjects." *American Journal of Clinical Nutrition* 69, June 1999, pp. 1117-22.

28 T. Wadden et. al. "Exercise in the Treatment of Obesity: Effects of Four Interventions on Body Composition, Resting Energy Expenditure, Appetite, and Mood." *Journal of Consulting and Clinical Psychology* 65, April 1997, pp. 269-77.

29 J. Rodin et. al. "Weight Cycling and Fat Distribution." *International Journal of Obesity* 14, April 1990, pp. 303-10.

30 Wadden, op. cit., *International Journal of Eating Disorders*.

31 G.D. Foster et. al. "Psychological Effects of Weight Cycling in Obese Persons: A Review and Research Agenda." *Obesity Research* 5, September 1997, pp. 474-88.

32 Ibid., p. 478.

33 R. McAllister and M.L. Caltabiano. "Self-Esteem, Body Image, and Weight in Non-Eating Disordered Women." *Psychol Rep* 75 (3 Pt 1), December 1994, pp. 1339-43.

34 P. Ernsberger et. al. "Consequences of Weight Cycling in Obese Spontaneously Hypertensive Rats." *American Journal of Physiology* 270, April 1996, pp. 864-72.

35 A.E. Field et. al. "Weight Cycling, Weight Gain, and Risk of Hypertension in Women." *American Journal of Epidemiology* 150, September 15, 1999, pp. 573-9.

36 M.T. Guagnano et. al. "Risk Factors for Hypertension in Obese Women. The Role of Weight Cycling." *European Journal of Clinical Nutrition* 54, April 2000, pp. 356-60.

37 E. Muls et. al. "Is Weight Cycling Detrimental to Health? A Review of the Literature in Humans." *International Journal of Obesity and Related Metabolic Disorders* 19, September 1995, pp. S46-50.

38 E. Muls et. al. "Is Weight Cycling Detrimental to Health? A Review of the Literature in Humans." *International Journal of Obesity and Related Metabolic Disorders* 19 Suppl 3(1), September 1995, pp. S46-50.

39 K. Brownell and J. Rodin. "Medical, Metabolic, and Psychological Effects of Weight Cycling." *Archives of Internal Medicine* 154, June 27, 1994, pp. 1325-30.

40 I.M. Lee and R.S. Paffenbarger, Jr. "Change in Body Weight and Longevity." *Journal of the American Medical Association* 268, October 21, 1992, pp. 2045-9.

41 D.M. Garner and S.C. Wooley. "Confronting the Failure of Behavioral and Dietary Treatments for Obesity." *Clinical Psychology Review* 11, 1991, pp. 729-80.

42 E. Sims. "Studies in Human Hyperphagia." in George Bray and John Bethune, *Treatment and Management of Obesity* (New York: Harper & Row), p. 29.

43 C. Bouchard et. al. "The Response to Long-Term Overfeeding in Identical Twins." *New England Journal of Medicine* 322, May 24, 1990, pp. 1477-82.

44 E. Sims. "Studies in Human Hyperphagia." in George Bray and John Bethune, *Treatment and Management of Obesity* (New York: Harper and Row, 1974), p. 29.

45 "Experimental Obesity in Man." *Transactions of the Association of American Physicians* 81 (1968): 153-70; Sims, interview (September 14, 1979).

46 T.A. Wadden and A.J. Stunkard. "Social and Psychological Consequences of Obesity." *Annals of Internal Medicine* 103, December 1985, pp. 1062-7.

47 A.J. Stunkard and T.A. Wadden. "Psychological Aspects of Severe Obesity." *American Journal of Clinical Nutrition* 55, February 1992, pp. 524S-532S.

48 J. Rodin et. al. "Psychological Features of Obesity." *Medical Clinics of North America* 73, January 1989, pp. 47-66.

49 F.X. Pi-Sunyer. "Comorbidities of Overweight and Obesity: Current Evidence and Research Issues." *Medicine and Science in Sports and Exercise* 31, November 1999, pp. S602-8.

50 Editorial, *New England Journal of Medicine* 338, January 1, 1998, pp. 52-54.

51 J.M. McGinnis and W.H. Foege. "Actual Causes of Death in the United States." *Journal of the American Medical Association* 270, November 10, 1993, pp. 2207-12.

52 D. Allison et. al. "Annual Deaths Attributable to Obesity in the United States." *Journal of the American Medical Association* 282, October 27, 1999, pp. 1530-8.

53 G. Gaesser. "Obesity, Health, and Metabolic Fitness." *Mesomorphosis* 1, June 1998 (an internet publication. To access this article, go to http://www.mesomorphosis.com/exclusive/gaesser/obesity01.htm

54 H.C. McGill et. al. "General Findings of the International Atherosclerosis Project," *Laboratory Investigations* 18, 1968, pp. 498-502.

55 *Milwaukee Journal,* March 20, 1994.

56 N. Mikhail et. al. "Obesity and Hypertension." *Progress in Cardiovascular Diseases* 42, July/August 1999, pp. 39-58.

57 I.S. Okosyn et. al. "Abdominal Obesity in the United States: Prevalence and Attributable Risk of Hypertension." *Journal of Human Hypertension* 13, July 1999, pp. 425-30.

58 O. Timar et. al. "Metabolic Syndrome X: A Review." *Canadian Journal of Cardiology* 16, June 2000, pp. 779-89.

59 "Sweet Eaters Weigh Less." *Obesity & Health*, September/October 1992, p. 92.

60 W. Bennett and J. Gurin. *The Dieter's Dilemma* (New York: Basic Books, 1982), pp. 108-10.

61 P. Lyons and W.C. Miller. "Effective Health Promotion and Clinical Care for Large People." *Medicine & Science in Sports & Exercise* 31, August 1999, pp. 1141-6.

62 G.D. Foster et. al. "What Is a Reasonable Weight Loss? Patients' Expectations and Evaluations of Obesity Treatment Outcomes." *Journal of Consulting and Clinical Psychology* 65, February 1997, pp. 79-85.

63 A. S. Beller. *Fat and Thin: A Natural History of Obesity* (New York: Farrar, Straus and Giroux, 1977), p. 74.

64 J. Sobal et. al. "Obesity and Marital Quality." *Journal of Family Issues* 16, November 1995, pp. 746-764.

65 V.J. Felitti. "Childhood Sexual Abuse, Depression, and Family Dysfunction in Adult Obese Patients: A Case Control Study." *Southern Medical Journal* 86, July 1993, pp. 732-6.

66 J. Anderson et. al. "Prevalence of Childhood Sexual Abuse Experiences in a Community Sample of Women." *Journal of the American Academy of Child & Adolescent Psychiatry* 32, September 1993, pp. 911-9.

67 M.E. Connors and W. Morse. "Sexual Abuse and Eating Disorders: A Review." *International Journal of Eating Disorders* 13, January 1993, pp. 1-11.

68 L.E. Edwards et al. "Pregnancy in the Massively Obese: Course, Outcome, and Obesity Prognosis of the Infant." *American Journal of Obstetrics and Gynecology* 131, July 1978, pp. 479-83.

69 H. Jensen et. al. "The Influence of Prepregnancy Body Mass on Labor Complica-

tions." *Acta Obstetricia et Cynecologica Scandinavia* 78, October 1999, pp. 799-802.

70 *Radiance* magazine, Fall 1989.

71 *Obesity & Health,* March/April 1994.

72 "Designer Diets Succeed When You Are the Architect." *Environmental Nutrition,* August 1992, p. 6.

Chapter 3 • bound by culture

1 A. Fallon. "Culture in the Mirror: Sociocultural Determinants of Body Image." In *Body Images*, ed. Thomas F. Cash and Thomas Pruzinsky (New York: Guilford Press, 1990), pp. 83-84.

2 A. Beller. *Fat and Thin: A Natural History of Obesity* (New York: Farrar, Straus, Giroux, 1977), p. 74.

3 Op. cit., Fallon, p. 82.

4 L.T. Sanford and M.E. Donovan. *Women and Self-Esteem* (New York: Penguin Books, 1984), p. 375.

5 "Where Fat Is a Mark of Beauty." *Los Angeles Times,* September 30, 1998, p. A1.

6 T. Cash. *Body Images* (New York: The Guilford Press, 1990).

7 H. Schwartz. "A History of Dieting." *NAAFA Newsletter,* July 1991, pp. 5-6.

8 *University of California, Berkeley Wellness Letter,* February 1991.

9 "You've Come a Long Way, Baby...Or Have You?" *Tufts University Diet & Nutrition Letter,* February 1994, p. 6.

10 D. Garner et. al. "Cultural Expectations of Thinness in Women." *Psychological Reports* 47, 1980, pp. 483-91.

11 S. Rubenstein and B. Caballero. "Is Miss America an Undernourished Role Model?" *Journal of the American Medical Association* 283, March 22, 2000

12 "Barbie's Missing Accessory: Food." *Tufts University Diet & Nutrition Letter,* January 1994, p. 1.

13 J. Price. "Dr. Dean Edell: Making a General Practice of Size Acceptance." *Radiance,* Spring 1990, p. 17.

14 T.F. Cash. "Body Images and Body Weight: What Is There to Gain or Lose?" *Weight Control Digest,* July/August 1992, pp. 169, 172-75.

15 "Kids Fear Fat Gain." *Obesity & Health,* March/April 1993, p. 31.

16 C.W. Callaway. *The Callaway Diet* (New York: Bantam Books, 1990), p. 17.

17 R.S. Strauss. "Self-Reported Weight Status and Dieting in a Cross-Sectional Sample of Young Adolescents." *Archives of Pediatric and Adolescent Medicine* 153, July 1999, pp. 741-7.

18 "On the Teen Scene: Should You Go on a Diet?" Website of the Food & Drug Administration, www.fda.gov (from an article that originally appeared in the September 1993 *FDA Consumer* with revisions made in 1994 and 1997).

19 D. Neumark-Sztainer et. al. "Weight-Control Behaviors Among Adults and

Adolescents." *Preventive Medicine* 30, May 2000, pp. 391-91.

20 "The Burdens of Being Overweight: Mistreatment and Misconceptions." *New York Times,* November 22, 1992.

21 "Penny Wise, Pound Foolish." *NAAFA Newsletter,* December 1992, p. 2.

22 *The U.S. Weight Loss & Diet Control Market, 6th Edition,* Marketdata Enterprises, May 2000.

23 "Statistics Related to Overweight and Obesity." National Institutes of Health, www.niddk.nih.gov

24 *Elle,* July 1994.

25 K.D. Brownell. "Dieting and the Search for the Perfect Body: Where Physiology and Culture Collide." *Behavior Therapy* 22, 1991, pp. 1-12.

26 Sanford and Donovan. *Women and Self-Esteem,* p. 379.

27 S.L. Turner et. al. "The Influence of Fashion Magazines on the Body Image Satisfaction of College Women." *Adolescence* 32, Fall 1997, pp. 603-14.

28 L. Pinhas et. al. "The Effects of the Ideal of Female Beauty on Mood and Body Satisfaction." *International Journal of Eating Disorders* 25, March 1999, pp. 223-6.

29 A.E. Field et. al. "Exposure to the Mass Media and Weight Concerns Among Girls." *Pediatrics* 103, March 1999, p. E36.

30 M. Tiggemann and A.S. Pickering. "Role of Television in Adolescent Women's Body Dissatisfaction and Drive for Thinness." *International Journal of Eating Disorders* 20, September 1999, pp. 199-203.

31 "The 1997 Body Image Survey Results." *Psychology Today,* January/February 1997, pp. 30-44, 75-84.

32 Plastic Surgery Information Service, Media Center, www.plasticsurgery.org

Chapter 4 • acceptable discrimination

1 "Fat Senior Allowed to Graduate." *NAAFA Newsletter,* August 1991, p. 2.

2 "Media and the Fifth Freedom." *NAAFA Newsletter,* October 1989, p. 5.

3 "Father Shoots Daughter for Being Too Fat." *NAAFA Newsletter,* September 1989, p. 1.

4 N. Angier. "Why So Many Are Prejudiced Against the Obese." *New York Times,* November 22, 1992.

5 *Men's Health,* April 1999, p. 58.

6 *Men's Health,* April 1998, p. 38.

7 J.R. Staffieri. *Journal of Personality and Social Psychology* 1967;7:101.

8 Experiment conducted in 1964 by the audio-visual department of Grandview Hospital, Dayton, Ohio.

9 S.L. Gortmaker et. al. "Social and Economic Consequences of Overweight in Adolescence and Young Adulthood." *New England Journal of Medicine* 329, September 30, 1993, pp. 1008-12, 1036-37.

10 A.M. Venes, L.R. Krupa, and R.J. Gerard. "Overweight/Obese Patients: An Overview." *Practitioner.* 1982, 226:1102.

11 H. Canning and J. Mayer. "Obesity: Its Possible Effects on College Admissions." *New England Journal of Medicine* 1966;275:1172.

12 G. Foster. "Psychological Factors in Overweight: Cause or Consequence?" *Weight Control Digest,* July/August 1991, p. 74.

13 L. Karris. "Prejudice Against Obese Renters." *Journal of Social Psychology* 1977; 01:159.

14 G. Kolata. "The Burdens of Being Overweight: Mistreatment and Misconceptions." *New York Times,* November 22, 1992.

15 "California Supreme Court Decides Weight Not Protected." *NAAFA Newsletter,* October/November 1993, p. 1.

16 K. Mayer. *Real Women Don't Diet* (Silver Spring, MD: Bartleby Press, 1993), pp. 37-38.

17 W.C. Goodman. *The Invisible Woman* (Gurze Books: 1995), pp. 46-49.

18 "Why Don't Magazines Show Clothes on More Real-Size Women?" *Glamour,* November 1998, pp. 244-48.

19 "Hallmark Apologizes." *NAAFA Newsletter,* April 1992, p. 4.

20 A. Myers and J.C. Rosen. "Obesity Stigmatization and Coping: Relation to Mental Health Symptoms, Body Image, and Self-Esteem." *International Journal of Obesity and Related Metabolic Disorders* 23, March 1999, pp. 221-30.

21 E. Rothblum. "Results of the NAAFA Survey on Employment Discrimination, Parts I and II." *NAAFA Newsletter* 17, April 1989 and May 1989.

22 M.V. Roehling. "Weight-Based Discrimination in Employment: Psychological and Legal Aspects." *Personnel Psychology.* 1999:52(4):969-1016.

23 B. Larsson et. al. "The Health Consequences of Moderate Obesity." *International Journal of Obesity* 5, 1981, pp. 97-116.

24 R.A. McLean and M. Moon. "Health, Obesity, and Earnings." *American Journal of Public Health* 70, 1980, pp. 1006-9.

Chapter 5 • creating your own ideals

1 A. Stunkard. *The Pain of Obesity* (Palo Alto, CA: Bull Publishing, 1976), p. 179.

2 M. Hower. "Imagine: Loving Yourself the Way You Are." *Radiance,* Summer 1991, p. 14.

3 R. Freedman. *Bodylove* (New York: Harper & Row, 1988), p. 8.

4 Fallon. *Body Images,* p. 80.

5 From an article in *Ladies Home Journal,* November 1996.

6 S. Jacoby. "The Body Image Blues." *Family Circle,* February 1, 1990, p. 46.

7 M.G. Hutchinson. *Transforming Body Image* (Trumansburg, NY: The Crossing Press, 1985), p.32.

Chapter 7 • self-esteem comes in all sizes

1 N. Branden. *How to Raise Your Self-Esteem* (New York: Bantam, 1987), p. 6.

2 N. Branden. *The Art of Living Consciously* (New York: Simon & Schuster, 1997).

3 Op. Cit., Branden. *Raise Self-Esteem*, p. 9.

4 R. McAllister et. al. "Self-Esteem, Body Image and Weight in Noneating-Disordered Women." *Psychol Rep* 75 (3 Pt 1), December 1994, pp. 1339-43.

5 "The Bruised Ego: Can Self-Esteem Survive Prejudice?" *International Obesity Newsletter*, January 1989, pp. 1-2.

6 P. Lyons. "Fat in the Fitness World." *Radiance*, Winter 1991, p. 14.

7 S. Kano. *Making Peace with Food* (New York: Harper & Row, 1989), p. 98.

8 D. Quinn and J. Crocker. "Vulnerability to the Affective Consequences of the Stigma of Overweight." In *Prejudice: The Target's Perspective.* J. K. Swim and Charles Stangor, Eds. (San Diego: Academic Press, 1998), p. 125-43.

9 C.S. Crandall. "Prejudice Against Fat People: Ideology and Self-Interest." *Journal of Personality and Social Psychology* 66, 1994, pp. 882-94.

10 Op. cit., Quinn and Crocker.

11 Op. cit., Quinn and Crocker.

12 J. Pierce and J. Wardle. "Cause and Effect Beliefs and Self-Esteem of Overweight Children." *Journal of Child Psychology and Psychiatry and Allied Disciplines* 38, 1997, pp. 645-50.

13 T.F. Heatherton et. al. "The Stigma of Obesity in Women: The Difference is Black and White." Paper presented at the annual meeting of the American Psychological Association, August 1995, New York.

14 S. Parker et. al. "Body Image and Weight Concerns Among African American and White Adolescent Females: Differences that Make a Difference." *Human Organization* 54, 1995, pp. 103-14.

15 S. Kumanyika et. al. "Weight-Related Attitudes and Behaviors of Black Women." *Journal of the American Dietetic Association* 93, 1993, pp. 416-22.

16 C. Miller. "What Is Lost by Not Losing: Losses Related to Body Weight." in *Perspectives on Loss: A Sourcebook*, J. Harvey, Ed. (Philadelphia: Brunner/Mazel, 1998), p. 253-67.

17 J. Crocker et. al. "The Stigma of Overweight: Affective Consequences of Attributional Ambiguity." *Journal of Personality & Social Psychology* 64, January 1993, pp. 60-70.

18 Branden. *How to Raise Your Self-Esteem*, p. 46.

19 Sanford and Donovan. *Women and Self-Esteem*, p. 22.

20 Branden. *How To Raise Your Self-Esteem*, p. 46.

21 A. Rumney. "Beyond the Looking Glass." In *Full Lives: Women Who Have Freed Themselves from Food and Weight Obsession*, ed. Lindsey Hall (Carlsbad, CA: Gürze

Books, 1993), p. 231.

22 *Radiance,* Fall 1991.

23 M.G. Hutchinson. "To Be Recovered and Fat." ibid., p. 102.

24 "Help Others, Help Yourself." *University of California, Berkeley, Wellness Letter,* December 1989, p. 1.

25 P. Ernsberger and P. Haskew. *Rethinking Obesity* (New York: Human Sciences Press, 1987), pp. 13-29.

26 "Less Pain." *Obesity & Health,* March/April 1994, p. 25.

27 B.A. Bruno. "One Therapist's Advice: Do Something Original—Be Yourself." *Radiance,* Fall 1992, p. 43.

28 A.B. McBride. "Fat Is Generous, Nurturing, Warm." in *Overcoming Fear of Fat,* eds. Laura S. Brown and Esther Rothblum (Binghamton, NY: Harrington Park Press, 1989), pp. 99-100.

29 C. Schroeder. *Fat Is Not a Four Letter Word.* (Minneapolis: Chronimed Publishing, 1992), p. 281.

30 Kano. *Making Peace with Food,* p. 101.

31 Op. Cit., Branden. *Living Consciously.*

32 Price. "Dr. Dean Edell," p. 16.

33 M.J. Sorensen. *Breaking the Chain of Low Self-Esteem* (Shorewood,OR: Wolf Publishing Co., 1998), pp. 184-85.

34 *The Art of Training,* Whole Person Associates, Duluth, MN.

35 C. Cardinal. *The Ten Commandments of Self-Esteem* (Kansas City: Andrew McNeel Publishing, 1998), p. 80.

36 S. Shapiro et. al. "Fear of Fat, Disregulated-Restrained Eating, and Body Esteem: Prevalence and Gender Differences Among Eight- to Ten-Year-Old Children." *Journal of Clinical Child Psychology* 26, December 1997, pp. 358-65.

37 J.R. Staffieri. "A Study of Social Stereotype of Body Image in Children." *Journal of Personality and Social Psychology* 1967;7:101.

38 A. Goldfield and J.C. Chrisler. "Body Stereotyping and Stigmatization of Obese Persons by First Graders." *Perceptual & Motor Skills* 81, December 1995, pp. 909-10.

39 S.Y. Kimm et. al. "Self-Esteem and Adiposity in Black and White Girls: the NHLBI Growth and Health Study." *Annals of Epidemiology* 7, November 1997, pp. 550-60.

40 R.G. Phillips and A.J. Hill. "Fat, Plain, but Not Friendless: Self-Esteem and Peer Acceptance of Obese Pre-Adolescent Girls." *International Journal of Obesity & Related Metabolic Disorders* 22, April 1998, pp. 287-93.

41 R.S. Strauss. "Childhood Obesity and Self-Esteem." *Pediatrics* 105, January 2000, p. e15.

42 B.K. Mendelson and D.R. White. "Relation Between Body Esteem and Self-Esteem of Obese and Normal Children." *Perceptual & Motor Skills* 54, June 1982, pp. 899-905.

43 Ibid., Strauss.

44 C.M. Grilo et. al. "Teasing, Body Image, and Self-Esteem in a Clinical Sample of Obese Women." *Addictive Behavior* 19, July-August 1994, pp. 443-50.

45 S. Martin et. al. "Self-Esteem of Adolescent Girls as Related to Weight." *Perceptual & Motor Skills* 67, December 1988, pp. 879-84.

46 J.W. Pierce and J. Wardle. "Cause and Effect Beliefs and Self-Esteem of Overweight Children." *Journal of Child Psychology and Psychiatry* 38, September 1997, pp. 645-50.

47 T. Anesbury and M. Tiggemann. "An Attempt to Reduce Negative Stereotyping of Obesity in Children by Changing Controllability Beliefs." *Health Education Research* 15, April 2000, pp. 145-52.

48 A. Moreno and M.H. Thelen. "Parental Factors Related to Bulimia Nervosa." *Addictive Behaviors* 18, November-December 1993, pp. 681-9.

49 A.J. Hill and J.A. Franklin. "Mothers, Daughters, and Dieting: Investigating the Transmission of Weight Control." *British Journal of Clinical Psychology* 37, February 1998, (pt 1): 3-13.

50 L. Smolak et. al. "Parental Input and Weight Concerns Among Elementary School Children." *International Journal of Eating Disorders* 25, April 1999, pp. 263-71.

51 S.Y. Kimm et. al. "Self-Esteem and Adiposity in Black and White Girls: the NHLBI Growth and Health Study." *Annals of Epidemiology* 7, November 1997, pp. 550-60.

52 Op. cit., Smolak.

53 J. Fisher and L. Birch. "Restricting Access to Palatable Foods Affects Children's Behavioral Response, Food Selection, and Intake." *American Journal of Clinical Nutrition* 69, June 1999, pp. 1264-72.

54 J.A. O'Dea and S. Abraham. "Improving the Body Image, Eating Attitudes, and Behaviors of Young Male and Female Adolescents: A New Educational Approach that Focuses on Self-Esteem." *International Journal of Eating Disorders* 28, July 2000, pp. 43-57.

Chapter 8 • creating personal style—in a big way

1 N. Roberts. *Breaking All the Rules* (New York: Penguin Books, 1985), p. 90.

2 R. Freedman. *Bodylove* (New York: Harper & Row, 1988), p. 218.

3 R. Olds. *Big & Beautiful* (Washington D.C.: Acropolis Books, 1982), p. 65.

4 H.E. Marano. *Style Is Not a Size* (New York: Bantam Books, 1991), p. 275.

5 Freedman. *Bodylove*, p. 197.

6 Marano. *Style Is Not a Size,* pp. 106-7.

Chapter 9 • I'm only telling you this for your own good

1 J.R. Rabinor. "Honoring the Mother-Daughter Relationship." In *Feminist Perspec-*

tives on Eating Disorders, ed. By Patricia Fallon, Melanie Katzman, and Susan Wooley (New York: The Guilford Press, 1994), pp. 275-80.

2 Olds. *Big & Beautiful*, p. 46.

3 Price. "Dr. Dean Edell." p. 17.

4 C. Shaw. *Come Out, Come Out, Wherever You Are* (Los Angeles: American R.R. Publishing, 1982), p. 74.

5 J. Sobal, B.S. Rauschenbach and E.A. Frongillo, Jr. "Obesity and Marital Quality." *Journal of Family Issues*, 1995 Nov; Vol 16(6): 746-764.

6 T.N. Garrison. *Fed Up! A Woman's Guide to Freedom from the Diet/Weight Prison* (New York: Carroll & Graf, 1993), p. 289.

7 Mayer. *Real Women Don't Diet*, p. 171.

8 D. Zimmer. "Fat Admirers." *NAAFA Workbook*, Chapter 5, 1988, p. 9.

9 C. Taylor. "Sex Talk: Not the Usual Line." *Radiance*, Fall 1990, p. 51.

10 L.C. Higgs. *One Size Fits All—And Other Fables* (Nashville: Thomas Nelson Publishers, 1993), p. 157.

Chapter 10 • lose weight and call me in the morning

1 J. Packer. "Barriers to Health Care Utilization: The Effect of the Medical Stigma of Obesity on Women." Dissertation, the City University of New York, 1990 (publication #9108157 *DAI* 1991, 51 [12B]).

2 C.C. Wee et. al. "Screening for Cervical and Breast Cancer: Is Obesity an Unrecognized Barrier to Preventive Care?" *Annals of Internal Medicine* 132, May 2, 2000, pp. 697-704.

3 G.L. Maddox and V. Liederman. "Overweight as a Social Disability with Medical Implications." *Journal of Medical Education* 44, 1969, pp. 214-20.

4 J.H. Price, S.M. Desmond et. al. "Family Practice Physicians' Beliefs, Attitudes, and Practices Regarding Obesity." *American Journal of Preventive Medicine* 3(6), 1987, pp. 339-345.

5 C.S. Rand and A.M. MacGregor. "Morbidly Obese Patients' Perceptions of Social Discrimination Before and After Surgery for Obesity." *Southern Medical Journal*, 83(12), 1990, pp. 1390-1395.

6 L. Maiman et. al. "Attitudes Toward Obesity and the Obese Among Professionals." *Journal of the American Dietetic Association* 74, 1979, pp. 331-36.

7 "Medical Students Reduce Prejudice." *Obesity & Health*, March/April 1993, p. 31.

8 *Radiance*, Spring 1992.

9 L.M. Young and B. Powell. "The Effects of Obesity on the Clinical Judgments of Mental Health Professionals." *Journal of Health and Social Behavior* 26, 1985, 233-46.

10 D. Quinn and J. Crocker. "Vulnerability to the Affective Consequences of the Stigma of Overweight." In *Prejudice: The Target's Perspective*, eds. J. Swim and C.

346 • self-esteem comes in all sizes

Stangor (San Diego: Academic Press, 1998), pp. 125-143.

11 A.J. Stunkard. "Talking with Patients." In *Obesity: Theory and Therapy, 2nd edition,* eds. A.J. Stunkard and T.A. Wadden (New York: Raven Press, 1993).

Chapter 11 • movers and shakers

1 M. Pratt, C.A. Macera and C. Blanton. "Levels of Physical Activity and Inactivity in Children and Adults in the United States." *Medical Science Sports Exercise* 31 (11 Suppl), 1999, pp. S526-33.

2 P. Lyons and D. Burgard. *Great Shape: The First Exercise Guide for Large Women* (New York: Arbor Housse, William Morrow, 1988), p. 23.

3 S. Blair. "Weight-Loss Through Physical Activity." *Weight Control Digest*, Vol. 1, No. 2, January/February 1991.

4 *Family Circle,* October 16, 1990.

5 G. Johnston. "Tips for Discovering Your Personal Best: Play, Exercise, or Sport." *Radiance,* Spring 1991, pp. 38-39.

6 P. Hassmen, N. Koivula and A. Uutela. "Physical Exercise and Psychological Well-Being: A Population Study in Finland." *Preventive Medicine* 30(1) 2000, pp. 17-25.

7 S.R. Cramer, D.C. Nieman and J.W. Lee. "The Effects of Moderate Exercise Training on Psychological Well-Being and Mood State in Women." *J Psychosom Res,* 35(4-5) 1991, pp. 437-49.

8 R. Norris, D. Carroll and R. Cochrane. "The Effects of Aerobic and Anaerobic Training on Fitness, Blood Pressure, and Psychological Stress and Well-Being." *J Psychosom Res* 34(4) 1990, pp. 367-75.

9 K.R. Fox. "The Influence of Physical Activity on Mental Well-Being." *Public Health Nutrition* 2(3A) 1999, pp. 411-18.

10 R. Ross et. al. "Influence of Dirt and Exercise on Skeletal Muscle and Visceral Adipose Tissue in Men." *Journal of Applied Physiology* 81, December 1996, pp. 2445-55.

11 R. Ross et. al. "Effects of Energy Restriction and Exercise on Skeletal Muscle and Adipose Tissue in Women as Measured by Magnetic Resonance Imaging." *American Journal of Clinical Nutrition* 61, June 1995, pp. 1179-85.

12 R. Ross et. al. "Response of Total and Regional Lean Tissue and Skeletal Muscle to a Program of Energy Restriction and Resistance Exercise." *International Journal of Obesity and Related Metabolic Disorders* 19, November 1995, pp. 781-7.

13 Lyons and Burgard. *Great Shape,* p. 152.

14 K. McCoy. "Making Waves." *Radiance,* Spring 1988, pp. 24-27,45.

15 M.G. Perri, A.D. Martin et. al. "Effects of Group- Versus Home-Based Exercise in the Treatment of Obesity." *Journal of Consulting and Clinical Psychology* 65(2), 1997, pp. 278-85.

16 J.M. Jakicic, C. Winters et. al. "Effects of Intermittent Exercise and Use of Home

Exercise Equipment on Adherence, Weight Loss, and Fitness in Overweight Women." *Journal of the American Medical Association* 282(16), 1999, pp. 1554-60.

17 S. Blair et. al. "Relationship Between Low Cardiorespiratory Fitness and Mortality in Normal-Weight, Overweight, and Obese Men." *Journal of the American Medical Association* 282 (16), 1999, pp. 1547-53.

18 Study conducted by Institute for Aerobics Research in Dallas. Reported in *Family Circle*, July 23, 1991.

19 "Does Exercise Work in Short-Term Weight Loss?" *Obesity & Health*, January/February 1994, p. 11.

Chapter 12 • so you still want to lose weight?

1 D. Neumark-Sztainer et. al. "Weight-Control Behaviors Among Adults and Adolescents: Associations with Dietary Intake." *Preventive Medicine* 30, May 2000, pp. 381-91.

2 J. Brody. *New York Times*, November 23,1992.

3 A.H. Mokdad et. al. "The Spread of the Obesity Epidemic in the United States, 1991-1998." *Journal of the American Medical Association* 282, October 27, 1999, pp. 1519-22.

4 J.S. Stern et. al. "Weighing the Options: Criteria for Evaluating Weight-Management Programs." *Obesity Research* 3, November 1995, pp. 591-604.

5 J. Hebebrand et. al. "Epidemic Obesity: Are Genetic Factors Involved via Increased Rates of Assortative Mating?" *International Journal of Obesity & Related Metabolic Disorders* 24, March 2000, pp. 345-53.

6 S. Wooley and W. Wooley. "Should Obesity Be Treated at All?" In *Eating and Its Disorders*, Eds. A.J. Stunkard and E. Stellar, New York: Raven Press, 1984. pp. 185-92.

7 D. Garner and S. Wooley. "Confronting the Failure of Behavioral and Dietary Treatments for Obesity." *Clinical Psychology Review* 11, 1991, pp. 729-80.

8 J. Price. "Food Fixations and Body Biases: An Anthropologist Analyzes American Attitudes." *Radiance*, Summer 1989, p. 46.

9 W. Bennett. "Dietary Treatments of Obesity." *Annals of the New York Academy of Sciences* 499, 1987, pp. 250-63.

10 Op. cit., J.S. Stern.

11 W. Callaway. *The Callaway Diet*, p. 43.

12 "Linking Gallstones with Weight Loss." *Obesity & Health*, May/June 1993, pp. 45-46.

13 "As Pounds Melt Away, So May Bones." *Environmental Nutrition*, December 1992, p. 7.

14 A. Stunkard. *The Pain of Obesity*, p. 88.

15 W.S. Agras. "Binge-Eating Disorder: Its Significance in Weight Control." *Weight*

Control Digest, September/October 1993, pp. 281, 284-90.

16 E. Satter. *How to Get Your Kid to Eat...But Not Too Much* (Palo Alto, CA: Bull Publishing, 1987), pp. 69-70.

17 F.M. Berg. "Binge-Eating Disorder: What's It All About?" *Obesity & Health,* March/April 1994, pp. 26-27.

18 R. Wing. "Binge Eating Among the Overweight Population." *Weight Control Digest,* March/April 1992, pp. 139-44.

19 J. Polivy and C.P. Herman. "Dieting and Binging: A Causal Analysis." *American Psychologist* 40, 1985, pp. 193-201.

20 M.D. Marcus et. al. "Binge Eating and Dietary Restraint in Obese Patients." *Addictive Behavior* 10(2), 1985, pp. 163-8.

21 M.M. Pederson et. al. "A Comparison of Binge Eating versus Dieting in the Development of Bulimia Nervosa." *International Journal of Eating Disorders* 21, May 1997, pp. 353-60.

22 "Dieting and the Development of Eating Disorders in Overweight and Obese Adults." *Archives of Internal Medicine* 160, September 25, 2000, pp. 2581-9.

23 A. Drewnowski. "Metabolic Determinants of Binge Eating." *Addictive Behaviors* 20, November-December 1995, pp. 733-45.

24 S.Z. Yanovski. "Biological Correlates of Binge Eating." *Addictive Behaviors* 20, November-December 1995, pp. 705-12.

25 T.E. Weltzin et. al. "Serotonin and Bulimia Nervosa." *Nutrition Reviews* 52, December 1994, pp. 399-408.

26 D.E. Wilfley and L.R. Cohen. "Psychological Treatment of Bulimia Nervosa and Binge Eating Disorder." *Psychopharmacology Bulletin* 33(3), 1997, pp. 437-54.

27 J.I. Hudson et. al. "Fluvoxamine in the Treatment of Binge-Eating Disorder: A Multicenter Placebo-Controlled, Double-Blind Trial." *American Journal of Psychiatry* 155, December 1998, pp. 1756-62.

28 S.L. McElroy et. al. "Placebo-Controlled Trial of Sertraline in the Treatment of Binge-Eating Disorder." *American Journal of Psychiatry* 157, June 2000, pp. 1004-6.

29 N.A. Shapira et. al. "Treatment of Binge-Eating Disorder with Topiramate: A Clinical Case Series." *Journal of Clinical Psychiatry* 61, May 2000, pp. 368-72.

30 Brody. *New York Times,* November 23, 1992.

31 F. Grodstein et. al. "Three-Year Follow-Up of Participants in a Commercial Weight Loss Program. Can You Keep It Off?" *Archives of Internal Medicine* 156, June 24, 1996, pp. 1302-6.

32 S. Sarlio-Lahteenkorva et. al. "A Descriptive Study of Weight Loss Maintenance: 6 and 15 Year Follow-Up of Initially Overweight Adults." *International Journal of Obesity & Related Metabolic Disorders* 24, January 2000, pp. 116-25.

33 S.J. Bartlett et. al. "Is the Prevalence of Successful Weight Loss and Maintenance Higher in the General Community than the Research Clinic?" *Obesity Research* 7, July 1999, pp. 407-13.

34 S.M. Shick et. al. "Persons Successful at Long-Term Weight Loss and Maintenance Continue to Consume a Low-Energy, Low-Fat Diet." *Journal of the American Dietetic Association* 98, April 1998, pp. 408-13.

35 S.S. Lehteenkorva and A. Rissanen. "Weight Loss Maintenance: Determinants of Long-Term Success." *Eating and Weight Disorders* 3, September 1998, pp. 131-5.

36 Wooley and Wooley. "Should Obesity Be Treated At All?" In *Eating and Its Disorders*, Eds. A.J. Stunkard and E. Stellar, New York: Raven Press, 1984. p. 187.

37 *Obesity*, Ed. Albert Stunkard (W.B. Saunders: 1989).

38 *International Obesity Newsletter*, October 1987.

39 *Obesity & Health*, May/June 1992.

40 T.A. Wadden et. al. "Exercise and the Maintenance of Weight Loss: One-Year Follow-Up of a Controlled Clinical Trial." *Journal of Consulting & Clinical Psychology* 66, April 1998, pp. 429-33.

41 M.L. Skender et. al. "Comparison of 2-Year Weight Loss Trends in Behavioral Treatments of Obesity: Diet, Exercise, and Combination Interventions." *Journal of the American Dietetic Association* 96, April 1996, pp. 342-6.

42 R.R. Wing. "Physical Activity in the Treatment of Adulthood Overweight and Obesity: Current Evidence and Research Issues." *Medicine and Science in Sports and Exercise* 31 (11 Suppl), November 1999, pp. S547-52.

43 W. McNeely and K.L. Goa. "Sibutramine: A Review of its Contribution to the Management of Obesity." *Drugs* 56, December 1998, pp. 1093-124.

44 S. Rossner et. al. "Weight Loss, Weight Maintenance, and Improved Cardiovascular Risk Factors After 2 Years Treatment with Orlistat for Obesity." *Obesity Research* 8, January 2000, pp. 49-61.

45 Memorandum, FDA, September 27, 2000, "Review of study protocol, final study report and raw data regarding the incidence of hemorrhagic stroke associated with the use of phenypropanolamine."

46 C. Haller and N. Benowit. "Adverse Cardiovascular and Central Nervous System Events Associated with Dietary Supplements Containing Ephedra Alkaloids." *New England Journal of Medicine*, advance release due to potential health implications, November 6, 2000.

47 S.M. Zaacks et. al. "Hypersensitivity Myocarditis Associated with Ephedra Use." *Journal of Toxicology. Clinical Toxicology* 38 (3), 2000, pp. 351-4.

48 T. Powell et. al. "Ma-Huang Strikes Again: Ephedrine Nephrolithiasis." *American Journal of Kidney Diseases* 32, July 1998, pp. 153-9.

49 A. Nadir et. al. "Acute Hepatitis Associated with the Use of a Chinese Herbal Product, Ma-Huang." *American Journal of Gastroenterology* 91, July 1996, pp. 1436-8.

50 *Tufts University Diet & Nutrition Letter*, July 1995.

51 "Popular Diet Supplement May Be a Cancer Risk." www.sciencedaily.com, March 24, 1999.

52 S.B. Heymsfeld et. al. "Garcinia Cambogia (Hydroxycitric Acid) as a Potential Antiobesity Agent: A Randomized Controlled Trial." *Journal of the American Medical Association* 280, November 11, 1998, pp. 1596-600.

53 M.H. Pittler et. al. "Randomized, Double-Blind Trial of Chitosan for Body Weight Reduction." *European Journal of Clinical Nutrition* 53, May 1999, pp. 379-81.

54 Center for Nutrition Policy and Promotion, USDA, May 30, 2000.

55 L. Hark and L. Stollman. "The Reincarnation of the High-Protein Diet." Heart Information Network, www.heartinfo.org, Center for Cardiovascular Education, October 1997.

56 B. Liebman. "Carbo-Phobia, Zoning Out on the New Diet Books." *Nutrition Action Health Letter*, Center for Science in the Public Interest, July/August 1996.

57 "The Threat of Insulin Resistance to Your Heart and How to Prevent It." *Environmental Nutrition*, August 2000.

58 M. Shah and A. Garg. "High-Fat and High-Carbohydrate Diets and Energy Balance." *Diabetes Care* 19, October 1996, pp. 1142-52.

59 A. Garg et. al. "Effects of Varying Carbohydrate Content of Diet in Patients with Non-Insulin-Dependent Diabetes Mellitus." *Journal of the American Medical Association* 271, May 11, 1994, pp. 1421-8.

60 M. Chandalia et. al. "Beneficial Effects of High Dietary Fiber Intake in Patients with Type 2 Diabetes Mellitus." *New England Journal of Medicine* 342, May 11, 2000, pp. 1392-8.

61 J. Hallfrisch et. al. "Mechanisms of the Effects of Grains on Insulin and Glucose Responses." *Journal of the American College of Nutrition* 19(3 Suppl), June 2000, pp. 320s-25s.

62 Callaway. *The Callaway Diet*, p. 12.

63 J. Price. "The Fallacy of Height and Weight Tables." *Radiance*, Summer 1989, pp. 35-36.

64 Price. "Food Fixations and Body Biases." p. 47.

65 J. Foreyt and G.K. Goodrick. "Choosing the Right Weight Management Program." *Weight Control Digest*, September/October 1991, p. 81.

66 G. Blackburn. "Effects of Degree of Weight Loss on Health Benefits." *Obesity Research* 3 (suppl 2), September 1995, pp. 211s-16s.

67 Callaway. *The Callaway Diet*, p. 51.

68 "Chocolate in Perspective: Cocoa Butter, a Unique Saturated Fat." Symposium proceedings, Dallas, Texas, February 9, 1994, reported in *American Journal of Clinical Nutrition* 60 (6 Suppl), December 1994, pp. 983S-1072S.

69 "How Do Artificial Sweeteners Affect Appetite, Intake, and Weight?" *International Obesity Newsletter*, June 1988, pp. 5-6, 8.

70 M. Faith, D. Allison and A. Geliebter. "Emotional Eating and Obesity: Theoretical Considerations and Practical Recommendations," p. 439.

71 Ibid., p. 441.

72 Ibid., p. 442.

73 D. Allison and S. Heshka. "Emotion and Eating in Obesity? A Critical Analysis." *International Journal of Eating Disorders* 13(3), 1993, pp. 289-95.

74 D. Remington and G. Fisher. *How to Lower Your Fat Thermostat* (Provo, UT: Vitality House International, 1983), p. 68.

75 W. Bennett and J. Gurin. *The Dieter's Dilemma* (New York: Basic Books, 1982), p. 66.

76 "Michigan Sets Guidelines for Weight Loss Industry." *Obesity & Health*, March/April 1991, pp. 27-29.

chapter 13 • the size acceptance movement

1 W. Bennett and J. Gurin. *The Dieter's Dilemma,* New York: Basic Books, 1982., p. 4.

2 Ibid., p. 58.

3 S.C. and O.W. Wooley. "Should Obesity Be Treated At All?" In *Eating and Its Disorders*, Eds. A.J. Stunkard and E. Stellar, New York: Raven Press, 1984.

4 S.C. Wooley and D.M. Garner. "Obesity Treatment: The High Cost of False Hope." *Journal of the American Dietetic Association* 91, October 1991, pp. 1248-51.

5 P. Ernsberger and P. Haskew. "Rethinking Obesity." *The Journal of Obesity and Weight Regulation* 6, Summer 1987, pp. 1-81.

6 G. Gaesser. *Big Fat Lies,* New York: Fawcett Columbine, Ballantine Books, 1996.

7 P. Lyons and D. Burgard. *Great Shape: The First Exercise Guide for Large Women* (New York: Arbor House, William Morrow, 1988), p. 10.

8 J. Hirschmann and C. Munter. *Overcoming Overeating,* Fawcett Books, 1998.

9 C. Erdman. *Nothing to Lose: A Guide to Sane Living in a Larger Body* and *Live Large: Ideas, Affirmations, and Actions for Sane Living in a Larger Body,* Harper San Francisco, 1995 and 1997.

10 G. Foster and C. Johnson. "Facilitating Health and Self-Esteem Among Obese Patients." *Primary Psychiatry* 5, October 1998, pp. 89-95.

11 X. Bosch. "Please Don't Pass the Paella: Eating Disorders Upset Spain." *Journal of the American Medical Association* 283, March 15, 2000, pp. 1409-10.

recommended reading

Self-esteem/body image

Bruno, Barbara Altman. *Worth Your Weight*. Rutledge: 1996.

Cooke, Kaz. *Real Gorgeous*. W.W. Norton: 1996.

Dixon, Monica. *Love the Body You Were Born With: A Ten-Step Workbook for Women*. Berkley Publishing Group: 1996.

Emme. *True Beauty: Positive Attitudes and Practical Tips from the World's Leading Plus-Size Model*. Perigee: 1998.

Erdman, Cheri. *Nothing to Lose: A Guide to Sane Living in a Large Body*. Harper-San Francisco: 1995.

Erdman, Cheri. *Live Large*. Harper-San Francisco: 1997.

Freedman, Rita. *Bodylove*. Harper & Row: 1988.

Garrison, Terry Nicholetti. *Fed Up! A Woman's Guide to Freedom from the Diet/Weight Prison*. Carroll & Graf: 1993.

Higgs, Liz Curtis. *One Size Fits All—And Other Fables*. Thomas Nelson: 1993.

Hirschmann, Jane, and Munter, Carol. *When Women Stop Hating Their Bodies: Freeing Yourself from Food and Weight Obsession*. Fawcett Columbine: 1995.

Hutchinson, Marcia Germaine. *Transforming Body Image*. The Crossing Press: 1985.

Lippincott, Catherine. *Well Rounded: Eight Simple Steps for Changing Your Life...Not Your Size*. Pocket Books: 1998.

Mayer, Ken. *Real Women Don't Diet*. Bartleby Press: 1993.

McKay, Matthew and Fanning, Patrick. *Self-Esteem*. New Harbinger Publications: 1987.

Rodin, Judith. *Body Traps*. William Morrow: 1992.

Sanford, Linda Tschirhart and Donovan, Mary Ellen. *Women and Self-Esteem*. Penguin Books: 1984.

Schroeder, Charles Roy. *Fat Is Not a Four Letter Word*. Chronimed Publishing: 1992.

Sward, Sharon Norfleet. *You Are More Than What You Weigh Workbook*. Wholesome Publishing Co: 1998.

Wann, Marilyn. *Fat!So?* Ten Speed Press: 1998.

Waterhouse, Deborah. *Like Mother, Like Daughter*. Hyperion: 1997.

Research

Atrens, Dale. *Don't Diet*. William Morrow: 1988.

Bennett, William and Gurin, Joel. *The Dieter's Dilemma*. Basic Books: 1982.

Gaesser, Glenn. *Big Fat Lies*. Fawcett Columbine: 1996.

Self-image/personal style

Arons, Katie. *Sexy At Any Size: A Real Woman's Guide to Dating and Romance*. Fireside: 1999.

Farro, Rita. *Life Is Not a Dress Size: Rita Farro's Guide to Attitude, Style, and a New You*. Chilton Book Co: 1996.

Marano, Hara Estroff. *Style Is Not a Size*. Bantam Books: 1991.

Nanfeldt, Suzan. *Plus Style: The Plus Size Guide to Looking Great*. Plume/Penguin: 1996.

Olds, Ruthanne. *Big and Beautiful*. Acropolis Books: 1982.

Roberts, Nancy. *Breaking All the Rules*. Penguin Books: 1985.

Nutrition/weight management

Callaway, C. Wayne. *The Callaway Diet*. Bantam Books: 1990.

Ciliska, Donna. *Beyond Dieting*. Brunner/Mazel: 1990.

Epstein, Diane and Thompson, Kathleen. *Feeding On Dreams: Why America's Diet Industry Doesn't Work and What Will Work for You*. Macmillan: 1994.

Fanning, Patrick. *Lifetime Weight Control*. New Harbinger: 1990.

Foreyt, John and Goodrick, G. Ken. *Living Without Dieting.* Harrison Publishing: 1992.

Hall, Lindsey. *Full Lives: Women Who Have Freed Themselves from Food and Weight Obsession.* Gürze Books: 1993.

Hirschmann, Jane and Munter, Carol. *Overcoming Overeating.* Fawcett Columbine: 1988.

Kano, Susan. *Making Peace with Food.* Harper & Row: 1989.

Omichinski, Linda. *You Count, Calories Don't.* Hyperion Press (Canada): 1992.

Remington, Dennis and Fisher, Garth. *How to Lower Your Fat Thermostat.* Vitality House International: 1983.

Children

Ikeda, Joanne and Naworski, Priscilla. *Am I Fat? Helping Young Children Accept Differences in Body Size.* ETR Associates: 1992. (To order, phone 1-800-321-4407)

Ikeda, Joanne. *If My Child Is Overweight, What Should I Do About It?* University of California: 1998.

Jasper, Karin. *Are You Too Fat, Ginny?* Is Five Press (Toronto): 1988.

Newman, Leslea. *Belinda's Bouquet.* Alyson Publications: 1991.

Passen, Lisa. *Fat, Fat Rose Marie.* Henry Holt: 1991.

Satter, Ellyn. *How To Get Your Kid To Eat, But Not Too Much.* Bull Publishing: 1987.

Teens

Brumberg, Joan Jacobs. *The Body Project.* Random House: 1997.

Cordes, Helen. *Girl Power in the Mirror.* Lerner Publications Co: 1999.

Friedman, Sandra Susan. *When Girls Feel Fat.* HarperCollins: 1997.

Nichter, Mimi. *Fat Talk.* Harvard University Press: 2000.

Exercise

Lyons, Pat and Burgard, Debby. *Great Shape: The First Exercise Guide for Large Women.* Arbor House/William Morrow: 1988.

Rice, Rochelle. *Real Fitness for Real Women: A Unique Workout Program for the Plus-Size Woman.* Warner Books: 2001.

Cultural perspectives

Chernin, Kim. *The Hungry Self: Women, Eating and Identity.* Perennial Library/Harper & Row: 1985.

Chernin, Kim. *The Obsession: Reflections on the Tyranny of Slenderness.* Perennial Library/Harper & Row: 1981.

Goodman, W. Charisse. *The Invisible Woman: Confronting Weight Prejudice in America.* Gürze Books: 1995.

Poulton, Terry. *No Fat Chicks.* Birch Lane Press, Carol Publishing Group: 1997.

Schwartz, Hillel. *Never Satisfied: A Cultural History of Diets, Fantasies and Fat.* The Free Press/Macmillan: 1986.

Seid, Roberta Pollack. *Never Too Thin: Why Women Are at War with Their Bodies.* Prentice Hall: 1989.

Stacey, Michelle. *Consumed: Why Americans Love, Hate and Fear Food.* Simon and Schuster: 1994.

Wolf, Naomi. *The Beauty Myth.* Anchor Books: 1992.

Directory of resources

Sullivan, Judy. *Size Wise: A Catalog of More Than 1000 Resources for Living with Confidence and Comfort at Any Size.* Avon Books: 1997.

NOTE: Many of these books can be found at **www.bulimia.com**, but some are out-of-print. They may be able to be located through Amazon's "out-of-print" service. Simply go to **www.amazon.com**, type in the name of the book and you will receive instructions on placing an out-of-print order.

plus-size resources

sted below are a variety of resources for large people. I have tried to the
est of my ability to verify that each is still in business, but I have found
at, especially with smaller companies, there tends to be a rather big turn-
ver. You may find, therefore, that some have gone out of business
etween the time I finished the list and the time you try to contact them.

lothing for plus-size women

, Coole Designs
ww.bcoole.com
)0-992-8924
> 4X, children's sizes to XL.

rownstone Woman
)0-221-2468
zes 14-28.

ane Bryant
)0-248-2000
> 5X.

aking It Big
ww.bigwomen.com
77-644-1995
6W - 44W, to 70" waist and 77" hip.

oaman's
-800-436-0800
> 5X.

enney's for 16W and Up
00-222-6161
izes 14W – 34W.

egalia
-800-362-8400
2W to 40W (1X to 5X).

Silhouettes
www.silhouettes.com
800-704-3322
Sizes 12 - 34.

Jessica London
800-784-1667
Sizes 14-34.

Ulla Popken
www.ullapopken.com
800-245-ULLA
Sizes 12 - 34.

Sweeter Measures
308-468-5156
P.O. Box 340
Gibbon, NE 68840
To 8X.

The Big, the Bad, and the
Beautiful
www.bigbadbeautiful.com
818-345-3593
Can make fashions for women
to 600 pounds.

Lingerie & loungewear

Barely Nothings
www.barelynothings.com
800-422-7359

Intimate Appeal
800-362-8400
Sizes 14W – 32W.

Barb's Large & Lovely
www.bll.com
636-939-4070
To 8X.

Alectra
www.alectra.com
888-755-9449

Large Size Lingerie
www.choicemall.com/
largesizelingerie

The Caftan Connection
www.caftanconnection.com
877-534-5533
Caftans to 5X.

Plus-size bras and undergarments

Decent Exposures
www.decentexposures.com
1-800-524-4949
Bras to size 54, underpants to size 16.

Sweeter Measures
1-308-468-5156
To 8X.
(Their skintouch and action knit
bras have been my favorites for
years.)

www.biggerbras.com
972-475-8110
To 56H.

Plus-size bridal

LeClaire Bridal
www.leclairebridal.com
561-394-8043

Plus Size Bridal
www.plussizebridal.com
866-757-2743

www.bigbeautifulbrides.com
(This site was said to be
"launching soon.")

Shoes in sizes above 10 and wide widths

Coward
800-362-8400

Maryland Square
800-727-3895

Masseys
800-627-7397

Plus-size mail order hosiery

Just My Size
www.justmysize.com
800-522-9567
Pantyhose to 6X, clothes to 4X.

No Nonsense
www.nononsense.com

Plus-size patterns

Great Fit Patterns
2229 N.E. Burnside, Suite 305
Gresham, OR 97030

Active wear and swimwear

Junonia
www.junonia.com
800-JUNONIA
14W to 40W (1X to 6X).

Full Bloom
303-873-9277
2172 So. Trenton Way, #8-104
Denver, CO 80231
To 12X.

Big Stitches (swimwear)
510-237-3978

Beautiful Skier
800-638-3334

By Ro!Designs
ByRoDesign@aol.com
310-221-0509
Workout clothes and swimwear.

Plus-size maternity

www.teleport.com/~rvireday/
plus/
PlusMat_clothingFAQ_index.html

PlusSize Maternity Store
www.plussizematernitystore.com

Baby Becoming
www.babybecoming.com
888-666-6910

Plus Size Mommies-to-Be
www.plussizemommies.com
877-956-6669

Pickles & Ice Cream
www.plusmaternity.com
888-44-PICKLES

Big, tall women

Amazon Designs
www.amazondesigns.com
501-963-6536

Plus-size belts and accessories

Bigger Bangles
830-629-2251

Children

See Chapter 7, pages 173-175

Teens

Girlfriends LA
www.gfla.com
800-617-4352

Extra Hip
www.extrahip.com
323-461-9506
Fashions and online "e-zine" for
teen girls.

Benina and Lu
www.beninaandlu.com
888-992-9899

The Plus Size Teen Directory
www.largerteens.com
413-586-2224
P.O. Box 60417
Florence, MA 01062-0417
Over 75 listings, including clothing
catalogs and websites for plus-size
juniors, plus-size modeling, magazines for big teens.

Men's large size clothing

JC Penney Big & Tall
800-222-6161

The King Size Co.
www.kingsizedirect.com
800-846-1600

Repp Big & Tall
www.reppbigandtall.com
800-690-7377

Sears Big & Tall
800-679-5656

Exercise/fitness videos

Big on Fitness
914-679-3316

The Larger Woman's Workout by
Idrea
Great Changes Boutique
818-769-4626
12516 Riverside Dr.
North Hollywood, CA 91607

Jan Thompson's "Getting Started
Right"
Showcase Productions
214-653-8352

Chair Dancing by Jodi Stolove
www.chairdancing.com
800-551-4FUN

Exercise/fitness online

www.kellybliss.com
Complete fitness site for plus-size
women.

www.cinderernst.com
Personal trainer.

Rochelle Rice
www.infitnessinhealth.com
877-XHERSIZE
Plus-size health club.

www.women-of-substance.com
Spa for plus-size women.

Knitting

www.ample-knitters.com
Email discussion list for plus-size
knitters, as well as free patterns and
resources.

Online shopping

Sandie's Boutique
www.zaftig-2000.com
Close-outs, samples, one-of-a-kind,
gently used and new clothing,
costumes, jewelry and accessories.

www.peglutz.com
Unique, original designs
including daywear, evening
wear, and couture. Sizes to 3X
(3X fits a waist of 65 to 73
inches and a hip measurement
of 78" to 86").

www.alight.com
Plus-size clothing with designer
style.
To 26W.

www.onlyreal.com
Gateway to popular retailers
that offer larger sizes.

www.longtallsally.com
For women 5-foot-9 and taller.

www.realsize.com
Delta Burke's clothes.

www.littleandlarge.com
Link to UK and US sites for
larger women and men.

www.sizeappeal.com
Trendy styles
To 3X, some 4X.

www.gypsymoon.com
Renaissance-inspired clothing.

www.abigattitude.com
Workout clothes.
To 4X.

www.plusshop.com
Swimwear and plus-size
clothing.
To 6X.

www.plussizeoutlet.com
1X to 10X.

www.mylesahead.com
Great selection of supersizes.
To 5X (5X is an 83-85" hip;
their "small" is a 50-52" hip).

Directories

The Directory of Resources for
Large-Sized Women
www.largedirectory.com
413-586-2224
P.O. Box 60417
Florence, MA 01062-0417
Over 100 listings of catalogs,
videos, magazines, organizations, support groups, and
health information.

Voluptuous Woman Directory
www.volupwoman.com
240-568-3890
P.O. Box 1172
Burtonsville, MD 20866

Kelly Bliss' Plus Size Yellow
Pages
www.plussizeyellowpages.com
Sewing, maternity, uniforms,
costumes, swimwear, organizations, newsletters, videos.

Online Plus Size Directory
www.plussizedirectory.com

www.faqs.org/faqs/fat-accep-
tance-faq/clothing/us/
55 pages of clothing resources.

Size acceptance websites

Radiance
www.radiancemagazine.com
510-482-0680
P.O. Box 30246
Oakland, CA 94604

Since 1984, Radiance has been a
leading resource in the worldwide
size acceptance movement with its
timeless interviews with plus-size
celebrities, articles on health,
media, fashion, politics, poetry, art,
book reviews, essays, and more. The
Radiance Kids Project helps children
feel seen, loved, and valued for who
they are, whatever their size or
shape.

www.sizewise.com
Includes information on books,
magazines, entertainment, kids,
health at any size, size discrimination, fitness clothing and equipment, size acceptance organizations.

www.grandstyle.com
Plus size fashions and accessories;
size-positive art, books, CDs, videos,
software; maternity; size-positive
columnists and articles; the best
plus-size apparel catalogs, websites,
and size-friendly resources; health
and fitness tips; calendar, bulletin
board, and recipes.

www.sizewithstyle.com
Shopping mall, élana fashions,
ezine, spa holidays.

www.bodypositive.com
Boosting body image at any weight.

www.sizenet.com
A variety of "channels" you can
tune in to for shopping and various
aspects of size acceptance.

Voluptuous Woman Company
www.volupwoman.com
Plus size events, resource guide,
plus-size e-cards, newsletter.

www.emmestyle.com
Supermodel Emme's website—focuses on "celebrating a woman's body."

Health at any size

Healthy Weight Network
www.healthyweightnetwork.com
701-567-2646

Healthy Weight Journal
800-568-7281
www.bdecker.com
The latest scientific information, insight, and vision on eating and weight issues; a critical link between research and practical applications.

Nondiet organizations and resources

HUGS International
www.hugs.com
204-428-3432

Overcoming Overeating
www.overcomingovereating.com
212-875-0442

"Body Trust: Undieting Your Way to Health and Happiness" (video)
www.schoolroom.com/mall
888-SCHOOLING

Wheelchairs of Kansas
www.wheelchairsofkansas.com
800-537-6454
Wheelchairs for larger people.

Amplestuff
www.amplestuff.com
845-679-3316
Airline seatbelt extenders, hospital gowns to 10X, books, fitness videos, digital scales to 1,000 pounds, hygiene and health products.

Size positive organizations

Largely Positive Inc.
www.largelypositive.com
P.O. Box 170223
Milwaukee, WI 53217
Newsletter *(On a Positive Note)*, Discussion Guide for self-esteem/body positive groups, brochures, video.

NAAFA (National Association to Advance Fat Acceptance)
www.naafa.org
916-558-6880
P.O. Box 188620
Sacramento, CA 95818
Online newsletter, annual convention, local chapters, information brochures, book service, special interest groups.

Council on Size and Weight Discrimination
www.cswd.org
914-679-1209
P.O. Box 305
Mt. Marion, NY 12456
Medical Advocacy Project, Kids Come In All Sizes Project, Media Project, International No Diet Day Coalition.

Largesse
www.eskimo.com/~largesse
Online international clearing-house for information on size diversity empowerment.

Abundia
630-963-0346
P.O. Box 252
Downers Grove, IL 60515
Retreats for "sisters of size"

Weight discrimination attorneys

Persons with Disabilities Law
Center, PC.
www.naafa.org/documents/
brochures/law_center.html
Phone: 404-892-4200
Fax: 404-892-0955
TDD: 404-892-6027
56 Seventeenth St. N.E.
Atlanta, GA 30309-3245

The Obesity & Law Advocacy
Center
www.obesitylaw.com
Phone: 619-656-5251
Fax: 619-656-5234
2939 Alta View Dr., Suite O-360
San Diego, CA 92139

about the author

Carol A. Johnson, M.A., is a research sociologist, certified psychotherapist and founder of *Largely Positive Inc.*, an organization that promotes health and self-esteem among larger people. She is also editor of *On a Positive Note,* a newsletter focusing on self-esteem and body image. Her chapter, "Obesity, Weight Management, and Self-Esteem," detailing the perspective of the larger patient, appears in the textbook *Obesity: Theory and Therapy (3rd Edition)* edited by Albert Stunkard, M.D., and Thomas Wadden, Ph.D. (Raven Press).

Her experience in weight-related issues is both professional and personal. She has been above average in weight since birth and has struggled with all the issues common to larger women in this society. For 15 years she has studied the research on obesity, and is now a leader in the crusade to disseminate accurate information on this subject, fight weight-based discrimination, and help women disconnect their self-worth from their weight.

Ms. Johnson has spoken extensively to both consumer and professional groups, including physician, dietitian, and nursing organizations, company wellness programs—and most recently at a Shape-Up America conference. She has also been a popular speaker at plus-size fashion events at stores such as Nordstrom, Macy's, and Liz Claiborne.

She has appeared on CBS This Morning, Ricki Lake, MSNBC, and a variety of local and national talk shows. She has been featured in *Woman's Day, Ladies Home Journal, Better Homes & Gardens, Elle,* and *BBW* magazines, and has given many television, radio, newspaper, and magazine interviews.

She is currently working with top obesity researchers on several weight-related projects including a campaign to fight weight-based discrimination.

To contact her, write to Largely Positive, P.O. Box 170223, Milwaukee, WI 53217; e-mail: positive@execpc.com. Website: www.largelypositive.com.

about the publisher

Since 1980, Gürze Books has specialized in quality information on eating disorders recovery, education, advocacy, and prevention. They also have published books on size acceptance, self-esteem, body image, and related topics. They distribute *The Eating Disorders Resource Catalogue,* which is used as a resource throughout the world. Their website (www.bulimia.com) is an Internet gateway to treatment facilities, associations, basic facts, and other eating disorders sites.

Order Form

Self-Esteem Comes in All Sizes is available at bookstores and libraries or may be ordered directly from Gurze Books.

FREE Catalogue

The Eating Disorders Resource Catalogue has more than 150 books on eating disorders and related topics, including body image, size-acceptance, self-esteem, and more. It is a valuable resource that includes listings of non-profit associations and treatment facilities, and it is handed out by therapists, educators, and other health care professionals throughout the world. The entire catalogue and much more is available online at *www.bulimia.com.*

___ FREE copies of the *Eating Disorders Resource Catalogue.*

___ copies of *Self-Esteem Comes in All Sizes*
   $14.95 each plus $2.90 each for shipping.

   Quantity discounts are available.

Name ————————————————————————

Address ————————————————————————

City, ST, ZIP ————————————————————————

Phone ————————————————————————

Gürze Books
P.O. Box 2238
Carlsbad, CA 92018
(800) 756-7533

Order online at *www.bulimia.com*!